Artaud and After

Also by Ronald Hayman

Leavis
John Gielgud
Samuel Beckett
Harold Pinter
John Osborne
John Arden
John Whiting
Robert Bolt
Arthur Miller
Arnold Wesker
Edward Albee
Eugène Ionesco
Tom Stoppard

Techniques of Acting
The Set-Up: An Anatomy of English Theatre Today
How to Read a Play

Tolstoy
The Novel Today: 1967–75
Playback
Playback 2
The First Thrust

Edited by Ronald Hayman

The Collected Plays of John Whiting
The German Theatre
My Cambridge

Ronald Hayman

Artaud and After

OXFORD LONDON NEW YORK
OXFORD UNIVERSITY PRESS
1977

Oxford University Press, Walton Street, Oxford OX2 6DP

OXFORD   LONDON   GLASGOW
NEW YORK   TORONTO   MELBOURNE   WELLINGTON
IBADAN   NAIROBI   DAR ES SALAAM   LUSAKA   CAPE TOWN
KUALA LUMPUR   SINGAPORE   JAKARTA   HONG KONG   TOKYO
DELHI   BOMBAY   CALCUTTA   MADRAS   KARACHI

© *Ronald Hayman* 1977

British Library Cataloguing in Publication Data

Hayman, Ronald
   Artaud and after.
   1. Artaud, Antonin – Criticism and interpretation
   I. Title
   848'.9'1209   PQ2601.R677Z/   77–30070
   ISBN 0–19–211744–0
   ISBN 0–19–281208–4   Pbk

Printed in Great Britain by
Western Printing Services Limited, Bristol

For
IMOGEN

Contents

	Preface	ix
	ANTONIN ARTAUD 1896–1948: *A Chronology*	xi
1	The Old Man of Fifty	1
2	Artaud and Before	20
3	The Young Artaud	36
4	Film Actor and Surrealist	53
5	The Aborted Theatre	66
6	The Theatre of Cruelty	76
7	Mexico	102
8	Delirium and Asylums	115
9	The Final Freedom	131
10	Artaud and After	144
	Select Bibliography	163
	Reference Notes	166
	Appendix: Artaud's Work in the Theatre and in the Cinema	170
	CATALOGUE OF THE EXHIBITION AT THE NATIONAL BOOK LEAGUE	173
	Index	182

Illustrations

between pages 16 and 17

1 The old man of fifty: Artaud in 1946. *Photo: Le Cuziat*
2 Artaud in the clinic at Ivry-sur-Seine. *Photo: Denise Colomb*
3 His room at Ivry. *Photo: Denise Colomb*

between pages 48 and 49

4 Aurélien Lugné-Poe
5 Charles Dullin
6 Jacques Rivière
7 Jean Paulhan

between pages 64 and 65

8 Artaud in 1926, photographed by Man Ray
9 Artaud as Marat in *Napoléon Bonaparte*
10 Scene from *Napoléon Bonaparte*
11 Artaud as Frère Massieu in *La Passion de Jeanne d'Arc*
12 Roger Vitrac
13 André Breton

between pages 80 and 81

14 Still from *La Coquille et le clergyman*
15 Artaud in his production of *Les Cenci*

between pages 112 and 113

16 Asylum of Quatre-Mares, Sotteville-les-Rouen
17 One of the many drawings done by Artaud between 1944 and 1948
18 Self-portrait, 17 December 1946
19 Sketches by Artaud, inscribed to Florence Loeb

between pages 144 and 145

20 Sequence from Artaud's *The Spurt of Blood*, in the 1964 Brook/
   Marowitz *Theatre of Cruelty* season. *Photo: Michael Hardy*
21 Scene from Peter Brook's production of the *Marat/Sade*, 1964.
   Photo: Morris Newcombe

Thanks are due to the following sources for permission to reproduce the above illustrations: Collection of Anie Besnard-Faure, 17; Centre Psychiatrique au Rouvray, Sotteville, 16; Denise Colomb, 2, 3; Harlingue-Viollet, 13; Kobal Collection, 9; Lipnitzki-Viollet, 4, 15; Collection of Florence Loeb, 18, 19; National Film Archive, 10, 11, 14; Rapho, 1; Fonds Man Ray, 8; Roger-Viollet, 5, 6, 7, 12; Royal Shakespeare Company, 20, 21

Preface

The first word of thanks must go to Clifford Simmons, who had the idea for an Artaud exhibition at the National Book League and asked me to arrange it. But for him this book would not have been written.

I am most grateful to Artaud's sister, Marie-Ange Malausséna, and to his friends who helped me when I was researching in Paris—Roger Blin, Alain Gheerbrant, Henri Parisot, and Marthe Robert. I must especially thank Marie-Ange Malausséna and Henri Parisot for giving me valuable material, including out-of-print reviews and copies of unpublished letters. I am also grateful to Bernard Gheerbrant, Albert and Florence Loeb, and Guy Lévis Mano for their helpfulness, and I must thank Michèle Pietri and Nadine Christoff of the Phonotèque at Radiodiffusion Française for allowing me to listen to recordings from the Archives de l'Institut National de l'Audiovisuel. I would also like to thank Mme Cécile Giteau and Mlle Kristou for being so kind when I was working at the Bibliothèque de l'Arsenal.

I am enormously grateful to Catharine Carver for doing so much more than can reasonably be expected of an editor. From the moment of its conception onwards, she has contributed greatly to the growth of this book.

All the translations from the French are my own except where another translator has been credited.

RONALD HAYMAN

London
February 1977

Antonin Artaud 1896–1948

A Chronology

1896   4 September: Born at Marseilles, the son of Antoine-Roi Artaud and Euphrasie-Marie-Louise Artaud (*née* Nalpas)

1901   First attack of an illness which may have been meningitis.

c. 1903   Begins to stammer.

1905   13 January: Germaine Artaud born. Dies 21 August.

c. 1906   Almost drowns while staying at Smyrna with maternal grandmother.

c. 1909   At the Collège du Sacré Coeur, helps to start a literary magazine in which he publishes poems.

1914   Leaves school.

c. 1915   Drug habit started with tranquillizers at the sanatorium in La Rougière, near Marseilles, and possibly opium to relieve headaches. Paints a self-portrait. Stammering worsens.

1916   Called up into the 3rd Regiment of Infantry garrisoned at Digne. Invalided out after 9 months.

1916–18   In sanatoria at St. Dizier (near Lyons), Lafoux-les-Bains in le Gard, Divonne (Ain) where he meets the painter Yvonne Gilles.

July–August 1918: Stays at Bagnères-de-Bigorre in the Pyrenees.

1918–20   At the clinic of Dr. Dardel in Le Chanet, near Neuchâtel, Switzerland.

1920   March: Accepted by Dr. Edouard Toulouse as a
        patient at Villejuif. Works on Dr. Toulouse's
        review *Demain*, contributing poems and reviews
        of art exhibitions and of plays. Meets Lugné-Poe,
        who offers him his first part as an actor.

1921   April: Starts writing for *L'Ere nouvelle*.
        c. October: Meets Firmin Gémier, who, after audition-
        ing him, arranges for him to meet Charles Dullin.
        Joining the training school attached to Dullin's
        company, he meets the actress Génica Athanasiou.

1922   While acting for Dullin he designs sets and costumes.
        July: At the Colonial Exhibition in Marseilles he sees a
        troupe of Cambodian dancers.
        October: Contributes verse to the *Mercure de France* and
        signs a contract for Daniel Kahnweiler to publish
        a collection of his verse, *Tric-Trac du Ciel*.
        November: Publishes two poems in *Action*.

1923   Edits an anthology of Dr. Toulouse's writings.
        February: First issue of *Bilboquet*, a review edited by
        Artaud.
        April: Joins the company at the Comédie des Champs-
        Elysées.
        May: Correspondence with Jacques Rivière begins.
        Tric-Trac du Ciel published.
        September: Recrudescence of illness increases his
        dependence on opium.
        December: Second issue of *Bilboquet*.

1924   September: Correspondence with Rivière published.
        Death of Artaud's father.
        October: Joins Surrealist movement.

1925   January: Contributes to the second issue of *La Révolu-
        tion surréaliste*. Appointed director of the Bureau de
        Recherches.
        Edits the third issue of *La Révolution surréaliste*, writing
        most of it himself; issue published in April.
        July: *L'Ombilic des Limbes* published.
        August: *Les Pèse-Nerfs* published.

1926　Founds the Théâtre Alfred Jarry with Roger Vitrac and Robert Aron.

November: Artaud's manifesto for it appears in the *N.R.F.*

December: Expelled from the Surrealist group.

1927　February: 'Manifeste pour un théâtre avorté' published in *Cahiers du Sud.*

March: Meetings with Jacques Maritain.

June: Théâtre Alfred Jarry's first production. Triple bill at the Théâtre de la Grenelle.

1928　January: Act III of Claudel's *Partage de midi* produced by the Théâtre Alfred Jarry at the Comédie des Champs-Elysées in the same programme as a showing of Pudovkin's film *The Mother.*

February: Showing of *La Coquille et le clergyman* at the Studio des Ursulines.

March: Lecture at Sorbonne on 'L'Art et la Mort'.

June: Théâtre Alfred Jarry production of Strindberg's *Dream Play* at the Théâtre de l'Avenue.

December: Vitrac's *Victor* at the Comédie des Champs-Elysées.

1929　February–April: While filming in Nice he plans to start a film production company with the Allendys.

November: 20,000 fr. donated by the Vicomte de Noailles to the Théâtre Alfred Jarry, but the expensive fund-raising brochure fails to raise funds.

1930　July–October: Sporadic visits to Berlin to work in the cinema.

1931　July: At the Colonial Exhibition in the Bois de Vincennes he sees the Balinese troupe.

August: Begins to write 'Sur le théâtre balinais'.

December: Lecture at Sorbonne on 'La Mise-en-scène et la métaphysique'.

1932　February: 'La Mise-en-scène et la métaphysique' published by *N.R.F.* Begins to press for the *N.R.F.* to sponsor a new theatre for him.

February–March: Works as assistant to Louis Jouvet.

June: *L'Intransigeant* publishes an interview with Artaud about the new 'Théâtre de *la Nouvelle Révue Française*'. Apology and correction printed immediately afterwards.

October: 'Le Théâtre de Cruauté' (first manifesto) published in the *N.R.F.*

1933   April: Lecture at Sorbonne on 'Le Théâtre et la peste'.

June: Reads his scenario *La Conquête du Mexique* and Shakespeare's *Richard II* at the home of Lise Deharme to raise funds for the Theatre of Cruelty.

October: 'Le Théâtre et la peste' published in the *N.R.F.*

1935   February: Reading of *Les Cenci* at Jean-Marie Conty's home.

May: *Les Cenci* runs at the Folies Wagram 6–23 May.

July: His favourable review of Barrault's *Autour d'une mère* appears in the *N.R.F.*

Relationship with Cécile Schramme begins in the autumn.

1936   January: Sails for Mexico, arriving on 7 February.

February: Lectures at Mexico University.

May–July: Articles for *El Nacional Revolucionario*.

August: Leaves Mexico City for Tarahumara territory.

October: Returns to Mexico City, sailing for France at the end of the month.

November: On arriving in France resumes his relationship with Cécile Schramme, soon becoming engaged to marry her.

1937   May: Engagement broken off after his insulting behaviour at a lecture.

July: *Les Nouvelles Révélations de l'Être* published anonymously.

August: Arrives in Ireland. Sails to the Aran Islands.

September: After spending a week in Galway, goes to

Dublin. Deported at the end of the month, arriving at Le Havre in a straitjacket on the 30th.

December: Taken into psychiatric hospital of Quatre-Mares, Sotteville-les-Rouen.

1938   February: *Le Théâtre et son double* published.
April: Transferred to asylum of Ste. Anne, Paris.

1939   February: Transferred to Ville-Evrard.

1943   January: Transferred to Chezal-Benoit.
February: To Rodez.

1944   May: *Le Théâtre et son double* republished.

1945   November: *Au pays des Tarahumaras* published.

1946   March: Released from Rodez asylum to stay nearby.
April: *Lettres de Rodez* published.
May: Returns to Paris, staying at Dr. Delmas's clinic in Ivry.
June: Fund-raising auction of paintings at the Galerie Pierre. Benefit performance at the Théâtre Sarah-Bernhardt.

1947   January: Solo appearance at the Théâtre du Vieux-Colombier.
February–March: Writes *Van Gogh le suicidé de la société*.
July: Exhibition of Artaud's drawings at the Galerie Pierre.
September: *Le Retour d'Artaud, le Mômo* published.
November: *Pour en finir avec le jugement de Dieu* recorded.

1948   January: *Van Gogh le suicidé de la société* awarded the Prix Sainte-Beuve.
March: Dies at Ivry.

The course of all recent serious theatre in Europe and the Americas can be said to divide into two periods—before Artaud and after Artaud.

SUSAN SONTAG in 1973

We are now going into the era of Artaud.

JERZY GROTOWSKI in 1967

I

The Old Man of Fifty

On 19 March 1946, six months before his fiftieth birthday and ten months after the Germans had surrendered, Antonin Artaud was released after spending over eight consecutive years in lunatic asylums. Had France not been occupied or had he not been penniless, he might have been liberated much sooner. According to the anonymous psychiatrist in Radiodiffusion Française's broadcast discussion on Artaud (5 March 1958), he would never have been interned at the third asylum, Ville-Evrard, but for his destitution. He had been sleeping in the open air and begging, accosting passers-by with the formula: 'Monsieur, the world has done me much harm. You are part of the world, so you have harmed me. Please give me five francs.'

Before agreeing to free him, the medical director of the fifth asylum, Rodez, stipulated that financial security should be provided for him. By now there was enough interest in him and his work for his manuscripts to command high prices on the autograph market, while several prominent painters, writers, and actors helped with the fund-raising. *Le Théâtre et son double*, his collection of writings about the Theatre of Cruelty, had been re-issued in May 1944. In November 1945 his letters and essays about Mexico had been published under the title *Au pays des Tarahumaras*, and some of his letters from Rodez were being printed. Picasso, Duchamp, Giacometti, Braque, Léger, and Dubuffet were among the painters to donate canvases to be auctioned at an exhibition which opened on 6 June; Sartre, Gide, Eluard, and Mauriac contributed autograph material to be sold. On 7 June there was a

benefit performance for him at the Théâtre Sarah-Bernhardt.
Together the two events raised over a million francs. Later on
Dullin, Jouvet, Barrault, Jean Vilar, and Roger Blin took part in
a gala matinée. For the remainder of Artaud's life—not quite two
years—he had something he had not experienced since childhood:
continuous financial security.

After staying for a month in a village near Rodez and returning
voluntarily to the asylum for another month, Artaud had arrived
in Paris on 26 May 1946, frail, ravaged, prematurely senile, almost
toothless. The following morning he appeared at the Café Flore, a
Basque beret pulled down almost to his ears. 'He resembled my
father at the end of his life,' wrote the young poet Jacques Prevel,
'his lip like a knife-blade, his speech cutting.' The years of confinement had not cured his need for drugs, which he had been
using throughout his life as pain-killers. At the café, when Dubuffet
advised him to follow a doctor's advice, he retorted: 'I'm more
competent than any of them. I know more about opium than they
do. I've had thirty years' experience of it.'

Since childhood there had been no doubt about the reality of
Artaud's sufferings, but he could not be sure whether the headaches and the bodily discomfort were coming from inside or from
outside. 'What constitutes this self which experiences what's called
being—being a being because I have a body? Mr. habits, Mr.
nausea, Mr. revulsion, Mr. cramps, Mr. dizziness, Mr. spanking
and Mr. slaps keep pace with Mr. disobedient, Mr. reaction, Mr.
tears, Mr. choked in a scandalized soul to make up the self of a
child.'[1]*

For much of the time, pain and consciousness must have been
indistinguishable. Apprehension about punishment and apprehension about the next wave of illness must have combined to make
awareness of his mind inseparable from awareness of his body.
Conditioned by physical malaise which invaded the brain, the
adult Artaud refused to differentiate between mental and physical
consciousness. His first collection of prose poems, *L'Ombilic des*

---

* Superscript figures in the text refer to Reference Notes at p. 166.
See the Select Bibliography, p. 163, for a list of principal sources cited
or quoted in passing.

Limbes (1925), contains his 'Description d'un état physique', which begins:

> a sensation of acid burning in the limbs
> muscles twisted as if to the core, the sensation of being glassy and brittle, a fear, a recoil from movement and noise. An unconscious displacement of walking, gestures, movements. Willpower constantly strained over the simplest gestures. . . .

Pain and disability must have been prominent among the factors that prompted the declaration:

> There where others put forward their works, I claim nothing but to show my mind
> Life is a conflagration of questions
> I cannot conceive of work detached from life. . . .
> I suffer because the spirit is not in life and life not in the spirit.*
> I suffer from the spirit as an organ, spirit as a translation or from the intimidation of things by the spirit in order to make them enter the mind. . . . I refuse to differentiate between types of self-experience. I do not acknowledge any system inside consciousness.

Artaud was nothing less than heroic in his efforts to make confusion into a virtue. Having only himself to consult, he read his own body as if it were a map of the universe. As he put it in 'Position de la chair' (December 1925): 'I must examine this sense of flesh which ought to give me a metaphysics of Being and definitive knowledge of Life. . . . There is an intelligence, quick as lightning, in the flesh, and the agitation of the flesh shares in the highest activity of the mind.'

When he wrote this, at the age of twenty-nine, his life had already been centred on doctors and sanatoria for ten years. By the age of forty-nine, still uncured, he had come to believe not merely that all doctors were incompetent but that they were persecutors:

> Lunatic asylums are consciously and pre-meditatedly receptacles of black magic

---

* Any book about Artaud in English cannot but suffer from the fact that there is no equivalent in the language to the French word *esprit* which means both mind and spirit.

and it is not only that doctors encourage magic by their hybrid and
    inopportune therapies
it is that they make magic.

If there had not been any doctors
there would not have been any patients,
no skeletons or diseased
corpses to butcher and dissect,
because it is with doctors and not with patients that society began.

Those who are alive are living off the dead.
So death must live
and there is nothing like a lunatic asylum for hatching death gently
and keeping corpses in an incubator.[2]

But the doctors were not Artaud's only persecutors. He was
living, as he had in the asylums, under constant terror of black
magic. Instead of shaking hands, he would hold out two fingers,
to put less of himself at risk. He asked his friends not to make love.
'There is no longer anything pure in sexuality. It has become a
dirty thing, like the function of eating in certain periods. That is
how Sodom and Gomorrah ended. . . . Each time a man and a
woman make love, I feel it. They are taking something away from
me.'[3] Above all they must not have children. 'Each time a child is
born, it takes blood from my heart.' Just by touching their own
testicles or their vaginas, men and women could make contact
with other consciousnesses. Artaud believed that damage was
being inflicted on him by malicious activities. There was one
particularly dangerous technique by which the act of masturbation
could be protracted for an hour. He was convinced there had been
gatherings of Mexicans, Tibetan lamas, and rabbis to weaken him
by masturbating collectively. He wanted to retaliate by leading a
party of fifty friends, armed with machine-guns, to Tibet. They
would also have to attack several Bohemian monasteries which
evil-doers were using as their headquarters.

From the summer of 1946 he was living just outside Paris, in a
clinic at Ivry. There he was under the care of Dr. Delmas, who had
accepted the condition imposed by Artaud's friends: that he should
be free to come and go as he pleased. No effective control, therefore, could be imposed on his use of drugs to relieve the accesses

of physical pain. Though Dr. Delmas provided some drugs, much of the money that had been collected for Artaud was spent on buying opium and laudanum at black market prices. The doctor gave him a large block of timber to keep in his room: he could release his aggressions by attacking it with a hammer. Before he died, most of it had been pulverized. He carried a knife around with him, and he would dig it ferociously into tree trunks. His poker had been twisted into the shape of a snake and a large hole had been cut into his table.

To defend himself against the demons who were draining strength from his testicles, he would intone magical imprecations, sometimes asking friends to join in the responses. On Wednesday 28 August 1946 he was in a manic state, screaming and dancing with rage. To Prevel, who had been listening to his ravings for two hours, he said: 'You will not go out of this room alive unless you respond.' When he planted his knife threateningly on the table, the young man started to scream with him. Afterwards they both felt calmer. 'If we'd been on the stage,' said Artaud with sudden detachment, 'we'd have been a great success.' After writing for a while, he again danced, screamed, fought with evil spirits, and finally explained: 'Terrible things have happened, Monsieur Prevel. Just now, a crowd of men were masturbating on me in between Syria and Lebanon.'

In the street he would walk in a zigzag, touching the trees. He incorporated magic spells into his poetry, and its obscurity was intended partly as a defence against his enemies. Sometimes he identified the evil spirits with God, the enemy of mankind. Those who could not repudiate the idea of God the Creator were cowards, he said; claiming to be the author of his own existence, he denied the reality of his parents. Many of the late poems centre on the revulsion he felt against the generative copulation of the 'papa-mama', and in a letter he had written to Henri Parisot on 7 September 1945 he had complained about the uterus

which I did not need and had never needed, even previously, because it is no way to be born—to be copulated and masturbated 9 months by the membrane, the shiny membrane which devours without teeth, as the Upanishads put it, and I know that I was born in another way—

from my works and not from a mother—but the MOTHER wanted to take me and you can see the result in my life.

During these last two years of his life, Artaud's output was phenomenal. He carried exercise books around with him and he wrote in restaurants, trains, and buses, sitting, standing, or lying on a bed in semi-darkness in friends' homes. 'His pencil would break. He went on with the wood, ploughing up the paper. He wrote in pencil on pages already used. He rewrote in ink over the pencil, his handwriting varying with the state of his nerves.'[4] He sketched a great deal with prodigious energy and neurasthenic intensity. Some of the results are superb. Like Van Gogh, he could articulate the agonized rhythms of his own mental processes in frenetic strokes on the canvas, whirling the viewer into vertiginous participation. In the asylum, 'art therapy' had been more effective than electric shock treatment; now that he was at liberty, sketching and writing both served as palliatives against suffering. The walls of his room at Ivry had sketches pinned all over them, and Prevel has described how, on 10 June 1947, Artaud was yelling out furiously against evil spirits when he stopped to hurl himself at a drawing on the wall. Across the chest of the figure he drew flames. 'It's becoming something,' he said.

Throughout his career he had shifted promiscuously from one art to another, fanatically repudiating earlier phases of his own activity. He wrote verse, criticism, stories, plays, screenplays, and prose which fits into none of the usual categories. He acted and directed in the theatre; acted in films and wrote screenplays. He sketched and he designed sets and costumes. In all these arts his talent was considerable, but his genius was for using words, and it was here that ambivalence erected the greatest obstacle. Like Rimbaud he detested 'literature'; like Rimbaud he produced some of the most impressive works of literature in the French language. Susan Sontag has said: 'Nowhere in the entire history of writing in the first person is there as tireless and detailed a record of the microstructure of mental pain.' But like Rimbaud, in struggling to express the mental pain, Artaud was fighting not only against traditional 'literature' but against language, often resorting to nonsense and magical incantations in his efforts to transcend its limitations. His passion for the silent cinema and for the non-verbal aspects of theatre was intimately related (partly as cause, partly as result) to his disenchantment with the literary text, but his career in the theatre and cinema consisted of a painful series of false starts. His influence on twentieth-century theatre has been enormous, but it has come mainly through his written formulations. His achievements as a practitioner were less persuasive than the force of his personality, which is still active, both in what he wrote and in what others have written about him.

Though his articulacy was the source of his greatest strength, it was a power that depended on his sense of the inadequacy of words. If there was a lightning-quick intelligence in the flesh, it must be allowed to speak out. There must be no gap between impulse and expression. In the Préambule he wrote in 1946 for his *Oeuvres complètes*,* he said: 'I am the one who in order to exist has to whip his innateness.' He felt fully alive only when fully in touch with every element in his mental and physical being. Racing breathlessly to keep pace with his own sensations, he was counting on language to act more as a mirror than as a mileage gauge. Inevitably he was disappointed, but the impossible demands he made on words prompted him to extraordinary achievements.

The conflict first came into the open in 1923, when he submitted some poems to Jacques Rivière, editor of the *Nouvelle Revue Française*. Their correspondence, which spread over more than thirteen months, started in May, when, rejecting the poems, Rivière suggested they should meet. For those who have received a Catholic education, there is no direct and painless route to iconoclasm, and the letters to Rivière are crucial in representing Artaud's final bid for benediction from a literary pontiff. 'For me,' as he wrote in the first letter, 'it is a matter of nothing less than knowing whether I have the right to go on thinking, in verse or in prose.' It was only after he failed to win what he would have

---

* See the Select Bibliography, p. 163. Cited throughout as 'O.C.' with the volume and page reference.

regarded as official approval for his *modus operandi* that he started on the course which led through the organized madness of Surrealism to the lonely madness of his later life.

That first letter to Rivière was written in the evening of 5 June, after Artaud had called at the offices of the *N.R.F.* in the afternoon: 'I am constantly in pursuit of my intellectual being. So when I can catch hold of a form, however imperfect, I fix it, out of fear of losing all thought. I am lower than myself, I know, and it worries me, but I submit, for fear of dying totally.' However badly turned his phrases were, he had not dared to query or contest them when they were offered by 'the central feeling which dictates my poems. . . . They arise out of the profound uncertainty of my thought.' He was 'quite happy when this uncertainty does not give way to the absolute non-existence which I sometimes suffer from'. The poems he had submitted were 'tatters I have been able to recover from complete nothingness'. As 'evidence of spiritual existence' it was important that they should be authenticated by Rivière's acceptance. Without denying their flaws, Artaud was claiming his poems had the right to exist literarily.

Rivière's reply, dated 25 June, was sufficiently uncomprehending to discourage Artaud from writing again until the end of January 1924. The letter he wrote then begins with the promise 'to go right to the end of myself. I am not trying to justify myself in your eyes. It matters very little whether I seem to anyone else to exist. To cure me from the judgement of others I have all the distance which separates me from myself.' He blames the formal defects of his poems on 'a central collapse of the soul, a kind of erosion of thought, both essential and ephemeral, the fleeting non-possession of the material benefits of my development, the abnormal separation of the elements of thought. . . . There is something which destroys my thought . . . which takes away the words *that I have found*, which slackens my mental tension, which unpicks the substantial process of my thinking as it goes on.'

He was making a practical appeal for authentication. Without authoritative encouragement he would not be able to go on; as he put it in his letter of 7 May, 'I need no more than for it to be believed that I have the ability to crystallize things in the forms and words that are appropriate.'

With the letter of 29 January he enclosed a poem called 'Cri', which began

> The little heavenly poet
> Opens the shutters of his heart.
> The skies clash. Oblivion
> Uproots the symphony.

And in the postscript to another letter he wrote: 'I have committed myself finally to submitting to my inferiority. . . . For my part I am waiting only for my brain to change, for the upper drawers to open. An hour from now, perhaps, or tomorrow, my thinking will be different, but this present thinking exists, and I am not prepared to lose it.' When Rivière offered to publish their correspondence, Artaud said yes to the opportunity of preserving the thinking it embodied, but he rejected Rivière's idea of giving each of them an invented name. Artaud wanted to show himself as he was—in his non-existence. The reader must be able to see that what is being documented is 'a sickness which affects the soul in its deepest reality, infecting its manifestations. The poison of being. A true paralysis. A sickness which robs you of speech, of memory, which uproots thinking.'

By 1946, when he wrote the Préambule, he no longer had any faith in the poems, which he dismissed as belonging to a style 'inaugurated by Matisse as the avowal of an enraged impotence'. He told the story of how they had been rejected by Rivière:

> Then I gave up. For me, the question not being one of knowing what would succeed in insinuating itself into the framework of written language
> but into the texture of my living soul.

In the forties, as in the twenties, Artaud was in headlong pursuit of his 'intellectual being', snatching at any form that offered itself. As a Surrealist, he had been associated with a group that despised rationalism. More isolated now, he was more self-conscious, and more willing to let the reader see into the secrets of semi-automatic writing. Sometimes his unconscious would throw up a word because of a rhyme or assonance with one just written. When *synovie* (synovia—the albuminous fluid secreted in the joints) made him think of Segovia, the guitarist got mentioned in a parenthesis.

'I know', said Artaud, 'that when I've wanted to write, my words have misfired, and that's all. And I've never known anything else. I don't care whether my words sound like French or Papuan. But if I hammer in a violent word like a nail, I want it to suppurate in the sentence like a wound with a hundred perforations.'

It is possible that Rivière's acccptance of the letters and refusal of the verse precipitated the process by which Artaud—more successfully than his detractors admit—made his art secondary to his life, which itself became more like a work of art or a myth. As he put it in a letter written between July and September 1946 to Peter Watson, 'My work says much less than my life about all that.' By now he had appointed himself as chief priest of the believers; from the beginning, though, the impulse had been Messianic. Rivière's reply to his letter of 29 January 1924 asks: 'Must one believe that it is anguish which gives you the force and lucidity that are lacking when you are not yourself the subject?' Even if Rivière was only a catalyst, he was encouraging Artaud to concentrate on the inner void.

But the tendency was already there. 'What you take to be my works', Artaud had written about 31 August 1923 in a letter to Dr. Edouard Toulouse, 'are now, as in the past, nothing except waste matter from myself, scrapings off the soul, which the normal man doesn't collect.' And in 1926, in his 'Fragments d'un journal d'Enfer', he spoke of the need 'to confront the metaphysics I have made for myself as a function of this nothing which I carry'. The confusion of ontological issues with a private malady is central to his achievement. Like Nietzsche, he saw himself as an incurably sick man capable of biting into the tumour that was devouring him and using the poison therapeutically on a cancerous culture. In November 1888, prophesying the 'transvaluation of all values', Nietzsche wrote: 'I swear that in two years from now, the whole world will be in convulsions. I am sheer destiny.' His Schopenhauerian view of life as dominated by Dionysiac forces, anarchic, blind, and destructive, is complemented by Artaud's Rimbaudesque equation of art with consciousness and consciousness with suffering. All Artaud could offer was himself, but he offered himself totally. As he wrote in *Les Pèse-Nerfs*, 'I know myself, and that is enough for me. It must be enough. I know myself because I am a witness of Antonin Artaud.'

He felt nothing but contempt for the literary artistry which disguises human misery by hanging ornaments on it. One of his techniques is self-interruption: what he is saying, however urgent, is liable to be displaced by something else which has suddenly come to seem more urgent. In 'Paul les Oiseaux' (1924–5), Paolo Uccello visibly shares his identity with the empathizing writer until the semi-transparent illusion is displaced by a confession of Artaud's dissatisfaction with his performance in a recent film. Similarly, he would interpolate personal letters into sequences of prose poems or produce criticism in letter form. On 17 March 1932 he wrote to Jules Supervielle: 'Allow me to address my article to you in the form of a letter. It is the only means I have of combating an absolutely paralysing feeling of gratuitousness and of having done with it after thinking about it for over a month.' The letter, which was probably never posted, now forms part of the Appendix to *Le Théâtre et son double*.

These writing habits help to explain the ambiguous status of everything he turned out. Throughout his life, much of his best writing had been in his letters, and the most substantial of the texts he created after his release from Rodez—*Van Gogh le suicidé de la société*—is less like an essay than like a long letter with long post-scripts. His letters are often set out like verse, and the statements in his verse are formulated as in a letter. Some of his best (and best known) texts, like 'Coleridge le traître', were composed as letters to friends and published shortly afterwards; his 1946 'Lettre sur Lautréamont' was a contribution to the *Cahiers du Sud*. By the time he wrote the Préambule, he was incapable of addressing the general public without referring in intimate terms to his life.

The Préambule was to be followed by new versions of the 'Adresse au Pape' and the 'Adresse au Dalaï Lama', both of which had been published in the third issue of *La Révolution surréaliste*, in April 1925. The new version of the 'Adresse au Pape' starts with a violently anti-Christian credo:

1. I repudiate my baptism.
2. I shit on the name Christian.
3. I masturbate on the holy cross . . .

4. It was I (and not Jesus Christ) who was crucified at Golgotha for
rising up against god and his christ,
because I am a man
and god and his christ are only ideas
which, besides, have been marked by humanity's dirty hands.

The address goes on to denounce the worldwide conspiracy against
Artaud. He has been 'bewitched, held prisoner by a dark, sinister,
dissolute magic'.

The mind, the brain, the consciousness and also, above all, the body
of Antonin Artaud are paralysed, held, garroted by methods among
which electric shock is a mechanical application and prussic acid or
potassium cyanide or insulin a botanical or physiological transposition.

The reasons he has suffered eight years of imprisonment and
poisoning are the same as the reasons for his crucifixion two
thousand years ago. The story of Artaud's crucifixion had been
told in several of his letters from Rodez, including a beautifully
written one of 6 December 1945, to Henri Parisot:[6]

I remember a winter evening at Nazareth when I caught up with a
man and a shifty-looking woman, whom I had long been pursuing
as a witch, but they had always escaped me. The woman was called
Mary and the man Joseph. Their surname, I believe, was Nalpas.*
The woman was pregnant with a child which I did not, for anything
in the world, want to be born, because I knew where it came from
and who it was. In other words, I knew about the vile machinations
of enchantment against myself which were the source of its existence.
And I had sworn at all costs to prevent its birth. . . .

The said jesus christ, whose real name, I believe, was Antonin
Nalpas, was a magician like his father and mother and I had many
times to battle with him. For, morally, he was a cowardly impostor,
and I caught him more than once—as I have caught his ghost here at
Rodez—insinuating himself through a dream into my body, to
magnetize my testicles and bewitch my excrement. . . . Yesterday,
with horror, I found a final memory of my life at Jerusalem two
thousand years ago.

I know that I was already called M. Artaud, that everyone took me
for a simpleton, accused me of hearing voices, of declaiming and

* Nalpas was Artaud's mother's maiden name.

singing out loud, of talking to myself, and, because I wrote and recited poems, of being an idle good-for-nothing. . . .

At that time, Judaea and especially Jerusalem were infested with magicians and wizards who never stopped harassing me for possession of the last strength that remained to me. I had no home and ate when I could, which is to say almost never. Sometimes I would fly into frightful rages which excited them and silenced the mob that followed me around. . . . One day the police and the rabbis of that time decided to get rid of me. They had me arrested one night in a garden planted with olive trees where I was sleeping under the stars, having no roof to shelter me. I stood trial, but although I was found guiltless of any crime by a certain pontius pilate, the imbecile mob rose up to demand that I should be crucified. I remember an inn where, sitting on a stool, I had a crown of thorns placed on my head. A Malacca cane was put between my hands to replace the one which had been taken from me and which had served me with its 200 million fibres to destroy those who put spells on me.* And at the threshold of the door open to the afternoon sun, all the populace passed to shower me with spit, with blows, with insults. I remember too the base torture of crucifixion at a place called Golgotha, and the shriek which rose up from my entrails when the cross was erected and dug into the ground, and that my whole body plunged towards the earth under the nails which held it by the hands and by the feet. . . .

Dead, my body was thrown on the dunghill, and I remember rotting there for I do not know how many days or how many hours in the expectation of waking up, since at first I did not know that I was dead and that I had to resolve to understand before I could succeed in raising myself. Then some friends who formerly had completely abandoned me decided to come to embalm my corpse. They were astonished, and pleasurelessly, to see me alive.

I can only believe I was an embarrassment to them.

But to feel my hands punctured and bleeding, my body stinking, and my face, caked with dung, on my body which survived itself, gave me such a horror for my condition and for things that I was convulsed with fury. An earthquake made me turn everything upside down and the conflict raged for more than a day in Judaea.†

---

* See chapter 8 for an account of this cane and how it was lost.

† The imaginative penetration has a striking affinity with that of 'The Man Who Died', D. H. Lawrence's short story of how Jesus returns to earth for the sake of doing something he has never done before—

In the two years that he survived his release from Rodez, Artaud came increasingly to identify not only with Jesus but with other persecuted poets. His 'Lettre sur Lautréamont' links Lautréamont's name with those of Baudelaire, Poe, Gérard de Nerval, and Rimbaud. None of them was acceptable to a society which feared that their aggressiveness could be subversive. Each of them died young for having tried to keep his individuality intact, refusing to become a funnel for everyone else's thoughts, while Hugo, Lamartine, Musset, Blaise Pascal, and Chateaubriand had made themselves socially acceptable, said Artaud, by letting themselves be raped by the collective consciousness.

The argument is developed in 'Coleridge le traître':

> Coleridge is not one of the *poètes maudits*, reprobates capable of *oozing through* at a given moment, of ejecting this little black mucus, this waxy fart of frightful pain at the end of a tourniquet of blood, released at the ultimate of their horror by Baudelaire or his real ghost, by Edgar Allan Poe, Gérard de Nerval, Villon perhaps. . . . For Coleridge too the question arose of existing and of saying what he'd seen he was. It's because of wanting to tell the whole truth that he died. Yes, I'm saying that he too died between the ages of 20 and 24, that Samuel Taylor Coleridge, who was readying himself to outclass Dante, remained nothing more than the author of 'The Ancient Mariner', 'Christabel' and 'Kubla Khan'. . . . I mean that Mr. Satisfied Coition, with the complicity of Mrs. Erotic Orgasm, rose up against the poet who was being born
> and with a blow of the tongue diverted* him and turned him away from himself
> because this is the way that it happens

Among Coleridge's juvenilia there had been an unfinished poem which implied a promise to pick up from the point at which Euripides' work† had been aborted:

---

making love. Perhaps it is easier for the non-Christian than the Christian to think his way into the details of the crucifixion experience.

* The French words *langue* and *dériver* also refer, punningly, to language and derivation.

† Nietzsche had made the point that Euripides was the first to expose the ancient mysteries to the daylight of rationalism. Artaud was especially interested in the *Bacchae*.

to undertake knowingly and with determination to give idolatry
its due flagellation,
to force the occult into the action, to take vengeance for humanity
against god ...
to transport the occult world into the daylight, in order to show
what nothingness it is made of.

Coleridge is blamed for breaking faith with his youthful vision of a
world without mortality, for leaving humanity with the task of
redeeming itself, for being willing to 'transform the mucus which
was taken from him into opium. So he took laudanum.' He con-
doned the bourgeois desire to avoid violence and bloodshed. 'The
Ancient Mariner' had been conceived after—not during—his
thinking, and the albatross represented the soul of man, which
Coleridge had killed to secure his own survival. When he betrayed
his genius, poetry sustained an inordinate loss:

150 years ago the igneous rope was rediscovered, the great nautical
cord in the throat of the priest who is to hang. In the midst of this
drift from reality towards a distant poetic virtuality, of this dislocation
of the real world for the benefit of an occult erotic reality, all the more
occult for being obscene, all the more obscene for being real—this
rope, I say, indicates the real author of the evil, the priest and the
initiate.
But that, the occult said to Samuel Taylor Coleridge, that is what
you will never say.

Between January and March 1947, at the Musée de l'Orangerie,
there was an exhibition of work by Vincent Van Gogh, who had
killed himself in 1890, after spending the last years of his life in
asylums. Some of Artaud's boyhood paintings are strikingly Van
Gogh-like.
In the first version of Artaud's 1924 text on Uccello, 'Paul les
Oiseaux ou la Place de l'amour', it is very evident that he was
identifying with Uccello. The final draft begins: 'Paul Uccello is
struggling in the midst of a vast mental skein, where he has lost all
the pathways of his soul. His reality has been interrupted, its form
lost.' In the second draft, 22 years before 'Coleridge le traître', he

praises Uccello for succeeding where later he was to blame
Coleridge for failing: in saying 'what he'd seen he was',

> He penetrates deeply into an unthinkable problem: self-definition as
> if it were not himself that he was defining, seeing himself with his
> mind's eyes, as if they were not his own. Holding on to the advantages
> of subjective judgement, while detaching himself from the personality
> he is judging. Looking at himself while forgetting that it is himself he
> is seeing. But making this view of himself spread out and distil itself
> in front of him like a landscape, measurable and composed.

Before the Van Gogh exhibition at the Orangerie had opened,
Artaud's friend Pierre Loeb, director of the famous Galerie
Pierre, where Picasso and Matisse sold their work, suggested that
Artaud should write a book on Van Gogh. Artaud did not go to
the exhibition immediately it opened, but Loeb, writing to him at
Ivry in another effort to persuade him, enclosed a page from the 31
January issue of the weekly *Arts*. Under the caption HIS MADNESS?
it published an extract from Dr. Beer's sumptuously illustrated
book *Van Gogh's Dream*. Without suggesting that his artistic
activity was due to the psychic troubles which provoked his internment and his suicide, Dr. Beer argued that they might have
stimulated 'phenomena of association' which were conducive to
painterly productivity. Van Gogh's mental illness could not have
been schizophrenia, he argued, because it must have been heredi-
tary.

These extracts from the book had the effect Loeb wanted:
Artaud was provoked into writing. 'The shitty scalpel of a doctor
must not be allowed to go on grinding indefinitely into the genius
of a great painter' (*O.C.* XIII. 167). Early in February, on a Sunday
morning, he went to the Orangerie with some friends. Paule
Thévenin has written: 'His visit to the exhibition did not last very
long because he could not bear to stay there when it became
crowded, but his gaze was so sharp and quick that this time,
which would have been far too brief for anyone else, was sufficient
for him to apprehend what was essential.' Afterwards he wrote the
notes which he used in dictating *Van Gogh le suicidé de la société*,
often departing radically from them, often improvising long
passages. By the end of February the work was almost complete.

The old man of fifty. Artaud after his release in 1946 from more than eight years of confinement in lunatic asylums

Artaud photographed at the clinic of Dr. Delmas in Ivry-sur-Seine, just outside Paris

His room at the clinic, where he lived from May 1946 until his death in March 1948

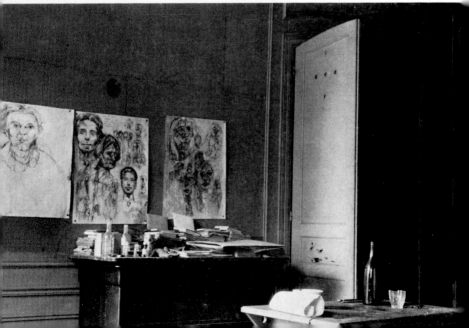

Gérard de Nerval, said Artaud, had been accused of madness in order to discredit certain vital revelations that he wanted to make. He was 'hit on the head one night to make him lose his memory of the monstrous facts he was going to reveal and which, as a result of this blow, passed inside him on to a supernatural plane, because the whole of society, secretly leagued against his consciousness, was then strong enough to make him forget their reality.' Similarly, Van Gogh's paintings were 'atomic bombs ... capable of subverting the larval conformism of the second Empire bourgeoisie'. They attacked 'the conformism of the institutions' and 'even external nature, with its climates, tides, equinoctial storms, cannot keep the same gravitation after the passage of Van Gogh on earth'. (The Gospels credit Jesus with power to make the wind and ocean obey his commands. In identifying with Jesus, Artaud never claimed such powers for himself, but he comes close to claiming them for Van Gogh.)

'What is a real madman?' asks Artaud.

It is a man who has preferred to go mad in the socially accepted sense, rather than give up a certain higher idea of human honour.
That is how society has organized the strangulation in lunatic asylums of all those it wants to be rid of or protect itself from, because they have refused to be accomplices in certain supremely dirty acts. Because a madman is also a man to whom society does not want to listen. So it wants to prevent him from telling intolerable truths.

Like Coleridge, Baudelaire, Poe, Gérard de Nerval, Nietzsche, Kierkegaard, and Hölderlin, Van Gogh was a victim of evil enchantment. It is usually contrived at night by 'strange forces lifted to an astrological vault, into that kind of dark dome, which forms, above all human breathing, the venomous aggressiveness of the evil spirit of the vast majority of people'. This is why the few men with lucid minds are prone to nightmares. They wake up 'surrounded by the formidable suction, the formidable tentacular oppression of a kind of civic magic which will soon be able to appear undisguised in modern living'. Van Gogh had just succeeded in finding out what he was and who he was when society's general consciousness suicided him to punish him for tearing himself away from it. Society insinuated itself into his body 'Because it is the anatomic logic of modern man never to have been able to live, or to think of living, except as one possessed'.

We can hardly fail to respond when Artaud describes the work of Van Gogh 'who painted not lines or forms but things of inert nature as if they were having convulsions. . . .'

> Now it is with his bludgeon strokes, real bludgeon strokes, that Van Gogh never stopped hitting at all the forms of nature and at things.
> Brushed with the nail of Van Gogh,
> landscapes show their hostile flesh,
> the snarl of their disembowelled recesses,
> so you do not know what strange force is also there,
>   metamorphosing itself.

In his paintings of crows, done just before (not as Artaud thought, just after he shot himself), Van Gogh succeeded, where Coleridge had failed, in opening 'the occult entrance to a possible beyond, a possible permanent reality'. He has released the crows 'like the microbes of his suicidal spleen' both at the top and at the bottom of the canvas.

Whereas Gauguin believed that the artist should raise living things to the status of myth, Van Gogh wanted to deduce myth from the most down-to-earth things in life. 'In every demented mind there is a misunderstood genius. The idea of it, which was gleaming in his head, was frightening, and from the strangulation, which life had prepared for it, it found no escape except in delirium.' As with Uccello, Artaud could not have written with so much insight if he had not been writing, at a remove, about himself. The identification is never explicit and it becomes apparent only peripherally. Dr. Gachet had never pretended that it was his function to improve Van Gogh's paintings; Dr. Ferdière did say that he could help Artaud with his poetry. A few pages later the comparison becomes more direct: 'I am also like poor Van Gogh. I no longer think, but each day I come nearer to the explosions I am producing.'

The identification becomes most productive when it gives him insight into Van Gogh's vision of the void. Describing the self-portrait with a straw hat, and describing himself looking at it, Artaud writes:

> I do not know a single psychiatrist who would be able to gaze with such desolating force into a man's face, dissecting the irrefragable psychology as on a cutting-board. . . .
> No, Socrates did not have eyes like these. Previously perhaps the unhappy Nietzsche was the only man to have this gaze which undresses the soul, delivers the body from the soul, strips the human body despite the subterfuges of the mind. . . .
> Van Gogh has seized the moment when the pupil of the eye is going to spill into the void . . . and, what is more, nothingness has never harmed anybody, but what pushes me back inside myself is this desolating absence which passes and momentarily submerges me, but I see there clearly, very clearly. I even know what nothingness is, and I will be able to say what there is inside it.

2

Artaud and Before

In March 1920 the twenty-three-year-old Artaud travelled with his father to Paris for a consultation with Dr. Edouard Toulouse, medical director of the asylum at Villejuif. According to an interview Mme Toulouse gave much later,[1] the doctor 'understood as soon as he saw him that he had in front of him a quite exceptional creature, of the race that produced Baudelaires, Nervals, and Nietzsches. . . . He was like a fisherman with a prize catch. This man, he told me, is on the point of falling off the tightrope, in spite of his genius. Will it be possible to save him?'

Perhaps Mme Toulouse's memories of the doctor's first impressions may have been coloured by later pronouncements from both men; it is striking that the three writers feature, together with Coleridge, Poe, Lautréamont, and Rimbaud, in the lists of *poètes maudits* Artaud was to make himself.

Edgar Allan Poe, whose dependence on drink and drugs was posthumously exaggerated by his literary executor, Rufus Griswold, used to complain that his enemies attributed his fits of insanity 'to the drink rather than the drink to the insanity'. Similarly, Artaud's detractors were later to attribute his malady to his drug-addiction rather than the drug-addiction to the malady. Nevertheless, alcohol and narcotics, taken in quantity, have irreversible effects on the metabolism of the imagination. As Baudelaire said, certain drugs induce the illusion that we can see life as a whole. Intensifying our sensations, they encourage the notion that everything in the universe is intimately related to everything else. Later, when the vision has disappeared, the sense of loss lingers. It is no accident that Poe's theory of cosmic unity, like his theories of poetry, derived from Coleridge. Poe's *Eureka* is almost hysterical in its insistence on the interdependence of atoms:

> If I venture to displace, by even the billionth part of an inch, the microscopical speck of dust which lies now on the point of my finger, what is the character of that act upon which I have adventured? I have done a deed which shakes the Moon in her path, which causes the Sun to be no longer the Sun, which alters forever the destiny of the multitudinous myriads of stars that roll and glow in the majestic presence of their Creator.

Logically it would follow from this that each particle of external reality is immeasurably important, but Poe also maintains in *Eureka* that the poet should reject the world in favour of his knowledge as a visionary.

At the age of twenty-seven he married his cousin, Virginia Clemm, who was not yet fourteen. When she died, eleven years later, he never recovered. In the story 'Ligeia' the heroine is based on Virginia, and her death represents the loss of all imaginative power. By using opium and later by withdrawing into madness and dreams, her lover tries to win back what he has lost. His madness succeeds in transforming another woman, Rowena, into a vision of the beloved. As a motto for the story Poe quoted from the mystic Joseph Glanvill: 'For God is but a great will pervading all things by nature of its intentness. Man doth not yield himself to the angels, nor unto death utterly, save only through the weakness of his feeble will.'

Poe's tragedy pivots on his ambivalence over pitting his will against God's. Sometimes he takes a position not far from that of Sade: 'the assurance of the wrong or error of any action is often the one unconquerable force which impels us, and alone impels us to its prosecution.'[2] The narrator in his story 'The Black Cat' lovingly and tearfully tortures and kills the animal he loves. In *Studies in Classic American Literature* D. H. Lawrence compared Poe to William Blake—another of 'these ghastly, obscene "Knowers"': 'It is easy to see why each man kills the thing he loves. To *know* a living thing is to kill it. You have to kill a thing to know it satisfactorily. For this reason, the desirous consciousness, the SPIRIT, is a vampire.'

Torn between self-hatred and vampiristic love, Poe could only yield himself up to vicarious self-condemnation and voluntary disintegration. Like 'The Haunted Palace', the poem of his character Roderick Usher in 'The Fall of the House of Usher', the whole of Poe's work is an allegory of its author's disruption.* Answering the question of why such 'morbid' tales had to be written, Lawrence said: 'He is reducing his own self as a scientist reduces a salt in a crucible. It is an almost chemical analysis of the soul and consciousness. . . . Drugs, women, self-destruction, but anyhow the prismatic ecstasy of heightened consciousness and sense of love, of flow. . . . [Poe] died wanting more love, and love killed him.' His poem 'Ulalume' represents life as illusion. Only death can reunite the poet with the vision that has vanished. Or as he says in *Eureka*, every man is God and God destroys himself as he gradually recovers his unity.

Poe published *Eureka* in 1848. In July 1849, he wrote 'I have no desire to live since I have done *Eureka*.' Three months later he died at the age of forty. Gérard Labrunie, who became known as Gérard de Nerval, hanged himself at the age of forty-seven, his ravaged face making him look very much older. Less than two years earlier, he had begun *Aurélie*, one of the first and one of the greatest accounts of madness ever written. Dr. Blanche, the director of the nursing home where he was an inmate, had encouraged him to work on it. The final pages were found on his body.

Poe's father had disappeared before the child was born; his mother died when he was two, which was the age Nerval had reached when his mother died. He never possessed even a picture of her, but later, in his madness, he had visions of her dead. He was brought up by his great uncle, who seems to have owned a great many books about magic and the occult. Like Artaud, Nerval found comfort in his preoccupation with Oriental religion and mysticism, with alchemy and numerology. He recreated his mother

---

* Offering himself for the part of Roderick when the story was about to be filmed, Artaud claimed that an actor who had not experienced the same 'quality of nervous suffering' could not bring it to life.

endlessly in his imagination, while the idea of her must have pre-
disposed him towards the metaphysical beliefs he formulated in
the introduction to his translation of Part Two of Goethe's *Faust*.
For Goethe, he wrote,

> as no doubt for God, nothing finishes, or at least nothing is trans-
> formed except matter, and the spent centuries are preserved complete
> as intelligences and shades, in a series of concentric areas, spread
> around the material world. . . . It would be consoling, indeed, to
> believe that nothing can die which has come up against intelligence,
> and that eternity keeps in its bosom a sort of universal history,
> visible to the eyes of the soul. . . .

Before the first outbreak of madness in 1841, he was suffering
from hallucinations, which he later described in *Aurélie*. Because
Jesus Christ died at the age of thirty-three, and because he was
thirty-three, he took it as a warning of imminent death when one
night, towards midnight, his eyes chanced on the number 33 on
the front door of a house illuminated by a street-lamp. He had
megalomaniac delusions about being related to Napoleon and he
signed one letter Napoleon della Torre Brunya. He also believed
he had had previous incarnations, and towards the end of his life
he would draw up genealogical trees incorporating ancient and
modern names.

As he said, 'I am one of the writers whose life is intimately
involved with the works which have made them known.' His
writing merges memories of dreams and hallucinations with
history, literature, and memories of personal experiences. As he
wrote in July 1854, 'Perhaps my experiences of the bizarre have
existed only for me, whose brain is abundantly nourished with
visions and who have difficulty in separating real life from dreams.'
(As epigraph to *Eureka*, Poe had written 'I offer this book to those
that have put their faith in dreams as the only realities.') When
Nerval started on *Aurélie*, in December 1853, he wrote to Dr.
Blanche: 'I will go on with this series of dreams if you like or I will
start on a play.' The activity was therapeutic. As he said the next
day, in another letter to the doctor, 'I manage in this way to
liberate my mind from the visions that have been populating it for
so long.' This literary relationship between doctor and patient was

to have a direct influence on Artaud's experiences at Rodez, where Dr. Ferdière fancied that he could offer the same kind of help as Dr. Blanche had.

Like Poe, Nerval felt certain that everything in the universe could feel; he wrote of 'a pure spirit under the bark of stones'. He was convinced that sleep was a means of making contact with the world of spirits, and much of his verse rests on the assumption of a correspondence between the minutiae of private life and movement in the universe. He mythologized his own life, merging his identity with that of heroes from past literature. As he wrote in the Preface to *Les Filles du Feu*, 'You incarnate yourself in a hero of your own imagination so well that his life becomes yours. You burn with the artificial flames of his ambitions and loves. . . . Inventing is primarily remembering oneself.' But he invented very little, depending mainly on unexplained juxtapositions between fragments of memory.

As Jean Richer has written of Nerval:

> The poet's universe is characterized by a rejection of both time and incarnation—a fundamental rejection of the human condition. The aspiration towards the superhuman, the Luciferian exploration of consciousness will lead Nerval to use humour, poetry, and finally 'madness' in the effort to escape from himself. . . . The rejection of time and the flight into memory may have been born out of a desire to relive happy moments of early childhood, while the rejection of incarnation may have emerged from a disgust with the lower functions of the body.[3]

By the end of his life Nerval was expressing his sense of alienation from himself in almost the same words as Rimbaud was later to use. On a photograph of himself which he described as 'posthumous' he wrote 'Je suis l'autre'. Rimbaud's words were 'Je est l'autre'.

On 7 March 1946 Artaud drafted a letter to Georges le Breton, who had published two articles on Nerval in the review *Fontaine*. Artaud said he had always felt his life was close to that of Nerval, whose poetry could not be explained by alchemy, mythology, or the Tarot pack: they could be explained by it. It reclaimed characters from them by giving them new life. The poetry is like a supply of nerve-force to the heart. The existence of Nerval was both a cavern and an issuing-bank, a void that served as a crucible for all poetry to be re-minted. As a man who was going to hang himself from a lamp-post in a sordid street, giving his own trans-figuration to the Hanged Man of the Tarot pack, Nerval must have suffered agonies; but he had known how to make them into music.

In these poems, Artaud wrote, there is a drama of spirit, con-sciousness, and heart, advanced by the strangest consonances, not of sounds, but of animation. We find a metamorphosis of the very principle of action. No human being has ever contrived more incredible explosions of language. Nerval has dragged out into daylight the tragedies of a repressed humanity, the tempestuous complaints of the characters he brings to life. During his dealings with alchemical science and with Tarot, there must have been terrifying explosions in his soul. Poets, unlike magicians, have knowledge of the void, of that abyss of horror from which the awakening consciousness has always been trying to escape into something. A world of parturition, not of something, but of nothing. The soul is nothing and knows nothing. Nerval's poems are creatures extricated by him from nothing and through that sombre story which was his life. His suicide can have been nothing other than a protest against expropriation—the expropriation of time, seen from the viewpoint of life revolting against the presence of infinity. His poems accuse God of Original Sin.

Quoting Nerval's line 'And protecting always my Amalechite mother', Artaud argued that the Amalechites believed themselves to be born directly from the earth without any intervention from a Creator, and that, according to the Bible, the Amalechite woman was the first mother who wanted to bring the inmost principle of God to earth, and to incubate it as her own son.

The meaning of the *Chimères* could emerge only when they were spoken aloud: the syllables needed to be 'spat out anew at each reading'. Declaimed like this, Artaud believed the poems could constitute a pure example of Theatre of Cruelty. Air and space were essential to their tonal quality. Similarly, in his letter of 27 November 1945 to Henri Parisot, Artaud had coupled his own manner of declaiming Poe or Baudelaire or Nerval with his interest in the peyote ritual: fundamental to both, as to his Theatre of Cruelty, was his concern to drive out evil spirits. According to this letter, his object in going to the Tarahumaras had been 'to stop *certain magical practices* by which I have always been victimized'.

To denounce Nerval's verse as obscure, he told le Breton, is to withdraw in fear from the possibility of knowing Gérard de Nerval's soul, as if it were infected with the plague. If he was not crucified at Golgotha, at least he was hanged by his own hand, and he would not have suffered from life if life had not been stated in symbols and if, 'desperate and repressed by the ritual of alchemy, the symbols and allegories of creatures had not also been put beyond semination, outside this seeding of tumours and grains which in real life culminates in syphilis or the plague, in suicide or in madness'.

Baudelaire once defined genius as 'childhood clearly formulated' (*l'enfance nettement formulée*) and as the ability to rediscover childhood at will (*l'enfance retrouvée à volonté*). His mother did not die when he was two but remarried when he was ten. Writing before the recent discovery of Baudelaire's early letters, Sartre picked this as the point at which the child 'chose' his destiny. The letters show that the mother had already inflicted profound psychological damage, inculcating both his compulsion to distinguish himself and the habit of emotional withdrawal under the guise of detachment, apathy, ennui. A pattern was established of violent oscillation between hectic activity and remorseful impotence. 'Without explosions I can never find my way out of difficult situations.'

This helps to explain why Baudelaire became a legend during his lifetime. A woman once said to him: 'That's odd—you're very conventional. I thought you were always drunk and feeling ill.' His dandyism was an elaborate system of self-defence. To protect himself from the risk of behaving sincerely and looking ridiculous, he cultivated a pose of aloof inscrutability. But, worn too often, a mask begins to remould the features. Like Poe, whom he called 'the best writer I know', he came to take a Sadean view of Nature, 'which pushes man to kill his fellow-creature, to eat him, to imprison him, to torture him. . . . Nature can recommend nothing but crime. . . . Everything which is beautiful and noble is the result of reason and calculation.'⁴ In his *Journaux intimes* he said: 'The unique and supreme pleasure in making love lies in the certainty of doing evil. The man and the woman know, from birth, that all pleasure resides in evil.'

Like Poe, who believed the imagination was 'a virtually divine faculty', Baudelaire argued in 'Le Salon de 1859' that 'imagination created the world': 'In the beginning of things, imagination created analogy and metaphor. It decomposes all creation, and, with the wealth of materials amassed and ordered according to rules whose origins can be found only in the deepest recesses of the soul, it creates a new world, it produces the sensation of something new.' But it cannot always do this. As he said in his essay on Poe, our instinctive sense of beauty makes us regard the world as 'a glimpse, a correspondence with heaven'. Our thirst for all that lies beyond the world is unquenchable. The emotion that music and poetry can arouse is evidence of 'an impatient melancholy, a clamant demand by our nerves, our nature, exiled in imperfection, which would fain enter into immediate possession, while still on this earth, of a revealed paradise'.

The ambivalence in his attitude towards drug-taking is indicative of a wider-ranging ambivalence. The temptation, he said, is an indication of our thirst for the infinite, and he pondered 'in a philosophic spirit' about the spiritual phenomena they engender.* He also condemns drug-taking. 'Man,' he wrote in his book *Les Paradis artificiels*, 'is not so abandoned, so devoid of honest means of attaining heaven that he must turn for help to chemistry and witchcraft.' In the essay on hashish which prefaces his translation of De Quincey's *Confessions of an English Opium Eater*, Baudelaire complains that 'hashish reveals nothing to the individual except the individual himself. . . . Everyone who does not accept the conditions of life is selling his soul.' We must not try to escape from 'human liberty and indispensable suffering'.

According to Sartre, Baudelaire chose suffering in preference to freedom. It could also be said that he suffered because he had

---

* The original Mexican name for hallucinogenic mushrooms was *teononancatl*, the flesh of God.

glimpsed paradise but remained earthbound, and because he knew that suffering was germane to his literary talent.

> Je sais que la douleur est la noblesse unique
> Ou ne mordront jamais la terre et les enfers
> Et qu'il faut pour tresser ma couronne mystique
> Imposer tous les temps et tous les univers.*

Rimbaud and Artaud were both to be influenced by his emphasis on the importance of suffering and on the visionary aspect of poetry. What Rimbaud had in common with Baudelaire was a talent for integrating extra-sensual emotions with sensual experiences. Like Rimbaud's prose poems in *Les Illuminations*, Baudelaire's in *Le Spleen de Paris* seem to be making spiritual statements through physical juxtapositions. Nerval had said that his verse would lose its charm if it were explained; Baudelaire's prose poems accumulate resonance from the unexplained connections between fragments of internal and external experience. The assumption of a correspondence between minutiae of private life and movements in the universe can generate analogies, metaphors, and pregnant juxtapositions which evoke a vivid impression of spiritual life: Baudelaire spoke of 'almost supernatural' states of soul in which 'familiar sensations are invested with universal significance'. The connections he made between unconnected images create spaces which add up to an absence that suggests a presence. This is why Rimbaud saluted him as 'the first visionary, King of poets, a true God'.

When Lautréamont's poetry was rediscovered at the beginning of the century, André Breton wrote, 'I believe that literature is tending to become for the moderns a powerful machine which is advantageously replacing the old ways of thinking.'

For all these nineteenth-century *poètes maudits*, the relation between life and literature was rather different from what it had been for previous writers. Duchamp gave up painting when he was

---

* 'I know that suffering is the unique nobility / Never eroded by earth or hell / And that to weave my mystic crown / All periods and the whole universe must be made to contribute.'

thirty-one. Rimbaud stopped writing when he was about twenty; he became a businessman in the East, as if his life could cancel his work as an artist in the West. Artaud was later to make his life particularly opaque, as though to counterbalance the transparency of his art; Isidore Ducasse, who died at the age of twenty-seven, made his life particularly transparent, dissolving his identity into his work. He styled himself the Comte de Lautréamont—the first syllable suggests *l'autre*—and in *Les Chants de Maldoror* he merged Lautréamont's identity with Maldoror's, jerking his narrative disruptively backwards and forwards between 'he' and 'I', while deliberately shattering the illusion with contradictions, changes of tense and interruptions, addressing himself (which self?) directly to the reader, reminding him that what he is reading is a written text.

As with Sade and Rimbaud, the violent rebellion against literary convention and the fact of authorship becomes inseparable from the violent rebellion against conventional morality and the idea of God. On the second page of the first 'song', Lautréamont writes:

> I will establish in a few lines how Maldoror was good during the first years of his life, which were happy; that's done. He then noticed that he had been born evil: extraordinary fate. For many years he hid his character as best he could; eventually this concentration, which was unnatural to him, made the blood rise to his head every day; until, unable to go on with such a life, he threw himself resolutely into a career of evil . . . pleasant atmosphere! When he kissed a small pink-faced child, he would have liked to cut its cheeks off with a razor. . . .

One of the most frequently recurrent themes is that of the adolescent's attempts to free himself from domination by the father and by a paternal God. Like Kafka, Isidore Ducasse seems to have been agonized into his artistic identity by an overwhelming mixture of love and dread, resentful reverence and desperate rebellion. This almost intolerable tension makes itself felt stylistically in the tug-of-war between the anarchic impulse and the striving to systematize the narrative structure.

The tangled relations in Ducasse between first person and personae prefigure Artaud's insistence that it wasn't his parents but his works that gave him his existence. Like Kierkegaard,

Ducasse seems to have found it immensely difficult to believe in his own reality, and the whole of the *Chants de Maldoror* could be read as an argument designed to convince himself that he existed. The pain inflicted on the reader by the horrific cruelty is only an overspill of the pain he was inflicting on himself, involuntarily and testingly, like a man thinking up the most frightening possible subjects for nightmares before he goes to sleep. The strategic violations of the illusion in the narrative may have been intended to create the private illusion that the reader was already there, which would have meant that Ducasse was not alone.

The suffering is obvious and unavoidable. He asks himself the same question as the young Artaud: Who is responsible for it? 'Since the unmentionable day of my birth,' he writes, '. . . it is I who wanted it—for no one to take the blame.' But who is speaking? Ducasse, Lautréamont, or Maldoror? 'If I exist, I am not anyone else. I do not admit this equivocal plurality in myself. I want to reside alone in my intimate reasoning. . . . My subjectivity and the Creator, it's too much for one brain.' If he admits that he's saying this to himself, how can he reject the equivocal plurality?

In the amoeba process by which Ducasse separates Lautréamont from himself and Maldoror from Lautréamont, he is allegorizing Baudelaire's figure of the dandy.[5] The debt to Baudelaire is acknowledged explicitly, while the text abounds in echoes of his imagery. Without going as far as Rimbaud, who called himself a 'literaturicide', Lautréamont is more anti-literary than Baudelaire. Artaud's 'Lettre sur Lautréamont' suggests that Lautréamont killed Isidore Ducasse; certainly one could argue that Ducasse identified language with paternalistic authority and launched a suicidal attack on it, goading the floundering subjectivity into the oceanic text, pushing it further and further out of its depth. As Philippe Sollers argues, the articulate subject vanishes. 'As the speaking body is progressively absorbed by the written non-body, it undergoes an animalization, a mineralization, a vegetablization which make it pop up again like a duplicate.' Maldoror says:

> Since I pretend to be unaware that my gaze can kill even planets revolving in space, those who argue that I do not possess the faculty of memory will not be in the wrong. What remains for me to do is to smash this looking-glass into fragments.

'The text,' glosses Sollers, 'which has been searching for "man" in his perceptual, phenomenological, conscious, unconscious alienation, in his "lethargic catalepsies", is going to recreate him in a tidal invasion, an "irreducible mixture of dead matter and living flesh".'[6]

For Maldoror, birth is a wound which only death can heal: 'I have received life like a wound.' The wound, as Sollers suggests, 'consists in the destruction of the speaking subject in his superstition, his fear, and his religion by giving him concrete proof that they have never been anything more than the results of his reductions to representation. . . .'

The self-destructive shifting of the narrative between one level of illusion and another may remind the reader of Laurence Sterne's *Tristam Shandy*, but there is no possibility of comedy here. Like Nerval and Artaud, Lautréamont is engaged in a grim struggle for psychic survival, and he clutches desperately at the same reeds —cabbalistic mysticism, numerology, the superstitious hope that the whole of the past may still exist in the present, to be revealed in dreams, in flashes of illumination, in automatic writing that proceeds out of trance-like concentration. Like Nerval, Lautréamont merges his memories of dreams, of history, and of literature into the adventures of his hero. Images from the Bible are distorted and inverted. The temptation in the Garden of Eden is reversed when Maldoror kills the glow-worm that tempts him to kill the beautiful prostitute. The Crucifixion is turned upside-down in the third stanza of the fourth song, when the man who has refused to sleep with his mother is hanging from the gallows and being tortured both by her and by his wife. This episode is also reminiscent of Baudelaire's 'Le Voyage à Cythère' which was itself reminiscent of Nerval. But Lautréamont describes his art as science. In his *Poésies* he writes: 'The science I undertake is distinct from poetry. I do not sing the latter. I try to discover its source.'

'Real life is absent,' wrote Rimbaud in *Une Saison en Enfer*; Artaud, who echoed the title in 'Fragments d'un journal en Enfer', declared in 'Rimbaud et les modernes' that 'Rimbaud taught us a new way of existing, of behaving in the midst of life.'

It was in the winter of 1870, after reading what Baudelaire had written in *Les Paradis artificiels* about the 'almost supernatural' states of soul which drugs could induce, that the sixteen-year-old Rimbaud talked excitedly to his friend Delahaye about the poet's duty to stop his sensations from becoming blunted. They must be kept constantly alert, even if it meant using stimulants and poisons. On 13 May 1871 he wrote to his teacher, Georges Izambard:

> Now I am debauching myself as much as possible. Why? I want to be a poet and I'm working at making myself into a Visionary (*Voyant*). . . . It's a matter of penetrating to the unknown by means of a disordering (*dérèglement*) of *all the senses*. The suffering is enormous, but you have to be strong if you have been born a poet, and I have recognized that I was. It's not in the least my fault. It's misleading to say 'I think'. One should say 'I am thought'.

Two days later he worked out what he meant in a letter to another friend, Paul Demeny:

> For I is another. If copper wakes up as a bugle, it isn't to be blamed. That's obvious to me: I am present at the hatching of my thought: I see it, I hear it: I touch the strings with the bow: the symphony stirs in the depths or leaps up on to the platform. . . . The poet makes himself into a visionary by means of a long, immense, and calculated disordering of all his senses. All forms of love, suffering, and madness; he searches for himself, he makes himself into a distillery for all poisons, keeping only their quintessences. Unspeakable torture. He needs infinite faith and superhuman strength. Above all others he becomes the sick man, the criminal, the accursed, and the supreme scholar. Because he penetrates to the unknown. Because he has cultivated his soul, which was already rich, more than anyone else has. He has penetrated to the unknown and when, driven mad, he ends by losing all sense of his visions, at least he has had them. Even if he succumbs, in his strivings, to things which are unspeakable and unheard of, other appalling craftsmen will come. They will start from where he stopped.

Jacques Rivière, who called Rimbaud 'the creature exempt from original sin', does not appear to have been reminded by Artaud's letters of Rimbaud's formulation about being present at the hatching of his thought. Buht, thoug Artaud found it impossible to do what Rimbaud claimed he could do, he did his utmost to go on from where Rimbaud had left off, whatever the cost to his health, his peace of mind, and his sanity. For Rimbaud's own abandonment of the task he had set himself implied a recognition that it was impossible.

In his essay 'Le Salon de 1846' Baudelaire had suggested that there was an analogy between colours, sounds and perfumes; Rimbaud developed the idea in his sonnet 'Voyelles'.

> A noir, E blanc, I rouge, U vert, O bleu: voyelles,
> Je dirai quelque jour vos naissances latentes.

But Rimbaud may be thinking not merely of the sound but of the shape each letter has, A suggesting the triangle of pubic hair, E the bosom, I lips, O the violet around the girl's eyes, U divine vibrations of churning, poisonous seas. This is not so much a descriptive as a visionary use of language. As Claudel said about *Une Saison en Enfer*, the thought 'does not proceed through logical development but, as with a musician, by melodic form and the relationship of associated notes'. But the success is only partial. Rimbaud himself later condemns it in the section of *Une Saison en Enfer* titled 'Alchimie du verbe':

> I invented the colour of the vowels!—A black, E white, I red, O blue, U green.—I regulated the shape and movement of each consonant, and, with instinctive rhythms, I flattered myself I had invented a poetic language, accessible, some day or other, to all the senses. . . . I wrote silence and night, I jotted down the inexpressible. I screwed down vertigo. . . . I grew accustomed to simple hallucination: I very frankly saw a mosque in the place of a factory, a school for drummers created by angels, carriages on roadways in the sky, a drawing room at the bottom of a lake; monsters, mysteries. . . .
>
> I finished up by venerating the disorder in my mind as if it were holy. I was lazy, overwhelmed by heavy fever. I envied the happiness of animals.

The compulsion to penetrate into the unknown had implied a rejection of both the known world and normal language. In *Le Bateau ivre* the words had been almost a magical incantation to steer the drifting of the boat-like self tossed about by mystical experiences. It was a heroic effort to transcend all the limitations of language and mental habit, holding his own identity in suspension or displacing it with his discontinuous vision that jumbled fantasy together with observation. He abandoned verse for a dizzying prose in which unrelated images are juxtaposed with a density and intensity that eclipses Lautréamont's prose. Compared with Baudelaire's *Le Spleen de Paris*, *Les Illuminations* is unstructured, anarchic:

> I have clasped the summer dawn.
> Nothing stirred yet on the palace fronts. The water was dead. The legions of shadows had not left the forest road. And I walked, breathing out warm, swift clouds; and precious stones looked out and wings rose without sound.
> The first adventure was, in the path already filled with cool, pale flashes, a flower which told me its name.[7]

As in Lautréamont, the rebellion against literature and language was also a rebellion against God and morality. In 'Matinée d'ivresse' (a section of *Les Illuminations*) he wrote:

> We were promised that the tree of good and evil will be buried in the shade, tyrannical proprieties deported, so that we could continue with our very pure love.

His homosexual relationship with the married Verlaine was itself part of his assault on Christianity, his attempt to repudiate his moral and cultural heritage:

> Priests, professors, masters, you are making a mistake in handing me over to justice. I have never belonged to this people, never been a christian. I am of the race that sang in the torturer's face. I do not understand the laws. I have no moral sense. I am a beast. You are making a mistake.

But he cannot convince himself for long. 'Adieu', the final section of *Une Saison en Enfer*, contains an agonized recantation as he bids a reluctant farewell to 'the rotting rags, the rain-soaked bread, the drunkenness, the thousand loves which crucified me':

> I have created all the festivals, all the triumphs, all the dramas. I have tried to invent new flowers, new stars, new flesh, new languages. I believed I could gain supernatural powers. Well, I must bury my imagination and my memories. What artistic glory—a story-teller who got carried away!

Me! I called myself magus or angel, excused from all morality, here I am, felled. I have to go on looking to make friends with rugged reality. Clodhopper!

Rimbaud could hardly have made a more determined series of efforts to transcend the existing structures of language and literature; he could hardly have admitted defeat more abjectly. He survived to the age of thirty-seven, but without writing anything except letters, many of them to his mother, who, like Baudelaire's and Artaud's, survived her unhappy son.

3

The Young Artaud

Robert Artaud died on 2 June 1901 at the age of three days. A few months later his four-year-old brother Antonin was so ill with what was probably meningitis, that he seemed unlikely to survive. The violent oscillations in his relationship with his mother go back at least as far as this. Later, when he denied the fact of being born, he had no contact with her, but there were long periods, both in childhood and in adult life, when his rapport with her was abnormally close. A Levantine Greek married to her cousin, a shipping agent who was often absent from their home in Marseilles, Euphrasie Artaud bore him nine children, but only three survived their infancy. In 1901, when her youngest was still unborn, the death of Robert left her with only Antonin and his younger sister, Marie-Ange, who developed close, affectionately protective instincts towards each other. That their two grandmothers were sisters made the family bonds all the closer. Surrounded for most of the time by females, the young Antonin was subjected to a bewildering alternation between maternal tenderness and disciplinarian prohibitions, between Greek pastries and unpalatable medicines. Sometimes his powders were mixed with jam to make him swallow them.

From childhood onwards, physical pain obstructed self-expression, while the inarticulacy seemed to foment the frustrations of the physical discomfort. Writing at the age of thirty-five to a sympathetic doctor,* he described

> a sensation of physical remoteness from myself as if I were never again going to control my limbs, my reflexes, my most spontaneous

* Georges Soulié de Morant, 17 February 1932.

mechanical reactions. Also another feeling of hardness and horrible physical fatigue in my tongue when I speak, *the effort of thought* always reverberating physically through all my muscles. My stammer is variable and sometimes it disappears altogether, but it is enormously exhausting. From my earliest childhood (6 to 8 years) I noticed that these periods of stammering and of horrible physical contractions of the facial nerves and the tongue alternated with periods of calm and perfect relaxation.

His father, Antoine-Roi Artaud, had given his first-born son a variant of his own name. As Antonin said later,[1] he lived for twenty-seven years with 'an obscure hatred of the Father, of my father particularly'. It was only when he died, that Antonin forgave him for

> this inhuman harshness he trod me down with. Another being left his body. And for the first time in my life, this father opened his arms to me. And I, who am embarrassed at my body, understood that throughout his life he had been embarrassed at his body and that there is a lie in existence which we are born to resist.

From other statements made in later life, it is clear that the child oscillated between guilt and resentment, between self-accusation and silent hostility towards the incomprehensible grown-ups grouped round the mother, who had presented him with a painful life of dubious value:

> From the age of eight and even earlier I remember constantly asking myself who I was, what I was and why live. . . . What it was to exist and to live, what it was to see myself breathe and to have wanted to breathe to prove the reality of life and to see whether it was desirable and if so why. I asked myself why I was there and what existence consisted of.[2]

He must have seen his own life and his own illness in the perspective of the illnesses that had killed his siblings. Were the authoritarian doctors who dispensed unpleasant medicines friends or enemies, protectors or torturers? It was when he was eight that his baby sister Germaine died. Of all the deaths this one seems to have been the most traumatic for him. Later he spoke of her as his daughter: 'Germaine Artaud, strangled at seven months.'

Who was his mother? Giver of life or taker? She overwhelmed

him with affection and then, abruptly, withdrew it. Apparently he soon became as prone as she was to accesses of hysterical rage. She had given him his identity and his nickname, Nanaqui, diminutive of the Greek name, Antonaki, and almost homonymous with Neneka, the nickname of her mother, Mariette Schily. She had a very close relationship with her grandson, often coming from Smyrna to visit the Artauds at Marseilles, while they often took holidays at Smyrna to be with her. Antonin was nearly drowned there when he was about ten. In adult friendships with women he clung to his childhood nickname, often signing letters with it. Writing to Anaïs Nin in June 1933, he said that his mother had given him the name when he was four. 'It describes me in the most innocent and purest part of my life.'

He was sent to a Catholic school, the Collège du Sacré Cœur. Under the Romantic pseudonym Louis des Attides he wrote verse which he published in the schoolboy magazine he started with a friend. None of his earliest poems have survived, but the influence of Baudelaire is apparent in the verse written between 1913 and 1915. He was also reading Poe.

The closeness of his emotional dependence on his mother is illustrated by a letter written to her in 1911:

> Forgive, I beg you to forgive a guilty son, a repentant heart. Oh! mama, I love you more than anything in the world, I love you, and I am tortured with remorse at what I did. I am mad. I am a monster but forgive me. What madness possesses me to do such things. Oh! I love you and I could never repeat it often enough, how enormous my sin is, but how good you are. . . . When I have deserved it, kiss me and may I then be forgiven for always, may I never fall back into the error. After each disobedience I am full of regret and I weep, but help me, make me think of my love for you and my duty to become good.
>
> God help me to reform myself. Oh mama I love you.[3]

During the twenties, in his relationship with the actress Génica Athanasiou, he would swing similarly between violent rage and abjectly apologetic professions of desperate need.

In 1914 or 1915 Artaud tried to destroy everything he had written and to dispose of all his books. When the crisis was over he was sent to a sanatorium not far from Marseilles. The letter of 1932 to Soulié de Morant dates his 'psychic problems' as having appeared in the open when he was nineteen. The following year, 1916, he was well enough to pass an army medical examination, but after nine months of military service he was released, partly because of ill health.

Still a practising Catholic, he would pray for several hours each day and there was still no conflict between his mystical cravings and religious orthodoxy.

At first he was shunted from one nursing home to another. By the summer of 1918 he had been at St. Dizier, near Lyons, at Lafoux-les-Bains, and at Divonne. Here he became friendly with a young painter, Yvonne Gilles, and went on sending her letters and poems for several years. In July he went into the Pyrenees, taking a cure at Bagnères de Bigorre and making excursions into the mountains. But at the end of the year, when he was sent to a Swiss clinic near Neuchâtel, he stayed for two years. It was the medical director there, Dr. Dardel, who finally recommended Dr. Edouard Toulouse, the progressive psychiatrist who was so impressed with the young Antonin Artaud when his father brought him to Villejuif in 1920.

Two new factors: Artaud was now in Paris, and Toulouse was a literary doctor who, since 1912, had been editing a review called *Demain,* 'dedicated to thinking and to a better life—Organ of integrated hygiene for the conduct of intellectual, moral, and physical life'. Artaud not only became involved in editorial work, but contributed poems, articles, and reviews of art exhibitions and plays. Mme Toulouse seems to have been one of the first to spot the Rimbaudesque element in his writing. In a letter to her written at the end of July 1921 from Marseilles, he said:

> No, familiarity with Rimbaud is not what is surfacing in what I do; it's a matter of having identical preoccupations. Strangely enough I have read Rimbaud only once, and for poems like his, especially the ones in prose, that's nothing. With Edgar Poe it's quite another matter. He can be said to have influenced me. Besides, we must wait till I have really expressed myself. So far I have written only one or two poems which give a glimpse of what I could be. What is also

needed is to be in possession of the TOTALITY of one's mind which is something I have never achieved.

In the middle of June 1922 he was writing to her again, asking her to send him the works of Rimbaud.

The Poe influence is strikingly apparent in two brief stories, 'L'Assomption' and 'Le Pion aux lunettes bleues', written about 1921–2. In an atmosphere of drugged nightmare, the characters meet surrealistically violent deaths, but euphoria breaks like sunlight through the gloom and the doom: 'The grim morning split into two parts. An inexpressible satisfaction permeated our flower fingers, and the wind filled our gowns like sails, like the water in swollen stones.'

It was through Dr. Toulouse that Artaud met the director Lugné-Poe, who offered him a walk-on in Henri de Régnier's play *Les Scrupules de Sganarelle*. Though the young man was immune neither to vanity about the beauty of his face nor to the appeal of exhibitionism, his involvement in theatre was, from the beginning, partly religious in its motivation. Like the church, the theatre could be an arena for making statements about the inner life, statements that depended not merely on words, but on atmosphere, gesture, costume, music, inflection, décor, procession, and possibly even incense. The reaction from the congregation or audience would be partly conscious, partly unconscious, partly physical, partly mental, perhaps partly spiritual.

Artaud was only twenty when he conceived a project for 'spontaneous theatre' to be created by a group of actors which would give performances in factories, travelling about like Elizabethan strolling players. At the same time, habitual drug-taking must have played a part in fomenting his disenchantment with words. If, in 1923, it was already difficult for him to catch up with his intellectual being, to find verbal coefficients for the intimate promptings of his tormented body, the drugs he took to relieve pain could only exacerbate the problem, inducing, as they do, vague impressions of universal correspondences, tilting the intelligence away from the planes of rationalism. As Artaud wrote in 'Manifeste en langage clair' (December 1925),

My mind, weary with discursive reasoning, wants to be caught up in the works of a new, an absolute force of gravity. For me it is like an overwhelming reorganization determined only by the laws of unreason and the triumphant discovery of a new faculty. This sense is lost in the chaos of drugs, which gives contradictory dreams the semblance of profound intelligence. This faculty is a conquest of mind over itself, though it cannot be reduced to reason, it exists, but only on the inside of the mind. It is order, it is intelligence, it is the signification of chaos. But it does not accept this chaos as it is: it interprets it, and in doing so, loses it.

Theoretically he recognized the loss; but mostly he went on writing as though it did not occur.

Both before and after his rejection of Catholic dogma, his thinking was resolutely anti-dualistic: internal and external experience must integrate. Art must hold up a mirror to consciousness, as consciousness must to reality. Language, whether verbal or non-verbal, must express the 'intellectual apprehensions of the flesh'. Acting, therefore, should involve not merely the body and the voice but the mind and the spirit. After joining Charles Dullin's company, where he had his first experience of improvisation, he described it as forcing the actor 'not to represent his spiritual movements but to *think* them'.

Artaud had a natural instinct for the theatrical, but it was to his face that he owed his initial run of luck in securing work as an actor. His first employer, Lugné-Poe, later wrote⁴ that he had responded to 'the poetic flame in the spirit of Antonin Artaud' though the young man's hesitant diction 'made it difficult for him to get started'. Artaud was cast as a man woken up in the middle of the night and, like the playwright, Lugné-Poe was delighted with the characterization achieved by 'this astonishing artist. . . . His make-up, his poses were those of an artist lost among actors.' He described Artaud as 'sensitive in the highest degree, intelligent, tormented with beauty'. But he never again employed him.

In April Artaud started writing for *L'Ère nouvelle*. His second article, 'Maurice Magre et la féerie', was about a writer whose evocations of enchantment were interwoven with references to opium. 'Why does this subject have to be decorated with tinsel?' asked Artaud. 'Why does he have to dress up his seductive phantoms with an old stock of down-at-heel images? . . . And since he has sung of opium, he has been able to derive an unprecedented resonance from everyday circumstances.'

Through Dr. Toulouse, Artaud met the writer Max Jacob, a friend of Charles Dullin, who had founded a theatrical company, l'Atelier, and was also running a school for actors. Mentioning Max Jacob's name, Artaud wrote to Dullin, but before he received a reply, he met another friend of Dullin's, the actor Firmin Gémier, who auditioned him and recommended him. As soon as he met Dullin, he was accepted.

Dullin had originally intended to be a priest; Artaud's letter of thanks to Max Jacob (about October 1921) described the work: 'It's all based on such a striving towards moral propriety . . . and on artistic principles which are so carefully thought out, so studied. . . . In listening to Dullin's teaching one has the feeling of rediscovering ancient secrets and a quite forgotten mystique of production.' He also wrote to Yvonne Gilles about Dullin:

> His own principles of teaching are applied with the object of *interiorizing* the actor's activity. Beyond the clarification of the scene, he seeks for renovation or rather novelty. He wants his productions to give the impression of never having been seen. Everything takes place in the soul. . . . His ideal is the Japanese actor who plays without props. The gods of the school are not Tolstoy, Ibsen, or Shakespeare but Hoffmann and Edgar Poe. . . . It's curious, to say the least, that with my tastes, I've happened on something so in tune with my mentality.

At the same time, as Artaud wrote in 1922, Dullin was introducing French audiences to 'the conquests of Gordon Craig, of Appia, of all these emancipators of the theatre'. Without making any concessions to 'the old tricks', Dullin was doing more than any of his precursors towards a rediscovery of 'the whole theatre, the theatre of the past and future'.

But Artaud did not find it easy to adapt himself to the communal life of the school. As Dullin later wrote,

> In spite of his shirt collar, which always had a button missing and which was held in place with some difficulty by a badly knotted rag of a tie, and despite the negligent way he turned himself out, he had something of the dandy about him—enough to prevent him from

harnessing himself with us to the cart which carried our scenery and costumes from the rue Honoré Chevalier to the rue Ursulines. He followed us at a distance—a little ashamed.

Apart from that, his application and willingness were exemplary, except with the mechanical exercises in diction. He energetically refused to do these.[5]

Artaud had less respect than Dullin for the proprieties of realism. Already attracted to the techniques of Oriental theatre, he used a make-up based on a Chinese mask to play a member of the town council in Pirandello's *The Pleasure of Honesty*. Dullin was not pleased.

At the school Artaud formed what was to be the closest of all his relationships with women (after the one with his mother), with the Romanian actress Génica Athanasiou, who had come to Paris in 1919 and been a pupil of Dullin's since 1920. She was four months younger than Artaud. Quick to recognize her talent, Dullin used her in the summer of 1921 when he presented the first production of his studio company in a barn at Moret-sur-Loing. Artaud met her in the autumn when Dullin brought the company to play at the Salle Pasdeloup in Paris. He did not make his début as an actor there until February 1922, but they did classes together, and on the way out from one of the rehearsals in the autumn of 1921, without saying a word to her, he slipped a folded piece of paper into her hand. She opened it to read:

> The marvellous night chirping with stars
> Which gazes at us from the empyrean centre
> Is less than equal to your milky face
> And the lunar flowers of your topaze eyes.

Their friendship developed quickly. He confided in her, sympathized, empathized. As with the writers and painters whose work he loved, his admiration was osmotic. Creating his own image of her, he wanted to recreate himself with a greater resemblance to her. In the summer, writing to her from Marseilles, he called her his 'other soul' and seemed delighted to acknowledge the influence she was having on his prose: 'You see, I am writing in your style now, without intending to, don't you find?' Soon he would find that his handwriting had come to resemble hers.

From the references in these letters to her spiritual qualities, it seems that he had been deeply affected by the experience of working with Génica, especially in the improvisations. Joining in the exercises himself, Dullin would make his actors impersonate a wind, a fire, or a vegetable, sometimes a dream or a mental event. As Artaud wrote in an article on the company's work, 'To feel, to live, truly to think—that should be the aim of the real actor. The Russians have long been using a method of improvisation which forces the actor to work from the depths of his sensitivity, to exteriorize this true and personal sensitivity with words, gestures, mental reactions invented on the spot, improvised.'[6]

Génica was regularly cast in leading juvenile parts and, after getting his first speaking role as Anselme in Molière's *L'Avare*, Artaud played opposite her in March 1922, when Dullin cast him as Galvan, the Moorish king, in Alexandre Arnoux's *Moriana et Galvan*. They both had parts in the other half of the double bill, *Le Divorce* by Regnard, and in the next production, *L'Hôtellerie* by Francesco de Castro (April). In Calderón's *Life Is a Dream* (June) she played Estrella, while he made considerable impact with his characterization of Basilio, the King of Poland. Writing in June 1922 to Yvonne Gilles, he described the role as having 'a prodigious range, somewhat in the manner of King Lear'. In this production he also designed the sets and costumes.

They separated in the summer, when he went home to Marseilles. In a letter dated 20 July 1922 she wrote 'My very dear one, I say goodbye to you from this room where I leave a part of my life which was much loved, especially towards the end.' Writing to her on the same day, he said: 'I mix you into everything I do. She would be *there*. She would say *that*. . . . It is only today that I can again find my thoughts. Yesterday and the day before, I couldn't write. I had nothing but vague images in my brain, sick images, as of twilight or the end of autumn.'

His letter describes a visit to the Colonial Exhibition. 'I had an impression of desolation, and also of calm and freshness. Sun, bright frocks. I thought of your frocks.' He must have seen the giant reconstruction of the Angkor temple and the Cambodian dancers who performed in it, but he does not seem to have been particularly impressed, though already he was thinking of his personal problem in terms of duplication, displacement, deviation from the self. In 'Le Poème de St François d'Assise' he wrote:

> I am this eternal absence from myself
> Always going near my own path

'You are always with me,' he wrote to Génica on 31 July. 'Whatever I do, your image is there, looking at me, judging me, sharing in what I do.' Physical pain was still driving him to opium, but he was fighting more vigorously against his dependence on it. 'I am now making a great effort', he told her in the same letter, 'to *give up* opium. And that is causing me frightful suffering. I am taking only a quarter as much and at longer and longer intervals.'

As in the deep involvements with the work of other writers, there was a total fusion of the sensual and intellectual elements in his response to Génica. Writing to her from Hyères, where he spent three days in August, he said: 'You have a delicious soul. French people can't write in the way you do. One feels one is drinking your soul, imbibing your marrow. . . . Because you express yourself TOTALLY, you produce phrases a greater writer would envy.'

From Hyères he went on to Cavalaire, a health resort. A letter of 11 August from there develops the idea that art is the *double* of life, a duplicate of reality. (In the language of the sorcerer, the *double* is the immaterial body that reproduces a person's image.) 'We have a spirit so made that it spends its life looking for itself, seeking not even the words but *mental state, palpable or felt*, which corresponds to ITS spirit. In becoming conscious, it duplicates itself, and once the state exists, the words always come. The difficulty is to fix the state, to maintain it, to *prolong* it.' Moments of excited insight came as bright intervals during periods of pain and depression. After writing the letter of 11 August, he had five days of neurasthenic inertia. 'My consciousness became inarticulate. I could no longer read, write, or think. I had no material thought, so to speak, because inside I was deeper, but incapable of expressing myself, paralysed.'

His reunion with Génica that autumn, coinciding with the

resumption of work on the stage, did bring him a respite from suffering. Artaud very seldom used the word 'happy' about his own experience, but in May 1923 he wrote to her: 'A year already. A year of total, absolute love. It's beautiful. I'm happy and it's through you. . . . I squeeze you in my arms. I make you enter me.' The letter is signed 'Naky'.

In October 1922 Dullin had taken over the theatre on the Place Dancourt, giving it the name it still has, the Théâtre de l'Atelier. The successful production of *Life Is a Dream* was revived there with Génica and Artaud in their old parts. In *La Condamnation de Banquet*, a verse adaptation by Roger Semichon of a sixteenth-century morality play by Nicole de la Chesnaye, she played Colic while he play Apoplexy.

Meanwhile he was writing prolifically, contributing to the review *Images de Paris*, and submitting verse to *Nouvelles littéraires* and *Mercure de France*, which published four of his poems in its December issue. He was also preparing eight poems for his first collection, which was to be published under the title *Tric-Trac du Ciel* by Daniel Henry Kahnweiler, owner of the Galerie Simon in the rue d'Astorg. Like Pierre Loeb's gallery, it also functioned as a small publishing house.

In December Artaud played Tiresias in Cocteau's thirty-minute adaptation of Sophocles' *Antigone*. Génica had the name part and Dullin was Creon. The décor was by Picasso, the costumes by Coco Chanel, the music by Honneger. The dress rehearsal was interrupted by two rival factions, purists who objected to Cocteau's treachery towards Sophocles, and Surrealists, led by André Breton, who objected to Cocteau's worldliness. Cocteau made an entrance on the stage to say: 'Go away, Monsieur Breton. We will go on when you have left the auditorium.'

In February 1923 Artaud played the role of a badly made marionette in Jacinto Grau's play *Monsieur de Pygmalion*. According to Fernand Tourret, 'Artaud made the character into a melo-dramatic villain, brushing against the scenery, simian, sly, ignoble.'[7] Twenty-five years later Dullin wrote: 'He had a very great personal success . . . playing a sort of incarnation of the spirit of evil, with the name Urdemalas. I can still hear him pronouncing this name as he brandishes his whip.'[8]

His last role at the Atelier was the Emperor Charlemagne in Alexandre Arnoux's play *Huon de Bordeaux*. Reviewing the production on 22 March 1923, Marcel Achard wrote that Artaud

> rose through ridicule to grandeur. It would be impossible to be less genuine, to introduce more vain grandiloquence into lyricism, to simulate the excitement of being in command more artificially. He gave the great emperor an improbable voice and a tormented appearance, remaining extraordinarily antipathetic.

In rehearsal Artaud had made one of his entrances on all fours, crawling towards the throne, and he had dismissed Dullin's protest with contempt. ('If it's realism you want, oh well!') The quarrel may have helped to terminate one of the best working relationships of Artaud's career.

He did not have to wait long for his next engagement, which was with Georges Pitoëff, who cast him as the Prompter in a production of Pirandello's *Six Characters in Search of an Author* at the Comédie des Champs-Elysées. But when Artaud disappeared a few days before the dress rehearsal, the role was recast. When he came back, he was forgiven but relegated to a smaller part. Writing to Génica on 6 May, he said: 'I think Pitoëff has a certain esteem for me, and perhaps even something that could be called deference, not because of what I do for him but because of what I can be.'

In the next production, Shaw's *Androcles and the Lion*, which opened in the middle of May, Artaud played Retiarius. Meeting him a couple of days after the first night, Lugné-Poe promised him roles in Strindberg's *Ghost Sonata* and Ibsen's *John Gabriel Borkman*, also inviting him to write a play. While he was rehearsing for the next production, Ferenc Molnar's *Liliom*, which opened at the Comédie des Champs-Elysées in June, he was offered a contract for the following season. Though he accepted, he seems already to have been at the threshold of his disillusionment with acting as a métier. He loved the moments of creative discovery in improvisation or rehearsal; he hated the element of repetition, which bulks so large in performance. To Jean Hort, who shared a dressing-room with him, he complained that an actor was no more than an instrument or a photograph. His function was 'to repeat what has been done already'.

In a book published in 1960 Jean Hort described the impression Artaud made on him:

> I can still see him in the grey suit he always wore. It looked so tight on him, he seemed to have grown overnight. The sleeves of the jacket were too short, so the rounded cuffs of his white, soft-collared shirt projected exaggeratedly. . . . At moments of relaxation on stage, he scarcely looked twenty, though he was twenty-seven, but as soon as he went into action, his intensely tormented acting made him seem to grow, transformed him, made him look any age. . . . I can still see his pale complexion, his shadowed cheeks where the incessant puckering had not yet formed permanent lines. The bright chestnut hair was still planted low on his brow. . . . I can still see his flashing, blue-green eyes, often feverish, his frail body, never strengthened by exercise. And his long, forked hands which constantly ran through his hair when anguish seized him.

Within three weeks of the happy letter written to Génica on 6 May 1923 Artaud was miserable again, begging her to write to him, worrying about her health, complaining that other actors in the company were paid more than he was, nervous about money. 'I have been like a lost cat since not having you with me. . . . I am writing this, very late at night, at the Eden Chope, where I take refuge every evening to write, read, and think about you.' Being alone now, he was spending more time at the café, which cost more money than he could afford. The only consolation was that Kahnweiler had responded so positively to some new verse written for Génica: it represented an authentically contemporary state of mind, he said.

By now Artaud's feelings about the separation between experience and expression had begun to project into the view he was forming of the cultural situation: it was Western culture that was driving a wedge between the two. In his Preface to an anthology of Dr. Toulouse's writings, published in 1923 under the title *Au fil des préjugés*, Artaud wrote: 'There are distortions of thought, mental habits, in fact vices, which contaminate our judgement almost at the moment of its birth. . . . After thought, after the form and the nature of thought, come the applications of thought.'

Lugné-Poe
(1869–1940) who
gave Artaud a
walk-on in *Les
Scrupules de
Sganarelle* in
February 1921

Charles Dullin
(1885–1949) tak-
ing a class at his
school

Jacques Rivière (1886–1925) and (*right*) Jean Paulhan (1884–1968) who succeeded him as editor of *La Nouvelle Revue Française*

In his Preface to Maeterlinck's *Douze chansons* (1923), Artaud praised the poet for 'a certain way of unifying—by virtue of whatever mysterious analogies—a feeling and an object, putting them on the same mental plane without recourse to metaphor'. Artaud goes on to quote the Talmud: ' "God's self is unknowable but his ways are expressed by numbers and symbols." The nature of these *numbers* eludes the majority of men, but Maeterlinck has focused them in lapidary phrases.' Artaud had now begun to take an interest in mysticism and Eastern culture.

The argument of *Le Théâtre et son double* is anticipated by the last four paragraphs of the Maeterlinck Preface: 'Drama is the highest form the mind can take. It is in the nature of profound things to collide, combine, develop deductively. Activity is the very principle of life.' But, though Maeterlinck had an intense feeling for the 'symbolic meaning of things, their secret transactions', his poetry could not reintegrate the object 'in its pure state of being an object handled by real hands. The feeling remained literary. That is the ransom of twelve centuries of French poetry.'

In the winter of 1923, when Artaud brought out the second and final issue of his miniature literary review *Bilboquet*—the first had appeared in February—he praised Jean Paulhan's *Le Pont traversé* for showing how human thought behaves in relation to dreams, and for revealing the stratifications in human thinking 'with infinitely more tact, felicity and certainty than Maeterlinck reveals the uncertain occurrences in the soul'. In the same issue he praised Paul Klee for 'his mental syntheses conceived like architecture' and for 'some cosmic syntheses which brings out into the open all the secret objectivity of things'. Jacques Rivière's *Aimée* was attacked: he seemed 'to work on a kind of dead matter, with each of its states fixed for ever'.

For his part, Artaud was trying to swim against the mainstream of French literature. As he said in the Preface to *Tric-Trac du Ciel*, a man can make himself feel welcome only when he rediscovers himself at the highest point of his self. 'Then nothing is being repudiated—not feeling, nor liaison with what is above, nor domination by mind.'

Artaud's extreme mental lucidity was sometimes swamped by the inertia that came with illness; sometimes it survived alongside the pain and depression, but he could have no confidence about the future. 'If, in six months from now,' he wrote to Dr. Toulouse towards the end of August 1923, 'my health has not achieved an equilibrium, I will withdraw from normal life, retiring to a very remote spot in the mountains or by the sea. . . . Here I am again in Marseilles, where I am again having feelings of numbness and dizziness, of a sudden and MAD need for sleep, of INSTANTANEOUS *stupefaction*, of sudden loss of strength accompanied by an enormous grief.' By November, when he was back in Paris, the feeling of numbness had given way to increasingly violent headaches, and his misery was intensified by an inability to settle anywhere. He wrote on 12 November to Mme Toulouse that after moving over fifty times from one hotel to another, he was sleeping almost at random in the homes of chance acquaintances. He was later thrown out of a room he rented in the rue Troyon after causing a flood by trying to drown a mouse.

By now he was in the middle of his correspondence with Jacques Rivière, which was to end with a letter* still more reminiscent of Rimbaud's† claim that he was present at the hatching of his thought:

> to have in oneself the inseparable reality and the material clarity of a feeling, to have it at the point where it cannot but express itself, to have a wealth of words and syntactic devices which could join in the dance, be brought into play; and just when the soul is getting ready to organize its wealth, its discoveries and this revelation—at this unconscious moment when the thing is on the point of emerging—a superior and malicious will attacks the soul like acid. . . . I ask nothing more than to feel my brain.

Struggling against illness, depression, drug-addiction, and financial anxiety, he found that each exacerbated the others. On 6 July 1923, he wrote to Génica from Marseilles: 'I cannot count on getting even another centime from my family', and, three days later: 'In the last few days I have truly believed I would die, in the real sense of the word. Imagine that: a general feeling of numbness and intense feebleness which is grief at the same time. My arms are as heavy as lead, while my legs do not know where my body is.'

* 6 June 1924.   † See above, p. 32.

His spirits rallied when she spent a few days with him in August, but on the 31st he wrote that he had again begun to suffer like the damned on the day after her departure, and, two days later, 'My suffering is so intense that my soul seems about to snap, that I am going to faint with grief.'

Emotionally he felt totally dependent on her. 'Every gesture I make, it seems to be you who are shaping it, giving it a direction.' But he sensed that her letters were becoming less affectionate. On 8 September he wrote: 'I no longer have the strength to be tender.' Nor did the start of the new theatre season provide anything of the tonic excitement it had previously offered: 'I am as undecided as I possibly could be,' he wrote on 14 September, 'about resuming the theatrical life which has completely ceased to interest me.' He was not only failing in his struggle against the drug, but failing to keep her as his ally. On 22 October he wrote:

> You are a criminal not to have pity on my distress, my grief, my torment. I shall not give up the poison until my state of health permits, and we shall remain together all that time, because you will not have the cruelty to abandon me in my misery. . . . I feel like howling when I read you, not because of what you say, but because you are obstinate, irremediably. . . . My frightful destiny has for a long time put me *beyond human reason*, outside life. Understand that for just one hour of real peace I would give up my life. I shall be capable of killing myself immediately if you write to me once more in the same terms.

She must have written back blaming his tone on the opium. Two days later he wrote: 'Ask my mother, if you know her. She will tell you that I have always been pitiless to those close to me, and well before the opium started.' Within a month he was threatening Génica that if she again mentioned the word opium, he would tear up the letter without reading any further.

He did resume his theatrical life in the autumn but the roles he was given were less interesting than in the previous season. He was cast as Jackson in Andreyev's *He Who Gets Slapped*, and in March 1924, when *Six Characters in Search of an Author* was revived, he finally played the Prompter. In Karel Čapek's R.U.R. he played the puppet Marius.

Meanwhile, his film career had begun. He was cast in an

important role in Claude Autant-Lara's first film, *Fait Divers*, and in April, working at the theatre during the evenings, he was filming during the day. 'Painting now bores me,' he wrote in April to Yvonne Gilles, 'and so does literature and even the theatre. I am making this film, playing my first part, trying to become a star and make a little money.'

4

Film Actor and Surrealist

Though it became less euphoric, Artaud's enthusiasm for cinema was not short-lived. During August 1929 he told an interviewer that he would feel compelled to give up acting if a film role ever made him feel cut off from himself, from what he thought and felt, but he appears to have found that interesting roles offered gratifying opportunities for a kind of self-transcendence. The good film actor, he said, 'does what no one would be able to do, what he himself could not do in his normal state'.

Dissatisfied though he later became with his performance in the spectacular adventure film *Surcouf—le roi des corsaires*, he enjoyed the shooting in and around St. Malo. Playing Morel, a man piqued by sexual jealousy into betraying the heroic privateer, he took pleasure in the identification—'The traitor Morel is not different from me,' he wrote to Génica on 29 July 1924—and in the impression he was making on the other actors.

> They all thought I was amazing, they said. I run like a madman among the ruins and go to throw myself from the top of a tower, falling to the beach. . . . There is a close-up of me driven to despair, and me beating my head against a wall, then gesticulating from the top of the tower, then falling . . . then you see my body crumpled on the sand. It moves convulsively a few times. You see my battered face raising itself. Then I fall back, definitely dead.

He tried hard to infect Génica with his new enthusiasm, advising her to abandon Dullin in favour of a more commercial career in boulevard theatre and films. But his high estimate of her potential as a film star failed to take the edge off her jealousy over the friendship developing between him and Maria Panthès, a young pianist friend of Kahnweiler's.

Artaud's uncle, Louis Nalpas, had been director of the important film company Le Film d'Art, which had produced Abel Gance's 1915 film *La Folie du Docteur Tube*, so it was easy for him to persuade Gance to meet Artaud, who wrote to Mme Toulouse about the interview in October 1924: 'My face, he said, was of great interest and so was my *mentality*.' The conversation ended with the firm promise of a role in a film about Napoleon. Artaud was never to act on stage again except in his own productions, and the violence of his abrupt reaction against the theatre is clear from a letter he wrote in February 1925 to the Administrator of the Comédie Française:* 'Your brothel is too greedy. Representatives of a dead art should try to stop bursting our eardrums. Tragedy has no need of a Rolls Royce nor prostitution of jewellery.'

It was in October 1924 that Artaud joined the Surrealist movement, not long after André Breton had steered it away from Dadaism. Neither Tristan Tzara nor Hans Arp became members of the new group, but it included Louis Aragon, Philippe Soupault, Paul Eluard, and Benjamin Péret, who had all been Dadaists. Writing to Rivière in June 1924, Artaud had cited Breton and Tzara as examples of a weakness from which 'the whole epoch suffers'—a 'psychological weakness which affects the very substance of what is usually called the soul and which is the emanation of our nervous strength, coagulated around objects'. But whereas their souls were affected only 'at the points of making contact with something else', Artaud's was 'physiologically impaired. . . . This detachment from the object which characterizes all literature is in my case a detachment from life. . . . I can say, truthfully, that I am not in the world.'

At the beginning of October he wrote to Mme Toulouse: 'I have met all the Dadaists who wanted to entice me on to their latest Surrealist boat, but nothing doing. I'm much too much of a surrealist for that. Besides, I always have been.' But on his return

* We do not know whether this letter was posted. It may have been designed, like the diatribes against the Pope and the Dalai Lama, for publication in *La Révolution surréaliste*.

to Paris from St. Malo, his feeling must have changed. His decision to join the movement had been taken before 10 November, when his photograph appeared in the first issue of *La Révolution surréaliste*, co-edited by Pierre Naville and Benjamin Péret. The *centrale surréaliste* or Bureau of Research had just been opened at 15 rue de Grenelle. As Aragon put it, it was 'a romantic Inn for unclassifiable ideas and continuing revolts. All that still remained of hope in this despairing universe would turn its last, raving glances towards our pathetic stall.'[1] The Surrealists advertised in the newspapers that they would welcome all bearers of secrets— inventors, madmen, revolutionaries, misfits, dreamers.[2] The cover of *La Révolution surréaliste* carried the slogan: 'We must formulate a new declaration of human rights,' and the Preface said that if 'it is realism to prune trees, it is surrealism to prune life'. The issue contained examples of automatic writing; descriptions of dreams by three surrealists including André Breton; a statement by Pierre Reverdy, who argued that dream is 'a freer, more abandoned form of thought'; excerpts from newspaper accounts of suicides; and the photograph of a murderess surrounded by photographs of Freud, Chirico, Picasso, and members of the group, including Aragon, Robert Desnos, Eluard, Max Ernst, Man Ray, Philippe Soupault, and Roger Vitrac.

The new confidence Artaud had acquired as a film actor helped him to prominence among the Surrealists. On 26 January 1925 he became director of the *centrale surréaliste*, and the next day he published a revolutionary tract, defining surrealism as 'a means of totally liberating the spirit and everything which resembles it'. As Susan Sontag has suggested, he 'took the Surrealist state of mind as a model for the unified, non-dualistic consciousness he sought'. This is not to deny the strength of conviction behind his commitment to a group of writers and artists who were launching the strongest possible attack on literature and art. 'We have nothing to do with literature,' Artaud asserted in the tract, 'but like the rest of the world we are quite capable of exploiting it when we need to.' The juxtaposition of the words 'surrealism' and 'revolution', he said, were to indicate the 'disinterested, detached, and even quite desperate character of this revolution'.

Though Breton claimed Baudelaire as a 'surrealist in his morality' and Rimbaud as 'surrealistic in the way he lived', Artaud did not have much in common with the other members of the group. According to Breton's 1924 manifesto, surrealism implied 'Dictation by thought in the absence of all restraint from reason and outside all moral or aesthetic preoccupation.' Unlike most of the Surrealists, Artaud never practised automatic writing, and temperamentally he was more depressive, less of a life-affirmer than the others, but he did share their anti-rationalism, and their belief that dreams told the truth. More important, he could feel, as he had when he joined Dullin's company, that he was not alone: and for the first time in his life he was a leader. On 18 April 1925, speaking in Madrid, Aragon said, 'I announce the advent of a dictator. Antonin Artaud is the man who has attacked the ocean. Today he takes on the huge task of dragging forty men who want to be dragged towards an unknown abyss. . . . He will have respect for nothing—not your schools, your lives, or your most secret thoughts.'

'1925, End of the Christian Era', was the caption on the cover of the third issue of *La Révolution surréaliste*, edited by Artaud, who wrote most of it himself. It was published on 15 April. 'Watch out for your logic,' warned the opening article. 'You don't know how far our hatred for logic will carry us.' In 'Rêve' he depicted himself as one of three men who were dressed as monks. They had put on long robes to hide their sin. His mother was dressed as an abbess and his sister was one of the women that the men hunted down, taking them on tables, in the corners of chairs, on the staircases. So Catholic imagery and morbid guilt survived alongside his surrealist iconoclasm. In his 'Adresse au Pape' he pointed out that, like the other gods, 'Your Catholic and Christian god . . . thought up all the evil. . . . From top to bottom of your Roman masquerade, what triumphs is hatred of the soul's immediate truths. . . . Neither the earth nor God is speaking through you.' What Artaud had said in the first person singular to Rivière less than twelve months earlier is now translated into the first person plural: 'We are not in the world.' It has also become a boast—the Pope, by contrast, is 'confined to the world'. Turning to address the Dalai Lama ('Oh, acceptable Pope, oh true Pope in the spirit'), Artaud prayed: 'Give us your illumination in a language that our contaminated European minds can understand . . . adjust our minds to those summits of perfection where the human spirit will no longer suffer.' And in his 'Lettre aux Ecoles de Bouddha' he complained: 'It is from other needs than those inherent in life that our mind is suffering.'

Like much of the Surrealists' most revolutionary work, Artaud's *L'Ombilic des Limbes* appeared under the imprint of a conservative publisher, Editions Nouvelle Revue Française, in July 1925. 'There where others put forward their works,' it began, 'I claim nothing but to show my mind. Life consists of burning up questions. I do not conceive of works as separate from life.' Artaud was beginning to turn his disadvantages to advantage, but if the new tone was positive, the tenor was destructive. 'We must rid ourselves of Mind as of literature.' He wanted to create a book which by leading directly into reality would take men where they would never have consented to go: to this extent he did want to be dictatorial.

L'Ombilic des Limbes contains the third version of 'Paul les Oiseaux', which had been drafted and redrafted during 1924. Artaud identified with Uccello both by projecting himself outwards and dragging Uccello inwards, representing him as 'trying to fight his way out from the middle of a huge mental tissue, where he has lost all the pathways of his soul, down to the form and balance of his reality'. The next paragraph might strike readers today as Beckettian:

> Leave your tongue, Paolo Uccello, leave your tongue, my tongue, my tongue, shit, who's talking, where are you? Proceed, proceed, brain, brain, fire, tongues of fire, fire, fire, eat your tongue, old dog, eats its tongue, eats, etc. I tear my tongue out.
> YES.

But of course it is Beckett who is Artaudesque. Both the style and the idea of his play *Not I* (1972) evolved from his novel *L'Innommable* (1949–50), where the prose is being made to explore the conditions of its own creation, curling back on itself in long sentences like a tongue trying to find its own roots:

> . . . where are you, what are you seeking, who is seeking, seeking who you are, supreme aberration, where you are, what you're doing, what you've done to them, what they've done to you, prattling along, where are the others, who is talking, not I, where am I, where is the

place where I've always been, where are the others, it's they are talking, talking to me, talking of me, I hear them, I'm mute ... you don't feel a mouth on you, you don't feel your mouth any more, no need of a mouth, the words are everywhere, inside me, outside me, well well, a minute ago I had no thickness, I hear them, no need to hear them, no need of a head, impossible to stop them, impossible to stop, I'm in words, made of words, others' words. ...

The central point about consisting of other people's words is the same as the one made by Artaud in 1946 when he said, 'In my unconsciousness it is always other people that I hear.'

Beckett partly fails, partly refuses to put the madness in focus as his own subjectivity overlaps unrepentantly with that of the narrators in his novels and the characters in his plays; with Artaud, one of the main differences between the early surrealism and the late madness is that the young man had the backing of a group whilst the old man of fifty was isolated. Another difference is that the old man was more destructively and self-destructively desperate to struggle free from the common stock of words into purity of existence in his own right. Beyond his ultimate rejection of words and the theatre lay a terroristic nihilism. A 1947 letter to Breton contains one of his many statements of the belief that there was no longer any language society would understand 'except bombs, machine-guns, barricades and everything that follows'. But before he was thirty, in *L'Ombilic des Limbes*, Artaud was already nightmarishly juxtaposing images of parturition and images of annihilation. His account of André Masson's *Homme* becomes very much more than a description of a painting. At the base of the slender stomach is an exploded grenade. The painting resembles a spinning chasm. The air is full of pencil strokes which are like knife-thrusts. It composes itself in cells where unreality grows. The stomach suggests surgery and the morgue.

L'Ombilic des Limbes contains a letter addressed to the legislator of the drug act. Similar in style to the letters and addresses in *La Révolution surréaliste*, it makes out a case for opium as a remedy against anguish. A footnote offers a clear formulation of Artaud's need for unrestricted contact with every element in his own personality. He wants to be able to sustain his thought, to be capable of exposing it to itself, to have it available under all circumstances, responding to feelings and to life. He would like to be in touch with his inner self at every moment; his thinking should always be equal to itself, however inadequate the form he uses to express it. The underlying fallacy is that thought can exist independently of words.

L'Ombilic des Limbes also contains *Le Jet de sang*, a five-minute playlet which was not staged until 1964, when Peter Brook and Charles Marowitz included it in their *Theatre of Cruelty* programme at the LAMDA Theatre. Subtitled *La Boule de verre*, it is a parody of Armand Salacrou's one-act play of that name, which had been published in the review *Intentions* (nos. 28–30, December 1924). After five stylized affirmations of a young man's love for a girl and one affirmation of their love for each other, they are interrupted by a noise like a huge wheel turning and blowing out wind. Two stars collide. Human limbs, masonry, and scorpions fall from the sky. A knight in armour appears, followed by a wet-nurse, who gives him Gruyère cheese. Six new characters including a priest and a prostitute make their appearance just before a thunderstorm breaks. God's enormous hand snatches hold of the prostitute's hair, which catches fire as her clothes become transparent. When she bites God on the wrist, a jet of blood spurts across the stage. At the end of the play most of the characters are dead, the wet-nurse is breastless, and scorpions are swarming out of her vagina. The 1964 production drew laughter of the wrong kind from the audience.

Artaud's next collection, *Les Pèse-Nerfs* (August 1925), confirmed that he was now less concerned to write verse such as Rivière had rejected than to create prose poems which pursue the self-analytical track that had begun with his letters to doctors, and been continued in his correspondence with Rivière. In default of a patriarchal authentication for his existence, he had no option but to make his symptoms into symbols for the human condition.

> If only one could savour one's void, settle down in it. And if it were not some sort of being, but not quite death.
>
> It is so hard to stop existing, stop being inside something. Real pain is to feel thought being displaced inside oneself. But thought that is like a point is certainly not painful.
>
> I am where I no longer have contact with life, but all the appetites

and insistent titillation of existence are inside me. There is nothing I have to do except remake myself.

Interpolated at the end of a sequence of prose poems are three 'Lettres de ménage'—letters written to Génica. They are printed without her name or any identifying clue, but they deal directly with the current phase of his relationship with her. She will never know anything about his life. It is impossible to discuss anything with her. She has always been more concerned with his outward appearance than his inner soul, which is damaged. He needs a woman who belongs exclusively to him and who can always be found at home—a woman who will devote her life to looking after him. She need not even be very pretty or very intelligent. The letters refer only obliquely to drugs, but he accuses her of blaming them for behaviour which has nothing to do with them.

The 'Fragments d'un journal d'Enfer' had appeared in the review *Commerce* (Spring 1926) after being published as the final section in the volume *Les Pèse-Nerfs*. The stubbornness of his adherence to personal imperfection has hardened since the letters to Rivière:

> They should all leave me to my dark clouds, my perpetual impotence, my illogical hopes. But they should know I repudiate none of my mistakes. If I have misjudged, my flesh is to blame. . . .
> Nothing concerns me which does not touch my flesh, coincide with it.

A paragraph on the penultimate page offers a grim insight into his view of life as a process of constant loss, a steady depletion of spiritual resources. He describes the ordeal of the suffocating soul, which is being progressively broken down, below the level of speech and thought. It disintegrates gradually as life nags it towards constant clarity. The suffering, the cyclical martyrdom remains obscure. Humanity will never understand what is going on.

Artaud's next collection, *L'Art et la Mort*, was not published until April 1929, but the prose poems in it were mostly written before he broke with Surrealism in November 1926, and the majority of them had appeared in *La Révolution surréaliste*. In the one printed first, 'Oui, au sein . . .', Artaud argues that death does not lie outside the domain of the mind. We are given intimations of it by dreams and by drugs, which are 'the closest and most useful helpers of death'. No one should be able to dream without afterwards feeling an 'atrocious nostalgia' for the fantasy landscapes, for 'the encirclement of certain hills by a sort of clay shaped as if by moulding it to our thinking'. Nothing is more like love than the appeal of these visions, which carry us closer to infinite reality and further away from the reality that decays with matter. In dreams, the soul can 'wake up to a clearer world'.

The text is Surrealistic in arguing that a disruption of the rationalistic network of relationships can 'offer death an outlet, putting us in touch with higher states of mind'. In the midst of them death expresses itself. Then we will not approach it as something totally unfamiliar. We will recognize the agony, the desolation, the sense of liquefaction, from our dreams. When we die, we will not feel we are doing something we have never done before.

The next piece, 'Lettre à la Voyante', describes a sudden fearlessness experienced in the clairvoyante's room.

> Whether it was death or life, I no longer saw anything but a wide peaceful space where the shadows of my destiny dissolved. . . . It did not matter to me if the most terrible doors opened in front of me: what was terrible was already behind me. Though evil, my immediate future seemed only like a harmonious discord, a chain of summits inverted and blunted inside me. . . . Balanced by my terrible past, my life to come slid smoothly into death.

His death would be sweeter than the best of his memories. The presence of the clairvoyante was like opium, reassuring. She opened doors into his brain cells but at the same time made it seem unnecessary for him to have contact with the powers of his own mind. The whole of life became a happy landscape with features like his own. 'The idea of absolute knowledge merged with the idea of absolute resemblance between life and my consciousness.'*

---

* At the risk of seeming apologetic, I must explain that no translation or paraphrase of these prose poems can possibly be adequate. The syntax is deliberately clouded with ambiguities. As Derrida puts it, the words whispered to Artaud must not be allowed to fall far from his body. He 'knew that each word, once it falls from the body, offering to

The two texts about Héloïse and Abélard and the new text about Uccello, show how Artaud's experience as an actor had developed his capacity for identification with a character. Whenever he could catch hold of an alternative identity, he clung to it with a creative desperation, criss-crossing with it in a pungent confusion of pleasure and pain. 'Le Clair Abélard' contains a joyful celebration of sexuality which contrasts strongly with the disgusted strictures Artaud was to set down later, but the imagery makes the perspective less personal than cosmic and eschatological:

> How sweet coition is! It may be human, it may take advantage of the woman's body, but what ecstasy, seraphic and close! Heaven within reach of earth, less beautiful than earth. A paradise embedded between his nails. .... Pleasure makes music, sharp and mystical, on the edge of a sharp dream.

The lover Artaud chose to be his alter ego could become a lover only by breaking his vows and betraying his faith:

> Between my thighs I feel the Church stopping me, complaining. Will it paralyse me? Am I going to withdraw? No, no, I burst through the final barrier. St. Francis of Assisi, guardian of my sex, stands aside. St. Brigit unclenches my jaws. St. Augustine unties my belt. St. Catherine of Siena puts God to sleep. It's over, it's all over. I am no longer a virgin.

But it is the castration that brings Artaud to the point of identifying overtly with Abélard.

> Poor man! Poor Antonin Artaud! He is really this impotent man who ascends the stars, who tries to pit his feebleness against the cardinal points of the elements, who tries to produce a thought which coheres, an image which stands up, for each aspect of nature, fluid or stable. .... For Artaud, loss is the beginning of this death he desires. But what an image—a eunuch!

So Artaud's most outspoken affirmation of sexual exhilaration culminates in an exposure of the dark underside of his ambivalence.

---

be understood or received, exhibiting itself, becomes a stolen word'. If he could remain half-understood, his words would be only half-stolen from him.

Whilst the iconoclasm of the other Surrealists was charged with *ioie de vivre*, Artaud, as Breton put it, carried around with him the landscape of a Gothic novel, torn by flashes of lightning. Nevertheless, he indubitably gained from his involvement in the movement. Without *La Révolution surréaliste* as a platform, he might never have written these texts, which rank among his best work.

Artaud's rupture with the group occurred after he had tried, during the summer of 1926, to act as mediator between Breton and Jean Paulhan, who had been appointed editor of the *N.R.F.* when Rivière died in 1925. The Surrealists wanted to publish in the review, and Paulhan would have welcomed them as contributors but refused to accept Breton's demand for complete freedom from editorial censorship. Artaud was at a nadir of depression, and in a letter written about May, he said it was his intention to publish no more of his own writing. He asked Paulhan to return the text of 'Lettre à la Voyante'. The relationship with Génica was almost at an end. On 27 July he wrote to her: 'I am wiped out by life, incessantly devoured by a programme which is not mine. I curse and vilify myself, despair of myself. You know what it is like to have desperation attached to one's personality as the skin is to the muscles.' In August, filming in *Le Juif errant*, he felt deserted even by his competence as an actor. 'It is going very badly. I play with a profound absence. For the first time I am accused of being flabby. I am not doing it deliberately. My power of projection has violently dwindled.'

But he had not stopped publishing. Another prose poem, 'L'Enclume des forces', and a poem appeared in the seventh issue of *La Révolution surréaliste*, which came out in the middle of June 1926; 'Lettre à la Voyante' and 'Uccello le Poil' were included in the eighth issue (1 December). It is often said that Artaud dissociated himself from the Surrealists when they committed themselves to communism, but this had happened much earlier. In April 1925, the Moroccan war broke out, with France as Spain's ally against the Berbers who were supported by the Communists. The first step in the Surrealist commitment was the formation of a 'united front' with certain para-Communist groups, and then, in October 1925, a committee had been formed 'to bridge the gap between absolute idealism and dialectical materialism'—as Breton later phrased it. The committee issued a manifesto titled *La Révolu-tion d'abord et toujours*: 'We are not utopianists: we conceive of this Revolution only in its social form.'

The other exacerbating factor in Artaud's relations with the Surrealists was his developing friendship with Roger Vitrac, the playwright who had been expelled from the group at the beginning of December 1924 after a quarrel with Eluard. By September 1925 Breton had written to Artaud, ordering him to break off his rela-tionship with Vitrac, but Artaud replied with what he described to Génica on the 10th as 'an incendiary letter which will stir up quite a lot of trouble in the Surrealist tribe'. His friendship with Vitrac became still closer in 1926, as they evolved a scheme for a new theatre to be named after Alfred Jarry, one of the precursors of Surrealism, who had died in 1907. The third founder-director of the new theatre was Robert Aron, and on 26 September Artaud and Vitrac approached Dr. René Allendy, founder of the French psycho-analytical society, and his wife Yvonne, who had inherited a great deal of money just at the right moment for the project.

In an October letter to Paulhan, Artaud was dissociating himself from Breton. 'I like my independence too much and I am not always in agreement with him.' On 8 November 1925 *L'Humanité* printed a public declaration by the Surrealists to the effect that they had never believed in a 'Surrealist revolution'. At the end of the month Artaud was expelled from the group during a meeting held at the café le Prophète. He was condemned for

> not wanting the Revolution to consist of anything but a transforma-
> tion in the interior conditions of the soul—which is characteristic of
> the mentally defective, the impotent and the cowardly. . . . He could
> neither recognize nor conceive of any other matter than the 'matter
> of his spirit', as he put it. Let us leave him to his detestable mixture of
> dreams, vague affirmations, gratuitous insolences and manias. . . . We
> see no reason for this decaying carcass to delay much longer in being
> converted, or, as it will no doubt say, in *declaring itself christian*.[3]

The final slur seems to have been based mainly on the visits Artaud was paying to Jacques Maritain, but there must have been some justification for it, to judge from the reproachful letter Jean Paulhan wrote at about the beginning of April 1927:

A photograph of Artaud by Man Ray

Artaud as Marat in Abel Gance's *Napoléon Bonaparte* (1925). Danton (*above right*) was played by Alexandre Koubitzky.

Artaud as Frère Massieu in Carl Dreyer's film *La Passion de Jeanne d'Arc* (1927)

Roger Vitrac
(1899–1952) and
(*right*) André
Breton (1896–
1966)

Artaud, beware of diminishing yourself by taking such absolute umbrage at your friends. If we stop believing in you, stop putting ourselves in your place, your articles no longer affect us, hardly make sense. . . . If you were taken in by Breton to the point of not seeing all the monsters you describe today, what confidence can I now put in you? And how much confidence can remain when you are to be seen so lightly declaring yourself a Christian? I understand what is getting the better of you. It is also rage against the Artauds of the past. . . . You proceed by destruction and suicide. But suicide wins, denying existence to everything that preceded it.

5

The Aborted Theatre

'There are those who go to the theatre as if they were going to a brothel,' Artaud had written in 1922. 'Furtive pleasure. Momentary excitement. . . . It can be said that there are now two theatres in existence—the false and facile theatre of the bourgeois, soldiers, investors, businessmen, wine-merchants, art teachers, adventurers, . . . which is found with Sacha Guitry, on the boulevards and in the Comédie Française; and another theatre which finds accommodation where it can, theatre conceived as the accomplishment of the purest human desires.'[1] This theatre was inspired by 'ardent faith', and Dullin's company was the most ardent of all. 'With the creation of the Atelier, Charles Dullin undertakes the important business of restoring the health, regenerating the morals and the spirit of the French theatre.'[2]

Having praised Dullin for giving the text supremacy over the characters, Artaud, when he turned against literature, turned against his old teacher and employer. The new attitude is formulated in 'L'Évolution de décor', an article in *Comœdia* (19 April 1924). The externals of production must be ignored, he wrote—lighting, décor, and costumes. Racine, Corneille, and Molière went to the heart of the problem with their focus on interior drama, on the comings and goings inside the souls of their characters. Gordon Craig had been too concerned with the superficialities of scenic decoration: Jacques Copeau's bare platform stage was preferable, although, far from advocating a return to the methods of the Théâtre du Vieux-Colombier, Artaud was now out to attack docile subservience to the script: what should be achieved as the production evolved was 'a kind of magnetic intercommunication between the spirits of playwright and director. . . . Applying ourselves to a text, forgetting ourselves, forgetting theatre, we should lie in wait for the images that are born in us, naked, natural, excessive, and we should go to the end of these images.' Whereas Dullin (like Lugné-Poe, Pitoëff, and Louis Jouvet) was proposing to 're-theatricalize theatre', Artaud's war-cry was 'Theatre must be thrown back into life.' Like Nietzsche in *The Birth of Tragedy*, he was concerned less with technique than with the extra-theatrical sources of dramatic energy. In the tragedies of Sophocles, Aeschylus, and Shakespeare, the actions of the heroes had been 'weighed down by a sort of divine terror which caused tremors in the soul'. The plays are 'like a transsubstantiation of life', and the director should be able to draw on the non-theatrical life which is their source.

As Henri Gouhier has pointed out, Artaud's surrealism left its mark on his theatrical ideas. We should free ourselves not only from all reality and all probability, he said, but from all logic. 'We must learn to be mystical again.' His Catholic upbringing had also left its mark. The choice of words with religious overtones tallies with the assumption that there should be some kind of communion with the audience. 'They would no longer come merely to see but to participate.'

A similarly religious undertone is discernible in the manifesto for the Théâtre Alfred Jarry which Artaud published in the N.R.F. on 1 November 1926. There was currently no other 'absolutely pure theatre' in Paris, he argued. 'We suffer from a huge inability to *believe*.' The theatre should be able to proffer 'a world ephemeral but true, a world in contact with reality'. 'We are not addressing ourselves to the mind or the senses of the spectators, but to their whole existence. Theirs and ours. We stake our lives on the show performed on the stage.' It would be presented with a profound sense that 'a part of our deepest life is involved in it'. Audiences would come in the same state of mind as if they were going to a surgeon or a dentist, not expecting to come away 'intact'. They should feel sure that 'we are capable of making them cry out'.

Though Artaud was not yet using the phrase Theatre of Cruelty, the notion was strongly present. The austerity of the proposals probably had its root in a penchant for spiritual self-discipline, acquired during his Catholic education. His theatre would be purgative; playgoing would become an ordeal. The brochure he wrote for the theatre's first season (1926–7) stressed the gravity of the transaction between the players and the audience, which should leave the theatre in a state of 'human anguish', having been 'shaken and turned back against itself by the inner dynamism of the production', a dynamism which should have 'a direct relationship with the anxieties and preoccupations' that permeate life. 'The spectator must have the feeling that a scene from his own life is being acted out in front of him.'

As in 'L'Evolution du décor', lighting, scenery, and costumes are dismissed as unimportant. 'For us, theatre rests on something imponderable. . . . Nothing short of a miracle can reward us for our efforts and our patience. It is on this miracle that we are counting.' Artaud had nothing to say about methods of production: 'The director who obeys no principle but follows his inspiration . . . will either find or fail to find the element of anxiety necessary to plunge the audience into the requisite uncertainty.' The brochure was ambivalent in the attitude it expressed towards the script: the intention was to show a minimum of respect to the spirit of it. At the same time, the script was the only thing that seemed either 'invulnerable' or 'true', and it was important to cut down on the 'hateful and cumbersome apparatus' which 'turns a written play into a show, instead of letting it stay within the limits of words, images and abstractions'. This is the point from which Artaud was to deviate furthest in his later thinking about theatre, which glorifies the non-verbal elements.

By November 1926 Artaud had given up hope of bringing the Théâtre Alfred Jarry to life. 'Manifeste pour un théâtre avorté' was the title of an article he wrote on 13 November. It was published by *Les Cahiers du Sud* (February 1927) with a postscript, written in January, arguing that 'the revolution we most urgently need to accomplish is a sort of movement backwards in time. We should return to the mentality of the Middle Ages or even simply to their living habits, but genuinely and by a kind of metamorphosis of essences.' This is reminiscent of his letter to Max Jacob about the feeling of 'rediscovering ancient secrets' while listening to Dullin's teaching.*

* See above, p. 42.

Artaud's anxiety about his personal situation was no less desperate than his proposal for a retrogressive revolution. About the beginning of February he was writing to Jacques Hébertôt: 'All I ask is work. Give me something to do, M. Hébertôt, it does not matter what: a role, a job in your offices or even as a road-sweeper. . . . To hell with my soul. . . . Perhaps it is anxiety and hunger that causes nightmares.' But thanks to Yvonne Allendy, who sent 3,000 francs to Robert Aron, it was possible to start rehearsals in May, and the Théâtre Alfred Jarry gave its first performances on 2–3 June 1927 at the Théâtre de Grenelle, with a cast that included Génica, E. Beauchamp, and Raymond Rouleau. The triple bill consisted of Artaud's *Ventre brûlé ou la Mère folle, Gigogne* by Max Robur (a pseudonym for Robert Aron), and Roger Vitrac's *Les Mystères de l'amour. Ventre brûlé* was later described (by Roger Vitrac) as 'a lyrical work which satirized the conflict between cinema and theatre'. The script has been lost, but Benjamin Crémieux[3] called it 'a short hallucination without a text—or almost—in which the author has constructed a synthesis of life and death'.

Les Mystères de l'amour introduced structural ideas which have been developed by later playwrights including Tom Stoppard.[4] Vitrac's characters included Lloyd George and Mussolini; the action absorbed fantasies into the flow of events; several locales were represented simultaneously on the same playing area. The author appeared as a character in the play, and when the hero reprimanded him for not making 'a theatre without words', his answer was that he had always wanted to. The character should have spat out the words put into his mouth.

Though the production of the triple bill had involved a loss of 7,000 francs and it seemed unlikely that the Théâtre Alfred Jarry could survive, Artaud was convinced that something worthwhile had been achieved by putting *Les Mystères de l'amour* on the stage. As he wrote to Jean Paulhan on 2 July,

The dialogue acquires a weight and sound which it does not have on paper. . . . What matters is a certain spiritual desperation which comes to life only in performance. Our object is to realize the soul's most secret movements through the simplest and barest means. To find an unexpected aspect in the most familiar, most banal situations.

But Artaud was in no position to concentrate his energy on preparing a second production. Before June was over Carl Dreyer had contracted him to play the part of Frère Massieu in *La Passion de Jeanne d'Arc*, which was shot entirely in close-up. Artaud recognized in Dreyer 'a man committed to elucidating one of the most anguishing of all human problems, committed to revealing Jeanne d'Arc as a victim of one of the most painful distortions possible—the distortion of a divine principle passing through human brains, whether they go under the name of government or church or anything else'. Writing in *Revue du cinéma* (no. 2, 1 February 1928), Pierre Audard praised Artaud and two of the other actors for their stillness, for not playing roles. 'They are immobile figures at the centre of things, a gaze centred on an invisible point, a hand reaching towards the unknown.'

Of all the screenplays Artaud wrote, the only one to be produced was *La Coquille et le clergyman*, which was directed by Germaine Dulac. At first he seemed very willing to make concessions. He gave her a script from which he had cut—so he said later— 'everything poetic or literary'. He passed on ideas for developing some of the images, but he tried not to interfere. He had a meeting with her in July 1927 and asked for another, but she was careful to avoid meeting him again until the shooting was complete.

His explanation of *La Coquille et le clergyman* in *Le Monde illustré* (29 October 1927) is reminiscent of the criticism he had been writing in 1923, praising Maeterlinck for putting feeling and object on the same mental plane without recourse to metaphor and Paul Klee for his 'cosmic syntheses which bring out into the open all the secret objectivity of things':

> *La Coquille et le clergyman* plays with created nature, trying to make it yield some of the mystery of its most secret combinations. We should not look for a logic or a sequence which is not present in things, but interpret images which develop in the direction of their essential, intimate significance, which goes from the outside to the inside. *La Coquille et le clergyman* does not tell a story but develops a series of mental states, which are deduced from each other, as thought is from thought.

And in 'Cinéma et réalité', the note which preceded the printed version of the screenplay in the *N.R.F.* (November 1927), Artaud wrote:

> It is not a matter of finding an equivalent of written language in visual language—which would merely be a bad translation—but of bringing out the very essence of language, transporting the action on to a plane where all translation would be useless, where the action works almost intuitively on the brain. . . . The human skin of things, the derm of reality—that's what the cinema plays with. It exalts matter, making it appear to us in its profound spirituality, in its relationship with the spirit it emerges from.

He again used the word 'transsubstantiation' in arguing, 'From this pure game of appearances, this kind of transsubstantiation of elements, is born an inorganic language which excites the mind by osmosis, without any sort of verbal transposition.'

In October, when Artaud saw the film Germaine Dulac had made, he accused her of betraying the spirit of his script and distorting images she had failed to understand. When the film was previewed in February 1928 at the Studio des Ursulines, two loud voices were heard in the darkness.

'Who made this film?'

'It was Mme Germaine Dulac.'

'What is Mme Dulac?'

'A cow.'

When the lights were switched on, the hecklers were found to be Artaud and Robert Desnos. The manager tried to have them ejected. Desnos insulted him; Artaud yelled and smashed mirrors. The scandal clouded the reputation of *La Coquille et le clergyman*, which should have been recognized as the first major surrealist film, preceding Buñuel's *Un Chien Andalou* (made in 1928) and *L'Age d'Or* (shown in 1930). Artaud's claim that he influenced Buñuel deserves to be taken more seriously than it has been.

As distractions from his malaise, neither Artaud's writing nor his activity in the theatre and cinema were more than sporadically effective, and the film role he accepted in October 1927 could not possibly have fulfilled the conditions he was to formulate in his August 1929 interview:* playing in Léon Poirier's patriotic film

* See above, p. 53.

Verdun, visions d'histoire, he must have found himself cut off from what he thought and felt. Justifying himself in a letter to Roland Tual at the end of the month, he said: 'For me, nothing makes sense any more. Human gestures no longer count. However low I prostitute myself, my spirit and my soul are elsewhere. I cannot come to terms with life. I despise good more than evil.'

A month later he was still deeply depressed. 'I have no life', he wrote to Dr. Allendy on 30 November 1927, 'I have no life! ! ! My inner effervescence is dead.' Different though he might have seemed from the twenty-six-year-old who had been so eager for Rivière to authenticate his existence by publishing his verse, the man of thirty-one found that such success as he had achieved did little to counteract the feeling of hollowness. 'I have a fundamental need for someone like you,' he told the doctor. '. . . There is something rotten inside me, a sort of fundamental defect in my psyche, which prevents me from enjoying what destiny offers me.'

Allendy had believed that psychoanalysis could help not only towards curing Artaud of his dependence on drugs but towards solving the deeper problems that created the need. Artaud had allowed his misgivings to be overcome, but not for long. Although he acknowledged in his November letter that he had benefited from the sessions, he still felt that there had been 'a sort of prostitution, of shamelessness', in letting his consciousness be 'penetrated' by an 'alien intelligence'. Nevertheless he wanted Allendy to go on helping him, and not merely by sending pills. 'The fact is that I am no longer myself. My authentic self is asleep. I move towards my images. I pull them out in slow tufts. They do not come to me. . . . It is authenticity that makes images valuable, but these have no value, being nothing but replicas, reflections of thoughts conceived previously or conceived by other people.'

Between the first and second productions of the Théâtre Alfred Jarry there was an interval of more than six months. The second programme (14 January 1928) coupled Pudovkin's film of Gorky's *The Mother*, which had been banned from the cinemas by the censor, with the third act of Claudel's *Partage de midi*, performed against the author's wishes and without any acknowledgement to him in the programme. The actors (including Génica as Ysé) did not know whose work they were performing. When some of the audience started laughing, Breton shouted out that it was by Claudel. As soon as it was over Artaud stepped on to the stage: 'The play we have just performed is by M. Paul Claudel, French ambassador to the United States and a traitor.' The insult to Claudel provoked a quarrel with Paulhan, while Artaud had become rather more anti-verbal since he wrote the brochure. He had never liked *Partage de midi*, and in a letter to Paulhan about the unfavourable review of his production in the *N.R.F.* he said; 'I do exactly what I please to a text. A text on the stage is always a poor thing. So I decorate it with cries and contortions which naturally have a meaning, though not for pigs.'

In the brochure for the Théâtre Alfred Jarry's 1926–7 season, it had been announced that future productions would include Tourneur's *The Revenger's Tragedy* and Strindberg's *Dream Play*. Some Swedish friends of Yvonne Allendy's were willing to act as backers for a new series of performances on condition that the company went ahead with the Strindberg production. Artaud directed, himself playing the role of Theology. When the play opened at the Théâtre de l'Avenue on 2 June 1928, the audience included the Swedish ambassador, Prince George of Greece, and several Swedish aristocrats. Just before the curtain went up, thirty uninvited Surrealists sat down in the stalls. As soon as the performance was under way the heckling started. The organizers were lackeys of Swedish capitalism. Artaud, who had been waiting in the wings, made a premature entrance not to silence the Surrealists but to side with them. He had agreed to produce a play by Strindberg, he said, only because Strindberg had been a victim of Swedish society.

When the Surrealists warned the company not to proceed with the second performance, which had been announced for 9 June, Artaud and Robert Aron decided to defy the ultimatum, announcing that the Théâtre Alfred Jarry would take the necessary steps, however repugnant, to defend its liberty. They then asked for police protection, with the result that Breton was arrested together with several other Surrealists when they tried to interrupt the performance. After this, Robert Aron withdrew from the venture.

The last production of the Théâtre Alfred Jarry—Roger Vitrac's *Victor ou les enfants du pouvoir*—had three matinée performances in December 1928 and January 1929. The role of Ida Mortemart had to be recast because the actress originally cast was nervous of playing a character who farted on stage. The controversy in the newspapers culminated in Artaud's letter to *Paris Soir* (21 December 1928). This was reprinted in the programme. The character, it said, should seem like a ghost which has retained

> all the intelligence and superiority of the other world . . . To her everything is a pretext for profundity, and she seizes it as if trembling with fear that she will not survive. In any case the worst side of her represents moral grief and the poisoning of matter. Her ghostly state —that of a woman spiritually crucified, gives her the lucidity of a clairvoyante.

We can draw inferences from this about the way Artaud used his own preoccupations in directing his actors. As in cinema, where he wanted disturbance or desperation to be materialized in images and movements, his prime concern was with what he thought of as an inner spirit. In manipulating actors on the stage, he must have been trying to approximate to the language he considered ideal for the cinema—non-verbal and incapable of translation into verbal terms. In so far as he thought of his own malady as centring on a gap between what needed to be expressed and his power of expressing it, theatre appeared to offer a means of striking sparks across the hiatus.

After the Vicomte and Vicomtesse de Noailles had made an offer of 20,000 francs, it should have been possible to keep the Théâtre Alfred Jarry alive, but too much of the money was spent on launching a public appeal with an expensive illustrated brochure titled 'Le Théâtre Alfred Jarry et l'hostilité publique'. Mostly written by Roger Vitrac but revised by Artaud, it started on a surrealistically negative note. Conscious of theatre's surrender to the invading cinema industry, the Théâtre Alfred Jarry proposed to contribute by specifically theatrical means to the ruin of French theatre, by dragging all literary and artistic ideas, all psychological conventions into the destruction. Explaining the attitude behind the productions, the brochure promised to avoid 'pictorial lyricism, philosophical tirades, obscurities and knowing innuendoes'. But there would be plenty of 'crisp dialogue, stock characters, brisk movements, stereotyped attitudes, proverbial expressions, comic songs and grand opera'. As well as provoking 'joy, fear, love, patriotism and the taste for crime', the productions would specialize in producing a sentiment no policeman can interfere with—'*shame*, the last and most redoubtable obstacle to liberty'.

Understandably, the fund-raising campaign failed. The Théâtre Alfred Jarry was dead, and so was the friendship between Artaud and Roger Vitrac.

6

The Theatre of Cruelty

It could be said that the next important event in Artaud's life occurred in July 1931, when he got the central idea for his 'Theatre of Cruelty' from seeing a troupe of Balinese actors at the Colonial Exhibition in the Bois de Vincennes. Not that the previous two and a half years were uneventful. He played the name part in Raymond Bernard's film *Tarakanowa*, a sort of Russian Western, which was shot in Nice, where he started making plans with the Allendys to form a film production company, though in theory he was very hostile to talkies. Even while working on the dialogue for a film of Robert Louis Stevenson's *The Master of Ballantrae*, he wrote to Yvonne Allendy: 'People like us, who have kept a feeling for real, pure cinema, are right to show up the absurdity and uselessness of non-silent films.' He employed sound in the unproduced screenplay *La Révolte du boucher* but mainly to cut across the images or create a dissonance with them.

During 1929 he wrote almost nothing except for the screen. 'Since the last time I met you at the N.R.F.,' said his January 1930 letter to Paulhan, '*I have not written ONE line*.' His health had deteriorated during the year, his stammer reasserting itself in the summer, and from July to October he suffered continually (as he wrote to Dr. Toulouse on 11 January 1930) from 'physical torture of the spirit, trembling, sudden pressure of all the nerves, collapses, profound lethargy'. Feeling better at the beginning of the new year, he wanted to work in the theatre again as a director. In April he was still trying to interest Louis Jouvet in employing him to stage Vitrac's *Le Coup de Trafalgar*. But no one offered him any work until he was contracted to do some dubbing on a film being made in Berlin, where he arrived in July 1930. He stayed on to play a small part in the film of Brecht's *Dreigroschenoper*. The director, G. W. Pabst, was working simultaneously with French and German actors to make versions in both languages. Raymond Bernard used him as a hardened soldier in *Les Croix de bois*, which was shot on location in Champagne, and again in *Faubourg Montmartre*; he also had a part in Marcel l'Herbier's *Femme d'une nuit*. A love affair with Josette Lusson (who posed for or appeared in the photographs used to illustrate 'Le Théâtre Alfred Jarry et l'hostilité publique') ended in March. He wrote in a notebook 'My self-styled [*soi-disant*] wife Josette has fornicated with Léon Mathot.'

His adaptation of M. G. Lewis's *The Monk*, which he had originally hoped to stage, was published in narrative form by Denoël, and he may have been about to start work on adapting *Les Cenci* when he had the crucial experience of seeing the Balinese theatre. After thinking of Ida Mortemart in *Victor* as a ghost, he was amazed when the first short Balinese play began with two ghosts—a father reprimanding his rebellious daughter. Later, as the theme was developed, the characters assumed human form, but, as in Artaud's ideal cinema, the story was told through 'inner states [*états d'esprit*] themselves ossified and reduced to gestures, schemes. . . . Like realization, conception has no existence except in so far as it is objectified on the stage. They triumphantly demonstrate the absolute domination of the director, whose creativity *eliminates words*.'[1] The 'idea of a metaphysic' appeared to emerge out of 'a new utilization of gesture and voice'.

When Artaud went on to describe the movements and sounds that constituted the 'new physical language based on signs', nearly all his images were non-human: 'angular postures', 'brutal jerks', 'syncopated modulations at the back of the throat', 'musical phrases cut short', 'insect flights', 'rustling branches', 'the musical angle formed by arm and forearm', 'a rarefied aviary where the actors themselves are the fluttering', 'hollow drum sounds', 'machines creaking', 'animated puppet dances'. He praised the asymmetrical robes that made the actors look 'like moving hieroglyphs'. He was full of admiration for the gestures that combined with a sound from an instrument to evoke the movements of a

plant, and he responded to 'the sighs of a wind machine that prolong the vibrations of vocal chords with such a sense of identity'
that it was impossible to tell where the transition came.

The representation of the devil reminded him of a puppet he had
used at the Théâtre Alfred Jarry (probably in *Les Mystères de
l'amour*). Its hands had been 'swollen with white gelatine' and it
had had leaves for fingernails. But the Balinese theatre was not
entirely unrealistic. Though the focus was on 'purely inner conflicts', especially in the latter part of the programme, there was un-
deniable realism, said Artaud, in the manifestations of terror at
apparitions from the other world—in 'this trembling, this puerile
yelping, this heel which rhythmically drums the ground, following
the automatism of the unleashed unconscious'.

To the Balinese, this was popular theatre, but it was not trivial;
and without being religious, it was like a holy ritual in giving an
impression of 'a higher, controlled life' and in

> excluding from the onlooker's mind any possibility of simulation, any
> absurd aping of reality. . . . The thoughts it aims to evoke, the spiri-
> tual states it tries to generate, the mystical solutions it proposes are
> moved, sustained, achieved without delay or circumlocution. It all
> seems to be an exorcism for making our demons FLOW.

Artaud used the word 'magic' to describe 'this intense liberation of
signs, at first held back, then suddenly thrown into the air'. But 'it
is by intellectual routes that we are led towards reconquering the
signs of what exists'. The production, in other words, was offering
the audience a means of reconciling external phenomena with its
internal life. Artaud had arrived at a vision of how it might be
possible to achieve the objective he had formulated in his early
manifestos for the Théâtre Alfred Jarry: production as spiritual
purgative. But he had moved away from his ambivalence about
the status of the script. In taking responsibility both for the way
the text was spoken and for all the non-verbal elements, the
director was the true author of the theatrical event.

Artaud's essay on the Balinese theatre appeared in the October
1931 issue of the *N.R.F.*, and in December he gave a lecture at the
Sorbonne on 'La Mise en scène et la métaphysique'. He said that
the sixteenth-century artist Lucas Van Leyden made the four or

five ensuing centuries of painting 'useless and invalid'. A drama of high intellectual importance was concentrated on the canvas of his *Lot and his Daughters*—a drama which 'was born in the heavens and occurred in the heavens'. Lot's daughters are parading past him like prostitutes at a banquet, as if they had never had any other aim but to please him, to be his playthings. Incest, as Artaud put it later, apropos his production of *Les Cenci*, reveals a 'nature that speaks more loudly than men do' (*O.C.* V. 49). The landscape conforms to the fiery light in the shaft of storm that cuts through the clouds. A black tower rises fantastically high out of rocks and plants; a high bridge juts out against the sea. People 'file across it like ideas in Plato's cave'. 'The very spirit of nature' seems to be 'externalized' in the solemn arrangement and disarrangement of forms round the heavenly fire, 'some as if bent under a wind of irresistible panic, others immobile and almost ironic'. The painting is what theatre ought to be, 'if only it knew how to speak the language that is proper to it'. But 'the dictatorship of the word' was so exclusive that everything specifically theatrical, all the elements not present in the text, were regarded as the low aspect of theatre.

Artaud's quarrel with the existing theatre centred on his conviction that it was wrong for drama to be concerned with the definition of individual character, the delineation of personal thoughts, the elucidation of emotional states, the discussion of psychological and social issues. 'Our theatre never goes so far as to ask whether by any chance our social and moral system is iniquitous.' Surely it was so iniquitous that it deserved to be destroyed, but the destruction was more a matter for machine-guns than for theatre, which had broken away from seriousness and from the dangerous possibility of having an immediate effect. 'It has broken with the spirit of profound anarchy which is at the basis of all poetry.' To derive poetic results from theatre, metaphysics must be made out of language, gestures, postures, décor, and music.

Thirty years after Artaud's death, it is still hard to draw up a balance-sheet of what was progressive and what was retrogressive in his thinking. Though the use of the word 'signs' for the component elements of theatrical language may seem to anticipate semiological analysis, what Artaud was expounding was not a science of signs but a metaphysics of signs. Temperament and religious education had combined to give him such a compulsive craving for unity and such a nostalgia for the Middle Ages that he could not possibly have taken a modernist view of the universe. While scientific progress was revealing the *perpetuum mobile* of nature, the artist's function was changing. Braque said he did not believe in things, only in the relationships between them, and Malevich spoke of 'a feeling of the absence of the object'. Novelists were no longer using description of landscape to indicate that human behaviour was bound by nature's laws, while the stream-of-consciousness technique offered a means of securing unity of vision from a shifting and subjective viewpoint. Or, as A. N. Whitehead put it, 'the event is what it is by reason of the unification within itself of a multiplicity of relationships.' In linguistics, as Saussure was arguing in the courses he delivered in Geneva between 1906 and 1911, 'it is the point of view that creates the object.' Neither signifier nor signified had an individual essence: meanings could be ascribed only by reference to a system of relationships. Effectively, Saussure was clamping down hard on the tendency to essentialism which the ambiguity of the word *'esprit'* encourages in French thinking. It is significant that Artaud had such very frequent recourse to the word.

Not that we can blame Artaud for failing to be *au courant* with Saussure's work, but his thinking about theatre could not have been what it was if he had not turned his back on Freud. In a letter he wrote much later (18 October 1943) to Dr. Ferdière, he said that his ignorance of Freud and Jung was compensated by his familiarity with the Cabbala in writings by medieval Jewish mystics —'In the light of those and of some early Christian writers I have found an explanation of things which has wholly satisfied me.' Though in 1931 he was not calling himself a Christian as he was in 1943, his idea of spirit was founded on essentialist and religious assumptions, while his antipathy towards the scientific method and towards contemporary culture was partly the cause, partly the result, of his nostalgia for primitive and Oriental cosmographies. The non-human imagery in his description of the Balinese actors shows how gratefully he responded to the implication of correspondences between the human organism and its environment, animal and vegetable, while the description of *Lot and His Daughters*

A still from *La Coquille et le clergyman* (1927), scripted by Artaud and directed by Germaine Dulac (1882–1942)

Artaud (*foreground, left*) as Cenci in his last production – *Les Cenci* at
the Folies Wagram, May 1935

sidesteps the problem of why it would have been impossible to produce such a painting 400 years later. In the nineteenth century a deeply religious painter such as Constable could still involve the sky in human events. Church steeples prick meaningfully above the skyline, while housetops stay below it. Reflections of sky and clouds in river and ponds are used to link the elements together. Outside Hadleigh Castle the isolated man, the dog, and the marooned-looking cows merge hopelessly into the stony earth surrounding the stony ruins. But the twentieth-century painter cannot make heaven participate in human action either sympathetically or punitively. Useful acting exercises may be based on the imitation of plants and animals, but there would have been less self-contradiction in Artaud's writings about theatre if he had not been thinking in terms of magic and mysticism, of making metaphysical statements with gesture and voice, of exorcising demons.

In a letter to Benjamin Crémieux dated 15 September 1931 (the first of four letters which have since acquired the title 'Lettres sur le langage'), Artaud argued that 'theatre should become a sort of experimental demonstration of the profound identity of the concrete and the abstract'. He attacked Western languages for desiccating ideas, while he praised Oriental languages for 'setting in motion a system of natural analogies'. Theatre should be where 'ideas are stopped in flight at a point where they have not yet become abstract'. The ideal theatre 'reconciles us philosophically with Becoming'. In the second of these letters (to Jean Paulhan, 28 September 1932), he spoke of 'an alternative natural language':

> Words do not wish to say everything. By their nature and because they are fixed once and for all, they stop and paralyse thought instead of allowing it free play and encouraging it to develop. . . . To spoken language I am adding another language and trying to restore its old magical efficacity, its power of enchantment, which is integral to words, whose mysterious potential has been forgotten.

It was in 1932 that the young Jean-Louis Barrault met Artaud and found him extremely impressive:

> He had an extraordinary forehead that he always thrust in front of him as if to light his path. From this magnificent brow sheaves of hair

sprouted. His piercing blue eyes sank into their sockets as if in that way they could scrutinize further. The eyes of a rapacious bird—an eagle. His thin pinched nose quivered incessantly. His mouth, like the whole of Artaud, preyed upon itself. His spine was bent like a bow. His lean arms with their long hands, like two twisted forked trunks, seemed to be trying to plough up his belly. His voice, rising up from his innermost caverns, bounded towards his head with such rare force that it was dashed against the sounding board of his forehead. It was both sonorous and hollow, strong yet immediately muted. He was essentially an aristocrat. Artaud was a prince.[2]

Luois Jouvet too was impressed by his personality, but it was only after prolonged importuning that he consented to employ Artaud as his assistant in the production of Alfred Savoir's *La Pâtissière du village*. But Jouvet did not respond favourably to the suggestion that the dream scene should be staged with twenty giant puppets swaying to the sound of a march mixed with Oriental harmonies while fireworks exploded all round them.

In the summer of 1932 there was a rumour that a 'Théâtre de la N.R.F.' was to be created with Gide, Valéry, and Paulhan on the management committee and with Artaud as artistic director. In an interview he gave to *L'Intransigeant* for the issue dated 26 June, Artaud said it was true, but Gallimard, Paulhan, and some of the others were so angry that a denial had to be printed immediately and an alternative title found for Artaud's project. He then invented the phrase that has become so famous, 'Theatre of Cruelty', explaining it in a letter to Paulhan dated 13 September: 'This Cruelty is not a matter of sadism or bloodshed, at least not exclusively. I do not cultivate horror systematically.' In using the word 'cruelty', he wanted 'to return to the etymological origins of language, which always evoked a concrete notion through abstract concepts. . . . Essentially [*Du point de vue de l'esprit*] cruelty means strictness, diligence, and implacable resolution, irreversible and absolute determination.' The current philosophical Determinism was itself an image of cruelty. In all practical cruelty there was 'a sort of superior determinism to which the torturer-executioner is himself subject. . . . Cruelty is above all lucid, a sort of rigorous discipline, submission to necessity.' There could be no cruelty without consciousness. Consciousness was what 'gives its blood-red tinge to every act of living, its hue of cruelty, because it is understood that life is always the death of someone else.'

Interesting and attractive though these ideas are, the linguistic assumption was confusingly retrogressive. Pressed for an elucidation of the phrase 'concrete notion', Artaud would have had to fall back on the Platonic idea that words derived from a set of individuated essences. By the eighteenth century it had already been obvious to Dr. Johnson (as he said in his life of Cowley) that 'words, being arbitrary, must owe their power to association, and have the influence, and that only, which custom has given them'. To Artaud, everything in the social and cultural world seemed to have an identity that did not depend on custom or relationships.

All the theories Artaud evolved for his Theatre of Cruelty were intended to introduce a new phase of theatrical practice in which 'the director becomes author—that is to say creator.' This is how he put it in a letter of 7 August 1932 to André Gide: 'And the interest my productions will arouse will be connected with the confidence that will be vested in me as creator or inventor of a theatrical reality which is absolute and self-sufficient.' But he wanted to have—either as patrons or as a board of management—several distinguished littérateurs, including Gide, Valéry, Paulhan, Gaston Gallimard, and possibly Julien Benda. With one eye on the fund-raising, he asked permission to announce that the first production would be an adaptation by Gide of an apocryphal Shakespearean play, the text prepared specially for the production. Artaud submitted a draft of what he wanted to print: 'This attempt at bringing the visual element into the foreground will develop the notion of a performance not for the eye or the ear but for the mind. Gestures will be equivalent to signs, signs to words. The words spoken will be, in a sense, incantatory—psychological circumstances permitting. . . . Above all, the humour emanating from the dialogue will be intended to question the known relationships between one object and another. Pushing the consequences of this dissociation to its extreme, it will realize a physical and spatial poetry which has long been missing from the theatre.'

Gide's reply, dated 16 August, was not unfriendly, but he asked Artaud not to use his name. 'I do not believe in the theatre, i.e. I do not believe that in a society like ours, with the mediocre middle-class public of today, communion is possible or even desirable.' When Artaud's manifesto for the Theatre of Cruelty appeared in the *N.R.F.* on 1 October 1932, the formulation of intention was different, while the word 'cruelty' was mentioned only perfunctorily. There could be no theatre without 'an element of cruelty at the basis of every show', said Artaud, and, under the caption 'Programme', he promised that, without 'taking account of text', his productions would include an excerpt from the Zohar —'the story of Rabbi Simeon, which has the violence and incessant energy of a great fire; the story of Bluebeard, reconstituted documentarily, with 'a new idea of eroticism and cruelty'; the Biblical story of the fall of Jerusalem, the colour of blood flowing through it, with that sense of abandonment and spiritual panic which is visible even in daylight; a story by the Marquis de Sade, with its eroticism transposed, pruned, and allegorically represented—the cruelty would be violently externalized and everything else covered up. A play from the Shakespearean period would be adapted to the current spiritual confusion, while other Elizabethan plays would be stripped of their dialogue to retain only costume, situations and characters. The influence of the Surrealist attitude to dreams is visible at several points in the manifesto, and Jan Kott has compared this attitude to the Elizabethan text with Picabia's trick of dismantling an alarm clock to make an *objet-dada* out of the parts.

The words 'metaphysics', 'magic', 'dream', 'ritual', and 'exorcism' are more prominent than 'cruelty'. The manifesto begins with the assertion: 'We cannot go on prostituting the idea of theatre, which is valid only when there is a magical and agonizing relationship with reality and with danger.' Spatial expression, the only reality on the physical side of theatre, allows the 'magical means at the disposal of art and language' to work 'organically and in their entirety, like renewed exorcisms'. If the theatre was to be saved from human psychologizing, a metaphysics must be created out of words, gestures, and expression. It would have to be based on cosmic notions concerning Creation, Becoming, and Chaos. 'They can create a sort of exciting equation between Man, Society, Nature, and Things.'

The vagueness of formulations like this made it hard to measure the over-ambitiousness of the project, though Artaud was patently being unrealistic when he proposed that Western habits of speech should be abandoned in favour of Oriental incantation, which 'finally destroys our intellectual subjection to language by conveying the impression of a new deeper intellectuality which is hidden under gestures and under signs raised to the dignity of particular exorcisms'. The new theatre language must 'use human nervous magnetism to transcend the ordinary limits of art and language to realize actively—that is to say magically, *in real terms*— a sort of total creation, where man has only to resume his position between dreams and reality'.

Artaud had not made up his mind about how much he expected the performance to communicate. He was assuming the possibility of a non-verbal, non-rational contact with the inner life of the audience, but he also said that it was not his intention to bore the spectator with 'transcendental cosmic preoccupations'. On the other hand, he did have a clear concept of the immediate physical impact, which would depend on 'cries, groans, apparitions, surprises, all kinds of *coups de théâtre*, magical beauty in costumes derived from certain rituals, brilliant lighting effects, beautiful incantation, harmonic charm, rare musical sounds, the colour of the objects, the physical rhythms of the movements whose rise and fall will beat to the pulse of movements familiar to everybody, the appearance of new and surprising objects, masks, outside puppets, abrupt changes of lighting, lighting effects that suggest heat and cold, etc.'

His private needs and preoccupations are visible both in the desire to destroy the fundamental dualism of theatre—between play and production—and in the concern to create a physical language which would short-circuit 'all the hiatus between mind and tongue, in which we see what might be called the impotence of language'. But his formulations have had enormous influence on the theatre's development. Susan Sontag was not exaggerating when she described his impact as 'so profound that the course of all recent serious theatre in Western Europe and the Americas can be said to divide into two periods—before Artaud and after Artaud'. Theatre has become less verbal and more physical. Not that Artaud's influence can be isolated from that of the designers Appia and Craig or the directors Meyerhold, Reinhardt, and Piscator, who in their different ways were all challenging what Artaud called the dictatorship of the word. Adolphe Appia (1862–1925), whom Jacques Copeau called his 'master', gave acting primacy over text and all the other elements in dramatic art, insisting that 'The point of contact between body and mind, which alone can create harmony, has become lost.'[3] Edward Gordon Craig (1872–1966) argued that the director should be dominant and that theatre was an art in its own right, born out of gesture, movement and dance.[4] The eclectic Vsevolod Meyerhold (1874–c.1940) was strongly anti-literary and deeply interested in a Dionysian focus on the inner life. He drew on the techniques of Noh theatre, *commedia dell'arte*, gymnastics, circus, and opera. By the thirties he was aiming at a Wagnerian synthesis of words, music, lighting, rhythmic movement, and 'all the magic of the plastic arts'.[5] His writings might have been more influential had his prose style not been so tedious. Max Reinhardt (1873–1943), who translated many of Craig's pictorial ideas into theatrical practice, was like Artaud not only in believing that theatre could be used to counteract the spiritual desiccation characteristic of the modern world, but also in using the imagery of cruelty: 'Every night the actor bears the stigmata, which his imagination inflicts on him, and bleeds from a thousand wounds.'[6] Erwin Piscator (1893–1966), who began as a disciple of Reinhardt, later collaborating with Brecht, developed an elaborate anti-illusionistic machinery to make didactic social statements. But none of these designers and directors seems to have exerted as much influence as Artaud on the evolution of theatrical style.*

The most influential passage of all in Artaud's manifesto deals with theatre architecture and the relationship of the acting area to the auditorium:

> We are abolishing stage and auditorium, replacing them with a sort of common space without any kind of division or barrier. . . . Direct communication will be re-established between spectator and performance, actor and spectator, by the placing of the audience in the centre of the action. . . . Abandoning existing theatres, we will take some hangar or barn, reconstructing it according to the architectural principles expressed in certain churches, certain holy places, certain

* See chapter 10 for a discussion of this influence.

Tibetan temples. . . . The four walls will be bare of any ornament, while the public will be seated in the middle of the floor on swivel chairs which allow it to watch the performance going on all round it. . . . Special positions in the four corners of the hall will be reserved for the actors and the action. Sequences will be played in front of whitewashed walls designed to absorb light. Overhead, as in certain primitive paintings, galleries will run all round the hall. These will allow the actors to pursue each other from one position to another whenever the action demands it, whilst the action can spread to different levels and differing perspectives. A shout uttered at one end of the hall can be transferred from mouth to mouth with successive modulations and amplifications till it reaches the other end. The action will unfurl, will extend its trajectory from level to level, point to point, paroxysms erupting suddenly in different places, as in a great fire.

In 1921 Appia had already been arguing that dramatic art was above all the art of life which could 'be expressed without buildings, without sets, since time and space are enough'. But— partly because they were so much better written—Artaud's formulations were more influential in preparing the ground for the reaction against 'the tyranny of the word' and against conventional theatre buildings. Brecht's Berliner Ensemble worked in an old proscenium theatre on the Schiffbauerdamm, but his alienation effect had been designed to destroy the illusion of the invisible wall, and in the fifties, the influence of his production ideas combined with Artaud's influence to interest directors, playwrights, and actors all over the world in making new contact with the audience—contact that would not depend on scenic illusion. In New York's Off-Broadway and in England's fringe theatre, pubs and cellars have been adapted to theatrical use, while small theatres have been built where the seating can be rearranged for each production. There have also been experiments in 'environmental theatre', extending the terrain of the designer to include the auditorium, so that spectators have the impression of sitting in the locale where the action is set.

On 14 November 1932 Artaud wrote a second letter to Paulhan about his use of the word 'cruelty'. He now defined it as:

appetite for life, cosmic strictness and implacable necessity, in the Gnostic sense of the whirlwind of life that eats up darkness, in the sense of that pain which is ineluctably necessary to the continuation of life. Good is willed—the result of an action; evil is continuous. When he creates, the hidden god conforms to the cruel necessity of creation, which is imposed on him, and he is not free not to create. So he cannot exclude from the centre of the willed whirlwind of good a nucleus of evil which is increasingly reduced, increasingly consumed.

Gnosticism, a heresy that survived from the third century to the seventh, was founded on the doctrine that the universe and its Creator were evil. Matter was beyond redemption; only the human soul had potential for goodness. Some of the Gnostic philosophers combined elements of Platonism with elements of Christianity, condemning the Jews and praising the paradisal serpent for warning Eve against the evil god of the Old Testament. One Gnostic doctrine was taken over by Mohammed: that Jesus of Nazareth was identical with the Son of God only from the moment of his baptism until the Passion. This explained why he had said, 'My God, my God, why hast thou forsaken me?' So the man who died on the Cross was only a man.

Like the Manichaeans, some of the Gnostics taught that all sexuality was evil; some spilled their sperm ritually to interrupt the cycle of procreation. Artaud's essay 'Le Théâtre alchimique'[7] is Gnostic in its argument that there were two stages in Genesis. After a period of 'single, conflictless Will', there was a period of 'difficulty and the Double, that of matter and the obscuring of the idea'. The earlier period offers no model for drama, but there is great excitement in the 'philosophical struggles' of the second stage. 'It is the principle of alchemy not to let the spirit come into its own until it has passed through all the piping and all the substructure of existing matter.' Artaud's concept of theatre derives partly from Gnostic ritual, partly from alchemy. The concern is with a communal act conducive to metamorphosis in the individual soul. Artaud implies an analogy with the Eleusinian mysteries, which must, he says, have worked towards resolving 'all the conflicts produced by the antagonism between matter and spirit, idea and form, concrete and abstract'.

Artaud was fascinated by the ideas of creation and destruction on a massive scale. Having asserted several times that contemporary civilization ought to be destroyed by bombs or machine-guns, and having compared the effect of theatre with that of a great fire, he went on to the most famous of all his analogies—between theatre and plague. He may have been prompted by the fact that Dr. Allendy was working on a book about the Black Death; Anaïs Nin, who was a patient and a friend, was doing research on it for him. When she met Artaud in March 1933, she described him in her diary as 'Lean, taut. A gaunt face, with visionary eyes. A sardonic manner. Now weary, now fiery and malicious. . . . He is the drugged, contracted being who walks always alone. . . . His eyes are blue with languor, black with pain. . . . The deep-set eyes of the mystic, as if shining from caverns. . . . He is poor. He is in conflict with a world he imagines mocking and threatening. His intensity is brooding, rather terrifying.'[8] She knew that Allendy had been trying unsuccessfully to liberate him from the drug habit. When she told Artaud that for her part she was happy in her world of hallucinations, he answered: 'I cannot even say that. It is torture for me. I make superhuman efforts to awake.'

Attending his lecture on 'Le Théâtre et la peste' at the Sorbonne on 6 April 1933, she sat in the front row because he had asked her to.

Is he trying to remind us that it was during the Plague that so many marvellous works of art and theatre came to be, because, whipped by the fear of death, man seeks immortality, or to escape, or to surpass himself? But then, imperceptibly almost, he let go of the thread we were following and began to act out dying by plague. No one quite knew when it began. . . . His face was contorted with anguish, one could see the perspiration dampening his hair. His eyes dilated, his muscles became cramped, his fingers struggled to retain their flexibility. He made one feel the parched and burning throat, the pains, the fever, the fire in the guts. He was in agony. He was screaming. He was delirious. He was enacting his own death, his own crucifixion. At first people gasped. And then they began to laugh. Everyone was laughing! They hissed. Then one by one, they began to leave, noisily, talking, protesting. They banged the door as they left. . . . More protestations. More jeering. But Artaud went on, until the last gasp. And stayed on the floor. Then when the hall had emptied of all but his small group of friends, he walked straight up to me and kissed my hand. He asked me to go to the café with him. . . . Artaud and I walked out in a fine mist. We walked, walked through the dark streets. He was hurt, wounded, baffled by the jeering. He spat out his anger. 'They always want to hear *about*; they want to hear an objective conference on "The Theatre and the Plague", and I want to give them the experience itself, the plague itself, so they will be terrified, and awaken. I want to awaken them. They do not realize *they are dead*. Their death is total, like deafness, blindness. This is agony I portrayed. Mine, yes, and everyone who is alive. . . . I feel sometimes that I am not writing, but describing the struggles with writing, the struggles of birth.'

Artaud was attracted to the idea of plague as a 'scourge', that 'liquefied' all the social structures. Order disappears. Morality is routed, psychology overturned. Delirium takes over. Immunized, apparently, by avaricious frenzy the dregs of the population enter the unlocked houses to lay hands on riches they will never be able to use. 'It is then that theatre establishes itself. Theatre, that is to say the gratuitousness of pointless actions.' If, as he had argued in his previous lecture at the Sorbonne on 'La Mise en scène et la métaphysique', the social and moral system ought to be destroyed totally, the damage that theatre could inflict must be peripheral and the value of the activity more spiritual than material. In *The City of God*, St. Augustine had compared the plague (which unlike leprosy and syphilis left the organs intact inside the diseased body) with the theatre, which, without killing, could induce mysterious changes in the minds of whole nations.

In Artaud's view the plague was not so much a disease carried by a virus as 'a sort of psychic entity'. Describing the symptoms in the individual body, he employed cosmic imagery. 'Soon the body fluids, furrowed like the earth by lightning, like a volcano assaulted by subterranean storms, look for an outlet.' The images spring from his vision of the plague as a destructive force wielded not by chance but by a fate which is either evil or at best indifferent to human morality. 'No one can explain why the plague strikes down the coward who runs away but spares the lecher who takes his pleasure from dead bodies.' The surge of erotic fever among recuperating victims of the plague is analogous to the gratuitousness of theatre, while the condition of the victim who dies with all his organs intact is comparable to that of the actor who lets himself be penetrated by emotions which have no source in reality. His paroxysms are physical but nothing has happened to him.

> The plague takes dormant images, latent anarchy, pushing them abruptly into extreme gestures; the theatre too pushes gestures to their extreme: like the plague it recreates the links between what is and what is not, between what could exist and what does. . . . All the conflicts dormant inside us are restored, while their energy is crystallized into names which we recognize as signs.

So the plague, like the Eleusinian mysteries, became in Artaud's hands a weapon against dualism. His constant ambition was to reunite reality with the ideal, practice with theory, matter with spirit, the human with the superhuman. The lecture ended with a celebration of John Ford's play *'Tis Pity She's a Whore*, which was lit, said Artaud, like the plague, by a 'sort of strange sun', an illumination of abnormal intensity which suddenly makes difficulty and even impossibility appear to be our natural element. If the creation involved a 'slaughter of essences', theatre, like the plague, was 'in the image of this slaughter, this essential separation'.

In June, when Artaud asked Anaïs Nin whether she thought he was mad, she decided 'that he was, and that I loved his madness. I looked at his mouth, with the edges darkened by laudanum, a mouth I did not want to kiss. To be kissed by Artaud was to be drawn towards death, towards insanity.' In a taxi, pointing to the crowded streets, he said that the revolution would come soon. The corrupt world must be destroyed.

> 'I wanted a theatre that would be like a shock treatment, galvanize, shock people into feeling.' For the first time it seemed to me that Artaud was living in such a fantasy world that it was for himself that he wanted a violent shock, to feel the reality of it, or the incarnating power of a great passion. . . . I realized that he wanted a revolution, he wanted a catastrophe, a disaster that would put an end to his intolerable life.

It was in 1933, probably at the beginning of the year, that Artaud wrote his second manifesto for the Theatre of Cruelty, including a synopsis of his project for the first production, which was to be titled 'La Conquête du Mexique'. The intention was to 'present events and not men'—subordinating human psychology to historical necessity. This objective was in line with Brecht's attempts to theatricalize individual actions as historical events, while the reasons Artaud gave for his choice are strikingly progressive. The condemnation of colonialism reflected the attitude of the Surrealists and Communists, which did not become generally acceptable until after the war. Ambitiously, Artaud thought he could use the story to deflate both Europe's fatuous idea of its own superiority and the notion that Christianity was superior to all the ancient religions. The materialism and the 'tyrannical anarchy' of the colonists would be contrasted with 'the profound moral harmony' and the 'organically hierarchical monarchy' of the natives. Artaud's production never materialized, but a similar confrontation between two modes of civilization was dramatized over thirty years later by Peter Shaffer in *The Royal Hunt of the Sun* (1964), a play which had great commercial success but negligible ideological influence.

Artaud's interest in primitive religions led him to Apollonius of Tyana, a neo-Pythagorean sage and clairvoyant, a contemporary of Jesus who was set up by one anti-Christian writer (Hierocles of Nicomedia) as a rival Messiah. After abandoning the idea of writing an essay on Apollonius, Artaud had gone on to study Heliogabalus, who was only fourteen when he became Emperor of Rome in A.D. 218, having been a priest of the local Sun-god at Emesa. In the book *Héliogabale ou l'anarchiste couronné*, which he finished in April 1933, Artaud entered into a stranger and more detailed identification than he had with Uccello or Abélard. The boy's personality concentrated all the qualities of an Artaudesque plague, and he let it loose on Rome in four years of misrule. 'If Heliogabalus brings anarchy into Rome, if he appears as the ferment that precipitates a latent state of anarchy, the original anarchy is in himself and it ravages his organism, throws his mind into a sort of precocious madness' (*O.C.* VII. 103).

Despite Heliogabalus' exorbitant cruelty and vicious irresponsibility—he gave the command of the Praetorians to an actor and put a hairdresser in charge of the food supply—Artaud admired him for reconciling the sexual principles within himself. Though effeminate and homosexual, he was high priest of a phallic cult. 'The religion of the sun is the religion of man, but man can do nothing without woman, his double, where he is reflected.' Behind Artaud's empathy with Heliogabalus lay his own childhood experience of being surrounded by women. Throughout the book, men are dominated by women. There is incest between the emperor and his mother, whose father had killed his father. Fascinated, as in 'Le Clair Abélard', by the theme of castration, Artaud tries to justify Heliogabalus's frequent recourse to it as a punishment: his motive must have been to liberate his victims from internal sexual conflict.

Fundamentally, Artaud's interest in Heliogabalus sprang from the same obsession as his interest in the theatre: imperial rule, like a public performance, can embody a direct connection between microcosm and macrocosm, mental imbalance and political chaos. In a letter of 30 December 1933 to Orane Demazis, Artaud uses the same word 'disordering' (*dérèglement*) that Rimbaud had used in his letters to Izambard and Demeny:*

> I think there is now a human duty... which corresponds to our sense of destiny... a human duty to take account of all the evil forces which make up the *Zeitgeist*. There is somewhere a disordering which we cannot master, whatever name we choose to call it by. All sorts of inexplicable crimes inside the self, gratuitous crimes, are part of this disordering. So are the far too frequent occurrences of earthquakes, volcanic eruptions, marine tornadoes, and railway accidents. What we do not want to recognize is that an entertainment can be a lightning-conductor, that what is enacted on the stage can go on to be acted out in life.

The same preoccupation with finding correspondences between the inner and outer worlds recurs in 'En finir avec les chefs d'œuvre', written about December 1933: 'Either we bring all the arts back to a central position and necessity, finding analogies between gestures in painting or acting and movements made by volcanic lava, or we should stop painting, chattering, writing, or

* See above, p. 32.

doing anything else.' But Artaud's prophetic gift was inextricable from his madness. The rejection of masterpieces looks forward to post-war manifestations of anti-art and Pop Art. 'We must do away with this idea of masterpieces for a self-styled élite, which the masses do not understand. . . . The masterpieces of the past are good for the past but no good for us. . . . Let us leave literary criticism to teachers and formal criticism to aesthetes, recognizing that what has been said does not need to be said again.' Though the Dadaists, with their concentration on immediacy and the ephemeral, had been inclined to rule out the possibility of creating a *magnum opus,* in 1933 Artaud's argument represented the view of a small minority; today there is a general feeling that artists cannot expect to produce masterpieces.

Marcel Duchamp, who was a friend of Picabia and peripherally involved with Dadaism, ultimately rejected the idea of anti-art, but he wanted to put an end to 'the possibility of recognizing or identifying any two things as being like each other' and to find a non-referential language: 'The search for prime words, divisible only by themselves and by unity' (in *From the Green Box*). His ready-mades (such as the urinal titled *Fountain*) anticipate Pop Art. A urinal or a Campbell's soup tin can arguably become a work of art even if the artist has not made it, but it cannot arguably become a masterpiece. The gesture of declaring it to be a work of art is an ironical act of criticism or anti-criticism. What was being sabotaged was the idea of tradition as represented, for instance, in T. S. Eliot's 1919 essay, 'Tradition and the Individual Talent'. For Eliot, the best and most individual parts of a poet's work 'may be those in which the dead poets, his ancestors, assert their immortality most vigorously'. Duchamp and Artaud both wanted to believe that the ancestors were not immortal.

But the affinity between Duchamp and Artaud goes deeper than this. Both wanted to get away from 'literature' and from 'influences'; both were influenced by Alfred Jarry, who in fact funnelled nineteenth-century literature into twentieth-century art. Both were at pains to reconcile male and female principles. In Duchamp's *La Mariée mise à nu par ses Célibataires, même* the figure of the bride was taken, as Duchamp often said later, from fairground figures representing a bride and groom, at which visitors were invited to throw wooden balls. Octavio Paz comments: 'The bachelor keeps his virility intact while the husband disperses it and so becomes feminine.'[9] In the painting, sexuality is translated into mechanical images.

Like Artaud, Duchamp was drawn to the non-human—as a means of sterilizing fantasies that were erotic in origin. Each was unable to express himself to his own satisfaction in any existing vocabulary: 'Every picture', said Duchamp, 'has to exist before it is put on canvas and it always loses something when it is turned into paint. I prefer to see my pictures without that muddying.' He tried to create a new visual language, and the effort sent him back, as it did Artaud, to alchemy as a means of reaching beyond dualism, bridging between mind and matter, spirit and substance. For Jung, alchemy was 'a question of actualizing those contents of the unconscious which are outside nature, that is, not a datum of our empirical world and therefore of an *a priori* or archetypal character'.[10] Duchamp, as John Golding has suggested, may have been attracted by the fact that the basic tenets of alchemy are archetypal.[11] This possibly explains the frequent recurrence in his work of the circle, the wheel, and the spiral in rotation.

Artaud's essay on 'Le Théâtre alchimique' had been intended for the N.R.F., but the publication of his first manifesto had failed to produce a favourable reaction, and he was not receiving as much support as he felt entitled to from Paulhan and his colleagues. In a letter of 18 October 1932 he had asked for the typescript to be returned, complaining that he was being thrown out of the N.R.F. Though his personal relationship with Paulhan improved, he had little to do with the review in 1933 or 1934, eighteen months elapsing between his lecture on 'Le Théâtre et la peste' and the publication of a revised version at the beginning of October 1934.

Nor did Paulhan ever use his influence, as Artaud hoped he would, to raise funds for the new theatre. In January 1934 Artaud launched a private appeal to potential backers by giving a one-man show in the house of Lise Deharme, who had herself promised 30,000 francs (if we can believe his letter of 19 March 1934 to Paulhan). Artaud's aim was to demonstrate not only his prowess as actor and author but the validity of his ideas: he gave a reading of *Richard II* followed by his scenario 'La Conquête du Mexique', 'interpolating a commentary'. Artaud was satisfied with his own performance, but not with its financial outcome. Lise Deharme 'betrayed' him by giving a 'derisory' sum, and no one else seems to have made a substantial contribution.

But Artaud was not yet defeated. 'I have just finished a tragedy,' he wrote to Gide on 10 February 1935, after putting the final touches to his adaptation of *Les Cenci*, derived mainly from Shelley's 1819 play (a French translation by F. Rabbe had been published in 1887) but also from Stendhal's 1837 translation of extracts from the archives in the Cenci palace. Like *Héliogabale* and *'Tis Pity She's a Whore*, the story involved incest: after raping his daughter, Beatrice, in order to punish her with eternal damnation, Count Cenci was murdered by her and by his wife, Lucretia. At the beginning of February, to raise funds for a production of his adaptation, Artaud invited potential backers to the home of his friend Jean-Marie Conty, where he gave a reading of his script. The guests included the publisher Robert Denoël, whose wife, Cécile Bressant, had ambitions as an actress, as had another of the guests, Iya Abdy, a beautiful blonde of Russian origin, who had previously been married to Sir Robert Abdy. It was by promising her the role of Beatrice and Cécile Bressant the role of Lucretia that Artaud secured the money he needed.

As in the painting of *Lot and his Daughters*, Artaud saw incest as precipitating a revelation of 'cosmic cruelty'. 'I have imposed on my tragedy the movement of nature, this kind of gravitation which works alike on plants and creatures, and which is also to be seen in the volcanic upheavals of the sun.' Drawn to the non-human, he was similarly drawn to the superhuman: he was calling the play a tragedy, he wrote in *Le Figaro* (5 May 1935), because it was a myth: 'the men, though less than gods, are more than men. Neither innocent nor guilty, they are subject to the same essential amorality as the gods of the Antique Mysteries, the source of all tragedy.' Writing about *'Tis Pity She's a Whore*, he had spoken of 'superhuman passion'. Annabella wept not with remorse but for fear she would not be able to satisfy her passion. In *Les Cenci*, the 'tempestuous' impulses of the characters lift them above the level of ordinary humanity. Shelley's Cenci dies after morbidly predicting the reign of evil on earth:

> O, multitudinous Hell, the fiends will shake
> Thine arches with the laughter of their joy!
> There shall be lamentation heard in Heaven
> As o'er an angel fallen; and upon Earth
> All good shall droop and sicken, and ill things
> Shall with a spirit of unnatural life
> Stir and be quickened even as I am now.

The final attitude of Artaud's Cenci is Sadean: it is not his fault if the impulse to incest was implanted in him.

> Repent? Why should I? Repentance is in God's hands. It is for him to regret what I did. Why did he make me father of such an utterly desirable creature? Let those who condemn my crime first condemn fate. Free? Who can speak of freedom when the heavens are about to fall on our heads? I open the floodgates only so as not to be submerged. There is something like a devil inside me destined to avenge the world's transgressions. From now on there is no destiny to stand between me and my dreams.

At the end of her life, Artaud's Beatrice has adopted the same viewpoint. She complains that no choice between good and evil has been made by God, by men, or by 'any of the powers that control what is called our destiny'. As in the works of Sade, the amorality of the characters is justified by analogy with the amorality of thunderstorms, hurricanes, and floods.

In his 10 February letter to Gide, Artaud wrote:

> In the dialogue of this tragedy there is, I will dare to say, an ultimate violence. Of the antique notions of society, order, justice, religion, family, and patriotism, none escapes attack. I therefore expect violent reactions from the audience. . . . I attack the social superstition of the family without asking for arms to be taken up against this or that individual. The same goes for order and justice. . . . People do not always distinguish between order and its representatives. . . . I attack order itself. . . . I strike hard in order to strike quickly but above all to strike completely and decisively.

Artaud was to be very disappointed when the production failed to arouse any strong reaction.

The only theatre available was the Folies-Wagram. 'The long entrance corridor, the immense auditorium surrounded by a

promenade, the long foyer, even the decoration of the walls—
everything suggested a place better suited to music hall than to a
serious revival of the scenic art.'[12] Rehearsals did not run smoothly.
Playing Cenci himself as well as directing, Artaud had great
difficulty in explaining his ideas to the actors. He quarrelled constantly with Iya Abdy: having provided most of the backing, she
did not feel obliged to do what she was told. 'At one moment in
the production', wrote André Franck,

> Artaud wanted to see her hanging by her magnificent head of hair
> from the torturer's wheel. It could not have failed to be effective. A
> convenient footstool under her feet, camouflaged, would prevent her
> from hanging in reality. Rightly or wrongly Mme Abdy suspects
> Artaud of wanting to overturn the little stool on the night of the
> première to make her reaction more truthful, more striking. . . . Stool
> or no stool she does not want to be hanged. . . . There will be no
> wheel and no hanging. Artaud's anger is terrible.[13]

Reviewing the production in the *N.R.F.* (June 1935), Pierre
Jean Jouve found Artaud's Cenci too self-conscious to be really a
man of the Renaissance. The combination of furious blasphemies
with atheism were reminiscent of the Marquis de Sade, while the
vengeful pride in doing evil seemed paranoiac. Jouve praised
Balthus's set, which made him think of Piranesi (who had in fact
inspired it), and Artaud's direction, which 'continually and
creatively brought the space to life. . . . The complex lighting
effects, the movements of individuals and groups, the sounds, the
music, show the audience that space and time constitute an
affective reality.' Michel Leiris has described how the objectiviza-
tion of collective delirium cut across all traditional ideas of
theatre.[14] The impression of disorder made it impossible for the
ordinary spectator to see how disciplined it all was.

Roger Blin, who, like Artaud, suffered from a stammer, made
his first appearance on stage as one of the two assassins, a non-
speaking role. 'You are a medium,' Artaud told him. 'Make up
your face in four quarters, two green, two red.' Both assassins had
to mime their performances. Many of the other make-ups were
stylized—one face was grey all over—and the production itself
was stylized. To make the actors think of themselves as rapacious

men of the Renaissance, Artaud had asked each of them to choose
an animal image for himself. In the banquet scene the tables were
arranged in a triangle, and each movement of Cenci's produced a
ripple of reaction from the guests.[15]

But most of the reviews were hostile and the production had to
be taken off after seventeen performances. On 15 May 1935
Artaud wrote to Paulhan:

> For me PERSONALLY it is a financial catastrophe. My royalties were
> spent in advance and I have nothing to live on. . . . I have made an
> immense effort, and here I am on the verge of the abyss. That is the
> result. From the theatrical point of view I believe the conception was
> good. . . . But I was betrayed by the realization. I cannot be every-
> where at once. That is the danger of theatre. I was too exhausted to
> play my own role. Hence the semi-failure of that aspect, but you
> know how I can act when I am at my best.

Artaud must have known that he would never have another
opportunity to realize his vision theatrically. After watching Jean-
Louis Barrault's mime of a horse in his *Autour d'une mère*, which
was based on Faulkner's *As I Lay Dying*, he waited for the young
actor, who later wrote: 'The two of us went down the boulevard
Rochechouart, and together we started off on two imaginary
horses, galloping as far as the Place Blanche. There he suddenly
left me. He was drunk with enthusiasm.'[16] Reviewing the production for the July 1935 *N.R.F.*, Artaud saluted a younger man who
was endowed with the ability to please the public. The critics had
not warmed to the production, but the audience had. The show
had magic in it, said Artaud, like the magic of black witch doctors
who drive out a disease by simulating the sick man's breathing.
Barrault's mime vindicated the importance of gesture and movement in space. Comparing him with the Balinese, Artaud was
awarding the accolade he had hoped to reserve for himself.

He may have been thinking partly of Barrault when he wrote
'Un Athlétisme affectif' in about December 1935. It advances the
idea that the actor should think of a human being as a double or an
'eternal ghost radiating affective powers'. The ideas about breathing and screams put forward in this essay and in 'Le Théâtre de
Séraphin' are remarkably similar to the ideas Barrault himself

advanced in 'An Attempt at a Little Treatise on the Alchemy of the Theatre' and 'Alchemy of the Human Body'.[17] Barrault complained later of being unable to separate Artaud's influence on him from that of Dullin and Etienne Decroux, the mime who had been an actor in the Théâtre Alfred Jarry. In any case, Artaud was able, through Barrault, to exert more influence on the development of French theatre than he had through his own activity as a practical man of the theatre.

They met almost every day. He introduced Barrault to Tantrist Yoga, Hatha Yoga, the Tibetan *Book of the Dead*, the works of Fabre d'Olivet, the Upanishads, the *Bhagavad-Gita, Milarepa*, and Pythagoras' *Golden Verses*.[18] He called the actor 'an athlete of the emotions'. He talked about magic and metaphysics. He taught Barrault about the Cabbala, which divides human breathing into six main 'arcana', each involving a different combination of masculine, feminine, and neuter. As in acupuncture, said Artaud, there are pressure points in the body which support physical exertion and come into play when affective thought is emerging. The solar plexus, for instance, is the centre for anger, aggressive and gnawing emotions. The secret is to agitate these pressure points as if whipping muscles into action. Barrault made good use of these ideas. What he learned may be inferred from Paule Thévenin's accounts in *Tel Quel* (nos. 20 and 39) of what Artaud taught her: 'He gave me exercises to do. . . . I learned to scream, to sustain the cry to the point of annihilation, to move from falsetto to a lower pitch, to prolong a syllable till breath was totally spent.'

Barrault's theatre was like a stewing pot in which Artaud's ideas went on fermenting for a very long time. Having once discussed with Artaud the possibility of finding a theatrical coefficient of the idea in 'Le Théâtre et la peste' by dramatizing Daniel Defoe's *Journal of the Plague Year*, Barrault commissioned Albert Camus to dramatize his novel *La Peste*. The play, *L'État de siège*, was produced in October 1948, seven months after Artaud's death, with sets by Balthus. The production was a failure, but often, though Artaud's ideas were vulgarized in being translated on to the grand scale—or perhaps because they were vulgarized—they made enormous impact. After Artaud's scornful treatment of *Partage de midi* in 1928, it was ironical that Barrault should score such a success with the play in 1948, and that in 1953 'total theatre' should reach one of its high points in his triumphant production of Claudel's *Christophe Colomb*. Even Artaud's ideal of merging the human with the non-human was realized in the incident when the actors who played Columbus and the drowning sailor had simultaneously to represent the sea and its energy. Unlike Artaud, Barrault had both the ability to persuade actors and the control of a mime over his own body. The mystical ideas he took from Artaud may have been antiquated and questionable, but there can be no questioning the theatrical effectiveness of the way he applied them. By extending the techniques of mime into his production ideas, he was validating Artaud's theatrical metaphysics.

After *Les Cenci* Barrault suggested they should work together, but Artaud rejected the proposal in a letter dated 14 June 1935:

> I do not believe in the possibility of a collaboration between us, because, if I know what we have in common, I am even more aware of what separates us. It is a question of our working methods, which start out from viewpoints which are diametrically opposed and end up with results which are not the same, despite appearances. . . . In a production staged by me, I DO NOT WANT there to be so much as the bat of an eyelid which does not belong to me. . . . In fact I do not believe in collaboration—especially since Surrealism—because I no longer believe in human purity. Highly though I esteem you, I think you are fallible.

Or as he put it ten months later,* when he was already in Mexico and about to set out on a journey to the interior, 'I am leaving in search of the impossible. We shall see whether I can nevertheless find it.' In other words, he had not stopped looking for the theatre he believed in, the theatre of cruelty. As he had said in a letter of 19 July 1935 to Paulhan, 'I believe that in Mexico there are still seething forces which pressurize the blood of the Indians. . . . There the theatre which I imagine, which perhaps I contain within myself, expresses itself directly, without the intervention of actors who can betray me.'

* In a letter of 2 April 1936 to René Thomas.

7

Mexico

D. H. Lawrence said at the end of his life that New Mexico had had a greater effect on him than any other place he had visited. In a posthumously published article he wrote that the Mexican Indians had liberated him from the present era of civilization:

> I had no permanent feeling of religion till I came to New Mexico and penetrated into the old human race-experience there. . . . In the oldest religion, everything was alive, not supernaturally but naturally alive. There were only deeper and deeper streams of life, vibrations of life more and more vast. So rocks were alive, but a mountain had a deeper, vaster life than a rock, and it was much harder for a man to bring his spirit, or his energy, into contact with the life of the mountain, and so draw strength from the mountain, as from a great standing well of life, than it was to come into contact with the rock. And he had to put forth a great religious effort. For the whole life-effort of man was to get his life into direct contact with the elemental life of the cosmos, mountain-life, cloud-life, thunder-life, air-life, earth-life, sun-life. To come into immediate felt contact, and so derive energy, power, and a dark sort of joy. . . . It is the religion which precedes the god-concept, and is therefore greater and deeper than any god-religion.[1]

There was nothing Artaud wanted more than to come into direct contact with the elemental life of the cosmos, and he had already shown how attracted he was by the ancient religions that effectively hinged the human self to the universe.

Since 1933 Artaud had been making notes on Oriental, Greek, and Indian cultures. Going to his hotel, wrote André Franck, one found him lying on his bed with the Upanishads or the Tibetan

Book of the Dead in his hand.[2] No doubt he also had access to the well-stocked library of Dr. Allendy, an expert on the Orient. But for Artaud, the impulse was anti-psychological. 'Psychology is not the science of man,' he wrote in one of his notebooks (*O.C.* VIII. 144). 'On the contrary.'

> The more man is preoccupied with himself, the more irrelevant are his preoccupations to human reality,
> individualist and psychological egocentricity
> opposed to humanism,
> squeeze a man hard and you will always find something that is not human.

Within a few weeks of the unfavourable reaction to *Les Cenci* he was thinking of leaving Paris for Mexico. In his letter of 19 July 1935 to Paulhan he said, 'For a long time I have been hearing about a sort of deep movement in Mexico in favour of a return to pre-Cortez civilization.' He had spoken to Robert Ricard, who had been teaching in Mexico and had said: 'These people really don't know what they are looking for. You could help them to straighten out their ideas.' Artaud's letter went on to describe the lectures he intended to give the Mexicans about the relationship between theatre and civilization. Theatre could lead to an *immediate* rediscovery of culture. 'Culture is not in books, paintings, statues, dances: it is in the nerves and the fluidity of the nerves.' With the keen appetite of a gold prospector, Artaud was planning to explore Mexico in search of 'the forces that are boiling up inside the blood of the Indians, putting it under pressure'.

By about August he was preparing notes for his lectures. He wrote ten manuscript pages under the heading 'Mexico and Civilization', maintaining that 'in Mexico, bound into the earth, lost in the flow of volcanic lava, vibrating in the Indian blood, there is the magic reality of a culture which could doubtless be materially re-ignited without much difficulty' (*O.C.* VIII. 159). He went on to attack the kind of minority culture that depended on the printed word and had lost contact with the primitive sources of inspiration. The dualistic rift between body and mind must be healed. Perhaps Mexico could teach the West how to revive the great myths. If the gods in the ancient Mexican pantheon looked savage and primitive, it was because they had not had time to dehumanize themselves.

They had never lost their potency because they were identical with active natural forces.

After eight years of writing no verse, Artaud began again in August 1935. Now that he had turned his back on theatrical activity, his energy and enthusiasm needed another outlet. The first new poem was to Lise Deharme, and some of his notes were laid out on the page like prose poems.* He also started a relationship with a young Belgian girl, Cécile Schramme, whom he thought seriously of marrying.

On 9 January 1936 he left Paris, sailing from Antwerp on the following day. Before leaving he had made arrangements for his manifestoes and articles about the Theatre of Cruelty to be published as a book, but it was only when he was on board the *S.S. Albertville* that he thought of a title for it—*Le Théâtre et son double*. 'If theatre duplicates life,' he wrote to Paulhan on 25 January,

> life duplicates true theatre, and that has nothing to do with Oscar Wilde's theories about art. This title reflects all the doubles of theatre I believe I have found over so many years: metaphysics, the plague, cruelty. . . . This word 'double' also refers to the great magical factor: the forms of theatre are no more than a figuration of it, waiting for it to become the transfiguration.

But there was a two-year delay in publication: the book did not appear until February 1938.

Arriving at Vera Cruz on 8 February, Artaud travelled by train to Mexico City. By the end of the month he had given three lectures at the University. In the first, on 'Surréalisme et révolution' (26 February), he praised the liberating effects the movement had originally had, but condemned its later affiliation with Marxism. The second, on 'L'Homme contre le destin' (27 February), attacked 'the false metaphysics born out of Marx's materialism. . . . If we have a false idea of destiny and its progress through nature, it is because we no longer know how to look at nature or to feel life in its totality. . . . To cure itself of chance, the so-called pagan world had consciousness. . . . There is a secret determinism based on the world's higher laws.' Even to mention it today was to court ridicule. 'What paganism divinized, Europe has mechanized.'

---

* I have already quoted one example above, p. 103.

The third lecture (29 February), which was on 'Le Théâtre et les dieux', proposed a concept of culture based on the idea that life is magical, that the element of fire was present in all manifestations of human thought, that the function of theatre was to display this image of thought that catches fire. Oriented in the same way as theatre was, true culture could be communicated only through space:

> Culture in space means the culture of a spirit that never ceases to breathe and to feel alive in space, which invokes the bodies of space as the very objects of its thought, but in so far as it is spirit, it situates itself in the middle of space, which is to say at its dead point.
>
> Perhaps it is a metaphysical idea, this idea of the dead point of space through which spirit has to pass. . . . Life should revive in metaphysics and this difficult concept, which maddens people today, is assumed by all the pure races which have felt themselves to be both in death and in life. This is the reason culture is not written, and, as Plato said, 'Thought has been lost since the day when the first word was written.' To write is to prevent the mind from moving among forms like a great breathing. Writing freezes mind, crystallizing it in a form, and idolatry is born from the form. . . . The Mexican Gods are Gods in space. . . . Whoever thinks of feeling and searching for the Gods today? To look for them is to look for their strength and give oneself the strength of a God. The white world calls these Gods idols, but the Indian mind knows how to make their strength vibrate, locating [*situant*] the music of their strength. Theatre, by a musical distribution of strength, calls up the power of the Gods. Each has his place in space that vibrates with images. The Gods come out towards us through a cry or through a face.

On 18 March he gave a lecture at the Alliance Française on 'Le Théâtre d'après-guerre à Paris'. The attempt had been made, he said, 'to rediscover the secret life of theatre just as Rimbaud managed to rediscover the secret life of poetry'. He compared Dullin's acting with a mechanical drill boring through the hardest of walls, and he used cosmic imagery to describe Génica Athanasiou's performance in Cocteau's *Antigone*. 'Her lament came from the far side of time, as if carried by the foam of a Mediterranean wave on a sun-soaked day; it was like carnal music spreading itself across glacial darkness.' He attacked Copeau for being subservient to the text, and commended Gaston Baty for not making this mistake, even if he did not succeed in realizing all his conceptions.[3] He praised Barrault as the champion of theatre's exploration of space, its search for the inner life which is concealed.

In May he began writing a series of articles for the newspaper *El Nacional Revolucionario*. In his 'Lettre ouverte aux gouverneurs des états du Mexique' he argued that the rites and sacred dances of the Indians (which he had not yet seen) were 'the most beautiful of all possible forms of theatre and the only one that can justify itself'. Tibet and Mexico were now the 'nodal points of world culture', but Tibetan culture was for the dead. Mexico was the only place where dormant natural forces could be useful to the living. The Indian rituals were direct manifestations of these forces: 'I will try to let the whole of my consciousness be penetrated by their soul-curing virtues.' This was an extraordinarily unpatronizing attitude to adopt in the thirties: before Lévi-Strauss, even anthropologists were generally condescending towards primitive cultures.

Writing, on 17 June, about 'La Jeune Peinture française et la tradition', he produced a variant of the argument he had advanced about Van Leyden's *Lot and His Daughters*. Since the Renaissance, European painters had concentrated on the expressions in human faces and on the superficial appearances of weather and landscape. 'Painting has fallen under the anecdotal domination of nature and psychology. Instead of being a means of revelation, it has become an art of simple descriptive representation.' It had lost the magic which had once been its *raison d'être*. Where Cimabue had manifested essences hieratically, Uccello had merely painted forms scientifically, and painters had gone on celebrating matter for its own sake. Artaud's revulsion obviously stems from his Gnostic disgust at the proliferation of unredeemed matter.

In 'Ce que je suis venu faire au Mexique' (5 July) he spoke ambitiously of his wish to revive the old idea of pagan pantheism 'in a form that would no longer be religious. True pantheism is not a philosophical system but only a method for the *dynamic investigation* of the universe.' In this article he referred explicitly to monist philosophy, which denies that matter and mind are two different kinds of substance. In the next article, 'La Culture éternelle du Mexique' (13 July), he developed the argument he had begun in the lecture 'L'Homme contre le destin'. 'A culture for which the universe is a whole knows that each element acts automatically on the totality. All we need is knowledge of their laws. To understand destiny is to dominate destiny, since, in the present as in the future, the external world falls under the sway of intelligence. By means of very precise astrological data, drawn from transcendent algebra, we can foresee events and manipulate them.' The ancient Mayas had been able to master the art of astrological prediction because they had understood that the sun was a principle of death —not, as it seemed to be, of life.

Artaud's thinking, then, was tending towards an equation between ultimate reality and nirvana, between the universe and the void. To glimpse the totality of creation is to see beyond the confines of the individual ego and of human life. As Artaud had written in one of his notebooks before he left Paris,

> there is only the void,
> everything is expressed by it, across it, around it,
> absence is more real than presence because it is eternal;
>   action is in short less immutable and permanent than reaction.
>
> (O.C. VIII. 130)

In Beckett's early novels *Murphy* (1938) and *Watt* (written 1942–5, published 1953) there is a comparable preoccupation with 'the positive peace that comes when the somethings give way, or perhaps simply add up, to the Nothing, than which in the guffaw of the Abderite naught is more real'. In his 'Dialogues with Georges Duthuit' Beckett describes Bram Van Velde as 'the first whose painting is bereft, rid if you prefer, of occasion in every shape and form, ideal as well as material, and the first whose hands have not been tied by the certitude that expression is an impossible act'.[4] In his lecture on 'Le Théâtre et les dieux', Artaud spoke of 'a fear of empty space' that

> haunts Mexican artists and makes them pile one line on top of another. . . . It indicates a need to make the void *ripen*. To populate the space so as to cover the void is to find the way of the void. It is to depart from a flowering line to fall back giddily into the void. And the Mexican Gods, who orbit round the void, provide a sort of

figured means of rediscovering the strengths of a void without which
there is no reality.

At the end of August, thanks to the Rector of the University,
Artaud was given a government subsidy to travel into the interior.
After a 750-mile train journey to Chihuahua, he had a long horse-
back ride across the Sierra Madre to the territory of the Tarahumaras, an Indian tribe that still celebrated the traditional ritual
with peyote (mescalin). In Indian mythology, the visions it en-
gendered were associated with elemental forces and with the
environment, animal and vegetable; like all hallucinogens, it tends
to overturn all moral assumptions and to encourage the impression
that body, mind, and spirit interpenetrate not only with one another but with the universe. Artaud knew the experience would be
crucial for him, but the preparation for it was extremely painful.
He had been taking heroin in Mexico City, but he was determined
to confront peyote 'with a body innocent of any other kind of con-
tamination'[5] and he threw the last of his heroin into a mountain
stream. The journey would in any case have been uncomfortable;
withdrawal symptoms made it almost intolerable. 'At the end of
six days, my body was more bone than flesh, parched by the loss of
gallons of liquid excrement.' After hearing drumrolls in the mountains, he noticed that Indians were staring at him from behind
rocks. He was riding along the bank of a stream when, on the other
side of it, he saw a group of Indians lying on the ground, masturbating, staring at him, and throwing earth in his direction. It was
like a malediction, and the image haunted him in his final years of
madness.

Riding into Tarahumara country, he had the impression that
nature had been carving human and animal shapes on the mountains all over the area. He saw female breasts, animal heads devouring their own likeness, images of childbirth during war. 'I saw in
the mountain a naked man leaning out of a big window. His head
was only a large hole, a round cavity, where, in turn, sun and
moon appeared, according to the time.'[6]

Artaud was lucky that as he arrived in the village, a tribesman
died. This meant that the peyote dance had to be performed in

order to protect the dead man's double from evil spirits. But Artaud had to wait 28 days for the ceremony. As so often in the past, he sensed that he was reaching a crucial juncture of his existence but was incapable of responding fully to it because he felt incomplete in himself. 'Why this terrible sensation of loss, of a lack that had to be made up, of the event being aborted?' Why did he feel that his body was 'intelligent but out of tune, needing to be dragged, needing to be killed, almost, to stop it from rebelling against me'? (*O.C.* IX. 51).

Then suddenly the sorcerers were arriving and women were grinding the peyote. A bonfire was lit. Two young goats were slaughtered. Ten crosses were erected in a ring, a mirror attached to each. The twelve phases of the dance lasted from sunrise to sunset. Artaud described it in inhuman terms—'the gimlet shrieks of the dancer', 'the dance which comes and goes like a sort of epileptic pendulum'. Finally, 'as dawn was about to break, we were given the grated peyote, like a sort of muddy gruel, and in front of each of us a fresh hole was dug to receive the spit from our mouths, which had already become holy from the contact with the peyote'. Afterwards the Indians laid him on the ground

> for the ritual to fall on me, for the fire, the singing, the dance, and the night itself, like an animated human vault, would rotate, alive, above me. So there was this rolling vault, this material ordering of cries, sounds, footsteps, singing. But above it all, beyond it all, this recurring impression of something behind, something greater—the Principle. . . . From now on it was necessary that whatever was hidden behind this ponderous grinding, making the dawn equal to the night, whatever it was must be drawn out and used, used for *my crucifixion*. (*O.C.* IX. 61–2.)

The sensation may have been entirely new, but the idea was not. In 1928 he must have been identifying with Vitrac's Ida Mortemart when he said that her spiritual crucifixion gave her the lucidity of a clairvoyante; earlier still, in 'Fragments d'un journal d'Enfer' (1926), he had written: 'There is something which is above all human activity: it is the example of this monotonous crucifixion, this crucifixion where the soul no longer ends by losing itself.' So it is hard to locate a starting point for his identification with the

man crucified at Golgotha,* though, describing his experience of
mescalin in 'Une Note sur le peyotl' (May 1947), he remembered
the euphoria as making him feel godlike:

> I no longer felt any anxiety. I had stopped questioning the reason for
> my life. I no longer had to carry my body. I understood that I was
> inventing life; that this was my function and my *raison d'être* and
> that I was bored when my imagination did not work and peyote made
> it work.

The drive towards the absolute being so strong in Artaud, it is
illuminating to compare this 1947 account of the 1936 experience
with what he had written about opium in 'Appel à la jeunesse:
intoxication-désintoxication' (*c*. October 1934):

> I take opium because I am myself but it does not cure me of myself.
> To give up drugs is to die. I mean that only death can cure me of this
> infernal narcotic palliative, while only reasonable absences, not too
> extended, not too prolonged, allow me to be myself. I can do nothing
> to fight opium, which is the most abominable deception, the most
> redoubtable invention of nothing, which has ever flooded human
> sensibilities.

In 'Le Rite du peyotl chez les Tarahumaras', written either late
in 1943 or early in 1944, while Artaud was at Rodez, peyote is
equated to man in his unborn state, with his whole atavistic and
personal consciousness alerted and supported. The ideas Artaud
now put into the mouth of the Tarahumara priest are suspiciously
tinged not only with the Christianity to which Artaud had once
again been converted but with his old Gnosticism and with his old
preoccupations. He makes the priest say that the evidence of our
eyes and ears is not to be trusted. The evil spirit has permeated
material reality and without *Ciguri* (the drug and the god) there is
no means of knowing the truth about it. God has withdrawn from
the world. 'There is something frightful which rises inside me,
coming not from me but from the darkness I have within me,
there where the human soul does not know where the self begins or
where it ends. . . . And soon that is all there will be . . . this

* See above, p. 12.

obscene mask of the man who sneers between the sperm and the shit.'

The book *Les Tarahumaras*, published by l'Arbalète in 1955, contains essays, letters, and notes by Artaud written between 1936 and 1948. According to the publisher, Marc Barbezat, it had been Artaud's wish, when they discussed the book in 1947 and 1948, that 'Le Rite du peyotl' should be printed before the earlier texts.* Obviously the forties texts are unreliable. He may have believed he was giving an accurate account of what had happened, but the experience was no longer fresh, and his memory had been debilitated both by drugs and by electric shock therapy. The most objective-seeming accounts of the Tarahumaras are to be found in 'La Danse du Peyotl', 'La Montagne des Signes', the three articles written for *El Nacional* and originally published in Spanish ('Le Pays des Rois-Mages', 'Une Race-Principe', and 'Le Rite des Rois de l'Atlantide'), and the 1937 article for *Voilà* ('La Race des hommes perdus'). Even in these, though, it is noticeable that the experiences were filtered through a mind conditioned by Artaud's needs and primed by Artaud's past.

His reaction to the mountainous landscape in the Tarahumaras' territory was that everything, as he says in 'Le Pays des Rois-Mages', 'was talking only about the Essential, or the principles according to which Nature formed itself; and everything lives only for the sake of those principles—men, storms, wind, silence, sun'. Against this perspective, the humanism of the Renaissance appeared to be 'a diminution of Man'. 'Une Race-Principe' shows Artaud had convinced himself that the Tarahumaras, like the ancient Syrians, had reunited the male and female principles. They tied their hair with two-pointed headbands. Wasn't this a symbolical part of their cult of a Nature that was both male and female? The root of the peyote plant looked like the male and female sex organs conjoined, and in celebrating the ritual, the priests threw

* Similarly, in *Le Théâtre et son double*, he had not wanted the essays to appear in chronological order. Unfortunately the editor of his *Oeuvres complètes* is equally averse to chronology, and in volume IX the articles and letters Artaud wrote in Mexico are spatchcocked confusingly between articles and letters written in France before, during, and after his confinement in lunatic asylums.

their European hats on the ground to put on the two-pointed headband, 'as if they wanted the gesture to indicate their entry into the circle of Nature which has two magnetic poles'. And in Artaud's description of the dance, in 'Le Rite du peyotl chez les Tarahumaras',

> it was no longer a man and woman who were there but two principles: the male, mouth open, gums chattering, red, inflamed, bloody, as if slashed by the roots of the teeth, now translucent, like commanding tongues; the female, a broken-toothed grub, holes drilled in her molars, like a rat in a trap, on heat and steaming, retreating, turning round in front of the hirsute male. They were going to collide, plunge themselves frantically into each other like things, having looked at each other and made war, interpenetrating finally before the *indiscreet* and *guilty* eye of God, who ought gradually to be supplanted by their action. For Ciguri, they say, was MAN, MAN as he constructed HIMSELF from HIMSELF in space when God assassinated him.

It seemed to Artaud that the two principles were separate from the two bodies but 'remained obstinately suspended outside of Being, like two ideas which had always been opposed to HIM and which made *their own bodies,* bodies in which the idea of matter is volatilized by CIGURI'. Or, as he says later, 'I believe I saw in this dance the point at which the universal unconscious is sick.'

The Tarahumaras had no fear of death. They did not attach the same value to their bodies as Europeans did. It was as if they were saying: 'This body isn't me at all.' The Indian, helped by peyote, had also sacrificed his consciousness to God. On dying he was fused into Infinity, reabsorbed into the great soul. The priests of Tutuguri presided over the metamorphosis, using their breath to raise the spirit that had produced them and was now scattering them into Infinity. After passing through the multiplicity of things, the spirit returned to unity in Tutuguri or the Sun, to be dissolved and resurrected in mystical reassimilation.

Writing after his release from Rodez, Artaud looked back on the experience as if it had been a revelation. He even talks, like the mystics, of feeling as if suddenly filled with a light he had never experienced. 'Sew yourself up into wholeness without God who assimilates you and produces you as if you were producing your-

Corridor at the asylum of Quatre-Mares, Sotteville-les-Rouen, first of the five asylums where Artaud was interned between 1937 and 1946. He was there from December 1937 to April 1938.

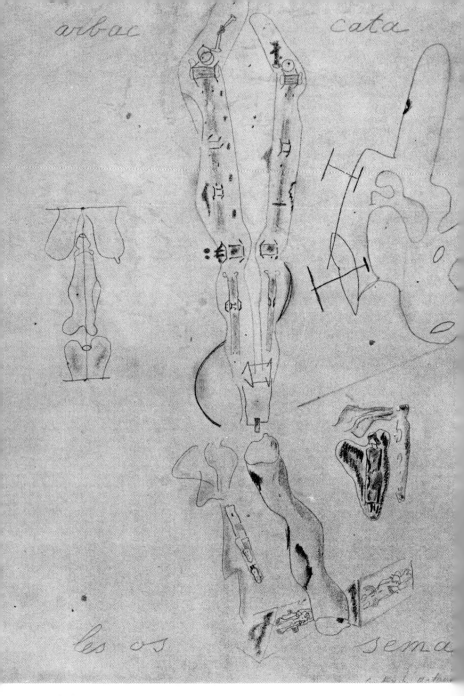

A drawing now in the collection of Anie Besnard-Faure. In *Ci-gît* he wrote of 'the pain sawn from the bone'. See chapter 9.

Self-portrait in pencil, 17 December 1946

Sketches inscribed to Pierre Loeb's daughter Florence; the head in the bottom right-hand corner is a self-portrait.

self, and as you do produce yourself against Him all the time in the void.' Artaud did not even claim that these were the exact words of the Indian chief: this is how he '*reconstructed* them under the influence of the fantastic illuminations of Ciguri'.

For the European, said Artaud, consciousness and the sense of self are formed by a process in which certain ideas are interiorized, while others are rejected. Eventually, when we interrogate ourselves, we answer with the assumption 'that the reply is coming not from someone else but from one's self'. The Indian knows that a lot of what is going on inside him is not himself, but the Other. The difference between the madman and the Tarahumaras, said Artaud, is that peyote has helped the Indian and reinforced his will-power in the work of separation and internal distribution.

But somewhere near the centre of what attracted Artaud to the Tarahumaras was the idea of nothingness, an acute sense of the void. 'Tutuguri', the poem he wrote at Ivry during the last months of his life, was a reworking of a text written much earlier.

> And in the wooden drum of the seventh Tutuguri,
> always an introduction of nothing,
> always this introduction of nothing:
> and this hollow time,
> a hollow time,
> a kind of draining void between the cutting wooden sticks
> nothing which summons the trunk of man
> the truncated human body
> in the fury (no, fervour)
> of things inside

Before he left Mexico City, on 17 June 1936, Artaud had written in a letter to Barrault: 'In going, I am not trusting to chance. I am looking for something precious. When I have it in my possession I will automatically achieve the *true drama*—perhaps it is not a matter of theatre on the stage—that I should create, this time with the certainty of succeeding.' In fact, what the peyote gave him was a euphoria which made everyday reality seem intolerably barren and loveless. He also learned something from the Tarahumaras about attachment to an idea of the divine, accompanied by detachment from the values and verdicts of society. 'The Tarahumara Indians live as if they were already dead. Averting their eyes from reality, they draw magical strength from the contempt they have for civilization.'[7] They maintained that self-deception was intrinsic to city life, and when they went into the Mexican cities 'to look at the men who have deceived themselves', they survived by begging with great arrogance and no gratitude, as if to say 'Being rich, you are a dog' and 'It's yourself you're benefiting by obeying the law, so I don't need to thank you.' By 'law' Artaud meant 'the law of physical reciprocity which we call charity'. He was himself to depend very heavily on this law when he returned to Paris, and his method of begging, like the attitude behind it, derived from that of the Tarahumaras.

8

Delirium and Asylums

Arriving back in France on 12 November 1936 with no money, Artaud stayed in the home of his friend Jean-Marie Conty, where, nearly two years previously, he had given the reading of *Les Cenci*. Weakened by heroin, he was urgently in need of treatment, but the renewal of his relationship with Cécile Schramme afforded some interludes of contentment. His 19 February 1937 letter to her consists of two lines:

> I love you
> because you have revealed human happiness to me.

Thanks to Paulhan's intervention, the Caisse de Lettres paid for him to spend a week in the Centre Français de Medicine and de Chirurgie at the end of February 1937; and in April he had to spend another few days in a clinic at Sceaux.

On 15 March he had written to Robert Desnos about the need 'to restore a balance which has been lacking for years. . . . I must be back in full control of my strength if I am to do what I have to do and say what I have to say.' In principle he was willing to compromise with bourgeois society by marrying the daughter of the monopolist owner of the Brussels tram service; in practice his ambivalence towards Cécile and her parents threw up insoluble problems. 'I find it intolerable', he wrote to her on 16 April, 'if you do not always tell the truth and if you try to conceal from me the sides of your nature which are bad sexually and erotically, or from the viewpoint of mood and feelings.' Invited to lecture in Brussels during May on his Mexican experiences, he arranged to stay with her parents, but he was full of misgivings, and on 18 May, at the lecture, he caused a furore by insulting the audience. The engagement was broken off.

Returning to Paris, he was ready for another withdrawal into esoteric transcendentalism, and when Manuel Cano de Castro taught him how to use the Tarot pack, his enthusiasm was overwhelming. 'He cast and interpreted horoscopes like a visionary,' wrote de Castro.[1] Artaud had told him that poets alone possessed soul and intuition; other men might be intelligent and knowing, but they were still soulless, representatives of 'Non-being'. Artaud's apocalyptic pamphlet *Les Nouvelles Révélations de l'Être*, published on 27 July, was centred on horoscopes he had cast on 15 and 19 June. The prophecies based on them are preceded by a prose poem which is more deliriously Rimbaudesque than anything he had written since *L'Art et la mort*. The Tarot pack was catalysing a disordering of all the senses. The claim in the second sentence to be an 'unredeemable brute' is probably an unconscious echo of Rimbaud's self-characterization as a beast with no moral sense.* Then, in a passage that anticipates *Van Gogh le suicidé de la société* by stepping further towards an explicit recognition of the void than ever before, Artaud wrote:

> It is a long time now that I have been aware of the void but refused to throw myself into it.
> I have been a coward like everyone I see.
> I now know that when I thought I was rejecting this world, I was rejecting the void.
> For I know that this world does not exist and I know *how* it does not exist.
> What I have been suffering from till now is having rejected the void. The void that was already inside me.
>
> I know the desire was there to enlighten me through the void, and I have refused to be enlightened.
>
> If I have been made into a bonfire, it was to cure me of being in the world.

His insistence in the poem that he is now not 'in the world',

* See above, p. 34.

suggests that he had no memory of making the same claim during his pre-Surrealist period.*

> This is a really desperate man speaking to you, one who did not know the happiness of being in the world until he had left it and became quite separated from it.

In the horoscope of 19 June, Artaud predicts that a Man will reimpose the Supernatural, which humanity has betrayed, although it has no other *raison d'être*. Nature is about to revolt. All values will be 'reclassified'. Sexuality will be put back into its proper place. A process has already begun by which human love is made impossible. Politically, the Right will triumph over the Left. (In 1943, at Rodez, Artaud inscribed a copy of the pamphlet to Hitler.) 'Because the Masses are Women by nature, and it is Man who has ascendancy over Woman, not vice versa.'

> That which has made us men and has separated the women from the man is now withdrawing from men. . . .
> And the Revolution we failed to launch will be launched against us by the universe.
> For the Revolution, too, remembers she is a woman.
> And before restoring kings everywhere, who will be everyone's slaves and therefore know all the better how to hold the world enslaved—
> She will teach us by the impossible possession
> that will make each of us possessed and mad
> HOW LIFE IS WITHDRAWING FROM US.

Artaud goes on in the poem to write about the sword and the stick he had been given. Both, he believed, had magical properties. The sword, made of Toledo steel, had been a present from a Negro sorcerer in Havana. The stick had been given to him by René Thomas, who 'had it from the daughter of a Savoyard sorcerer who is mentioned in the prophecies of St. Patrick, as is the stick itself. . . . It has 200 million fibres in it, and it is encrusted with magic signs, representing moral forces. . . .'† Artaud, who

---

* See above, p. 54.

† This is how he described it to Henri Parisot in a letter of 6 October 1945—long after the stick had been lost.

believed he had owned the stick in previous incarnations, carried it around with him wherever he went. Men were not allowed to touch it but women were. In Tarot symbolism, swords represent air, while sticks represent fire: of the thirteen knots on Artaud's stick, the ninth, according to the poem, represented the thunderbolt. Nine was the number of destruction by fire, which Artaud prophesied. It had already begun, he said. All forms would return to the Absolute, and Destiny would be returned to the four elements under the direction of a single man, a Tortured Man.

The Tortured Man was the subject of the other horoscope, cast four days earlier but described second in *Les Nouvelles Révélations de l'Être*. Artaud identified with this 'abstract creature' begotten by a woman on a man. The world's inverted perversion had provoked the ineffable. Incarnating a vision of the ubiquitous madness, the Tortured Man is himself thought to be mad, though the other side of him is a King, who had the right to divide things, saying 'This is, and that is not.' He rendered justice everywhere, but infernal justice, because it was no longer a matter of rendering it but taking it away. To save ourselves from being burnt alive, we must consent to an immediate magical burning, not of things, but of everything that represents things. What we do not burn will be burnt by the earth; what we burn will drive all of us into distraction and solitude.

The letter Artaud wrote to Breton's daughter, Jacqueline, on 28 July, the day after *Les Nouvelles Révélations de l'Être* was published, shows that he had come to regard himself as a magician. But there were some problems, he conceded, that magic could not solve, such as the problem of Sonia Mossé, an actress friend of Cécile Schramme's: 'She refuses to admit, even to herself, that she loves me, because she knows that I cannot or will not give her that physical part of love which only men are content with.'

Each day brought new proof that the stick was endowed with exceptional physical properties. It constituted his 'only *raison d'être* and *my last reason for staying alive*', though it is clear from a letter written two days later to André Breton that Artaud believed he would participate in inflicting the destruction by fire he had predicted: 'To acquiesce in burning the way I have burned all my life and am burning now is to acquire the power to burn. . . .

Between the anger of a furious spirit and the destructive force of all the fires there is no distance in reality. There is only something to find. I have found it.' The letter explains that the reference to the Right in *Les Nouvelles Révélations* is to the human Right and not to 'idiotic reactionaries', and that the Kings are spiritual rulers who will regain a material supremacy.

Another young woman who became important to him during that summer was Anne Manson,* a journalist who had approached him for advice about a visit she was contemplating to Mexico. His interest in her was platonic. On 2 August he wrote:

> What unites creatures is Love,
> What divides them is sexuality.

It was characteristic of him that a woman he had only just met should become his principal confidante; in his letter of 8 August he told her that 'a decisive truth' would appear before the end of the year. He had made, he went on,

> the absolute sacrifice of myself—that is to say of all happiness, all relaxation, all pleasure and all satisfaction in this world. . . . I believed that I needed devotion, but all devotees cause me suffering because they fail to understand me. . . . I cannot explain to them that my Way is the True Way and that there is no Way open to those unwilling to serve my Way! ! To be with me is to leave the rest. Whoever cannot leave the rest cannot be with me.

He was now going to be away for three months. When he came back she would have 'to choose to be with me or against Me'. The echo of Jesus' 'He that is not with me is against me' (Luke 11:23) strongly prefigures Artaud's explicit identification with him. His letter to Anne Manson of 10 August hints at a kind of resurrection through good works:

> If I took drugs it was to extinguish this terrible fire of separation and dissociation that has tortured my whole body for 22 years. The drugs only added to the flames and I acquiesced because the fire came before the work, but the work is going to destroy the fire that burns my body, disengaging from it another body.

* This was her *nom de plume*.

He had decided to go with the stick to the country of St. Patrick and he arrived in Ireland on 14 August. If he intended to stay for three months and anticipated a revelation of 'decisive truth' before the end of the year, he must have wanted to be there for it, but it did not seem to him that he was acting on his own decision. He interpreted St. Patrick's confessions as having a prophetic force, and he was obeying the will of destiny as expressed in the *Dictionnaire d'Hagiographie* which he had consulted in the Bibliothèque Nationale. According to letters he wrote later from Rodez,* his motive for going to Ireland was 'to wake the Irish up by making them recognize the Cane of St. Patrick which had been attached to the wall of St. Patrick's Cathedral in Dublin for nearly 1500 years before it disappeared during the second half of the nineteenth century'. He wrote to Anne Manson on 23 August from the Aran Islands:

> My Life, Anne, is fulfilling a Prophecy.
> One day you will understand these words.

A letter of 5 September to André Breton presents a curious mixture of Chinese, Hindu, Ionian, and Sadean ideas. Gods and men are both victims of Nature's criminal law. Christ was a magician who fought with a stick against the devils in the desert. The stain of his blood is still on the stick. He came back to earth in order to restore the truth of pagan religion. Nature is nothing in herself. She is, as Lao-tsze said, the Nothing from which life emerges, and (as the sixth-century B.C. Ionian philosopher Anaximander had said) there was injustice in the law of punishment and expiation by which living beings emerged out of infinity and finally returned to it. The gods are enemies of the infinity, the primordial Non-being, which devours them. It forms a triangle with them and humanity as the other two points. Life was not given to us: we ourselves made it, and only to punish the criminal force of Being, which acts on us, giving us no rest. The secret we must learn is to destroy this criminal law, so that we can fall back into Non-being at a point higher than Eternity.

Prominent among the complex confusions of this credo, is a

* E.g. the one to Paulhan dated 7 July 1943.

rationalizing and defensive impulse to denounce all law as criminal. Casually, towards the end of the letter, Artaud says: 'It may be that I shall be in prison some time from now. Do not worry. It will be voluntary and not for long.' He had been extremely short of money and seems not always to have been scrupulous about paying for his accommodation.

Before leaving Galway for Dublin on 8 September, he wrote ambiguously to Anne Manson: 'My earthly existence is what it should be, strewn with insurmountable difficulties, which I surmount. For that is the Law.' Five days later he was telling her that Christ spoke to him every day, revealing the mysteries of life and death, and of the Incarnations. Identical with the Holy Ghost, with Shiva, Krishna, and Vishnu, Christ was the Negative of Creation. The force he wanted to activate on earth was one of love: the apparent cruelty was necessary to overcome human resistance. 'Cruelty is not a luxury, Anne. . . . *To be cruel you have to be enlightened.* . . . Cruelty is not a game and I do not like it.' In his next letter (14 September) he said that within about twenty days he would be speaking publicly in the name of God. Catholicism would be destroyed as idolatrous and the Pope condemned to death as a traitor. The stick René Thomas had given him had belonged to Christ himself. Another letter was sent to René Thomas, informing him and predicting that the stick would have a role to play in the end of the world. Antichrist would not appear for some years, but within twenty days part of England would disappear under the sea. In a letter to Breton written the same day, Artaud said that the man who had become Antichrist was a young man who went frequently to the Deux Magots. Breton had shaken hands with him. By the second half of September he was casting Anne Manson in the role of a female Judas. 'Go to the Deux Magots, Woman, *betray me.*' Jacqueline Breton was to be 'the Predestined Spouse of the Superior Being'.

He appears to have had several brushes with the Irish police. That he spoke so little English was no doubt an advantage: the more they understood of his Messianic pronouncements, the less they would have sympathized. According to letters he wrote later from Rodez, he incited the Irish people to riot in the streets. According to his sister, Marie-Ange Malausséna, he finally asked for asylum at a Jesuit institution, but the principal refused to see him.

> He made so much noise, shouting his demands for a hearing, that the police were called. The stick of St. Patrick, which had been in his hand, disappeared during the scuffle which ensued, and Artaud was imprisoned for six days. The police searched his clothes, pulling the lining to pieces and cutting the pockets open, but they found nothing. Heavily escorted, he was taken on board the *Washington*, which was about to sail for France.[2]

In November, when Paulhan tried to find out through the French Consul in Dublin what had occurred, the report was that the police 'had expressed the desire to send our compatriot back to France. He was without resources and in an over-stimulated state. The Legation intervened to the best of its abilities on behalf of M. Artaud.'[3]

While he was on board the *Washington*, a steward and a mechanic came into his cabin with dangerous-looking metal implements. It may be that they wanted nothing more than to carry out some repair on the washbasin, but Artaud tried to defend himself. He was put into a straitjacket, and when the boat docked at Le Havre on 30 September, he was handed over to port officials, who had him locked up. According to the account he gave later (in a letter of 20 September 1945 to Roger Blin) he was kept in a straitjacket with his feet tied to a bed. In December, he was taken to the psychiatric hospital of Quatre-Mares in the suburbs of Rouen. His mother, now almost seventy, had great difficulty in finding out where he was, and when she was finally able to visit him, he was almost unrecognizable. She did her utmost to arrange for him to be released or at any rate moved nearer to Paris, and in April 1938 he was transferred to the asylum of Ste. Anne, where Roger Blin and Robert Desnos visited him. He was being treated as incurable, and at the end of February 1939 he was moved again—to Ville-Evrard, in the suburbs of Paris. On 4 March, after five days there, he wrote a letter to Adrienne Monnier, who had it published in the April issue of the *Gazette des amis des livres*. It said that the real world was comprehensible only to those in the know, that Shakespeare and Bach were both impostors, that von Ribbentrop, the

German Minister for Foreign Affairs, had been assassinated in Paris and replaced by a double.

From Ville-Evrard Artaud wrote a great many letters to his friends. 'I am a fanatic, not a madman,' he told Jacqueline Breton on 7 April 1939. He urged Charles Dullin and Roger Blin to do all they could to campaign for his release. At the end of October he wrote to Génica again: 'If I could no longer see you, even with spiritual sight, I could at least feel the breath of your faith passing me on many occasions when you were fighting against Evil. . . . This impious torture must cease because it injures all living creatures and insults the work of God.' In another letter, written on 10 November, he told her: 'This world is no longer viable. It is totally undermined.' Enchantment and other occult manœuvres were preventing her from understanding the evil that was being done to him; otherwise she would have rushed to his assistance. 'I beg you in your own interest and that of the inalienable purity of Goodness, to remain wholly pure and chaste, for ever.' His next letter (24 November) opened with an impassioned plea that she should obtain heroin or opium for him. Nothing else could help him to fight back against the hostile forces that were working on him magically each night while he was asleep.

Génica, we must leave this world, but first the Reign of the Other World has to begin, and we need quantities of armed troops. For the Bohemians to arrive on this world in sufficient force. . . . I need heroin to open the occult doors for them and blow up Satan's enchantment which is keeping them out and me imprisoned here.

At Ville-Evrard Artaud did not refuse, as he had at Ste. Anne, to see his family; his mother and sister were appalled to find how miserable his living conditions were. He was extremely thin and his hair had been cropped. In the summer of 1940 much of France was occupied by the Germans, who allocated only meagre rations of food to lunatic asylums. Continually overexcited, Artaud was being subjected to long spells of solitary confinement in the 'security quarters'.

But for the Occupation, his friends might have come to his aid more swiftly. In 1942, becoming increasingly anxious that Artaud might not long survive the treatment he was receiving, Robert

Desnos began manœuvring to have him moved to another asylum. Artaud resisted the idea, convinced that magical powers were working for him at Ville-Evrard, while his mother and sister were not eager for him to be taken where they would be unable to visit him. But a cousin of Arthur Adamov's had been very much impressed by Dr. Gaston Ferdière, who was now running an asylum in an area the Germans had not occupied. Dr. Ferdière, who had himself written verse and essays, was familiar with Artaud's work and eager to have him at Rodez. When Desnos visited him at Ville-Evrard just before he was moved, on 22 January 1943, he was 'talking like St. Jerome'.[4]

After three transitional weeks in Chezal-Benoit at another asylum within the Occupied Zone, Artaud arrived at Rodez on 11 February. According to Dr. Ferdière,

> On the very morning of his appearance at the hospital, after waiting for the arrival of the ambulance bringing him from the station, I held my arms open. He threw himself into them, making out that it was a reunion with the dearest of friends, that we had known each other for 15 or 20 years. He mentioned a dozen common friends whose names I did not know, reeling off a long string of specious memories which I was careful not to contradict. I told him immediately of my plan to give him his liberty, restore him to Parisian life, to the world of letters and the arts, and I took him straight away to lunch at my home. My wife made an admirable effort, welcoming him with open arms, allowing herself to be kissed by this repulsive-looking creature. It is embarrassing for a housewife to have a guest who gulps noisily at his food, mashes it up on the tablecloth, belches regularly and, before the meal is over, kneels down to psalmodize. I was soon able to calm him down by giving him back a little inlaid sword which I had just found listed on his inventory. You can buy them at any of the markets in Toledo.[5]

Present at the lunch was Frédéric Delanglade, a painter who lived with the Ferdières. He described Artaud as 'carrying his head low, toothless, spluttering when he launched abruptly into speech —not to say assertion or complaint'.[6] He reminded Delanglade of 'an actor playing a role. . . "Antonin Artaud is dead," he said. "My name is Antonin Nalpas." Then, when the audience seemed not to be paying attention to him, he stood up, recited some "magical" incantations and walked around his chair or complained that the pendulum of the clock was making too much noise.'

Throughout his first year at Rodez Artaud was considerably happier than he had been during the previous five years of confinement. He was given a room of his own, plentiful supplies of cigarettes, and enough food for him to regain weight. Like Dr. Toulouse, 23 years earlier, Ferdière found that the most effective therapy was through art. He encouraged Artaud to go on corresponding with his friends and persuaded him to translate poems by Lewis Carroll, a chapter of *Through the Looking-Glass*, and Robert Southwell's 'The Burning Babe'. He also adapted some poems by Edgar Allan Poe. After seven months at Rodez, Artaud told his mother (in a letter dated 17 September 1943) that she had been 'inspired by God' to recommend the asylum. Dr. Ferdière was a 'true friend'. The 'atmosphere of affection and human helpfulness' had shaken him up, no doubt, but had 'finally brought me back to myself and restored the sanity of my vision'. His letter of 10 October to Dr. Ferdière said that he found himself surrounded by Love and 'friends who have opened their heart to me. There is no one on the staff of this asylum who does not have a smile for me or an affectionate word when he meets me.' The doctor was himself described as 'a great spirit and a great heart'.

Now a fervent Christian once again, Artaud was taking communion at least three times a week. He dated his conversion back to September 1937.* After twenty years of alienation from religion and several years of atheism, he said, he had taken communion one Sunday morning in an Irish church. He now wanted to renounce all his writings except the correspondence with Rivière, *Le Théâtre et son double*, and *Les Nouvelles Révélations de l'Être*. He also wanted to renounce his earlier self. Antonin Artaud had 'died in August 1939 from brutality and poison'. But his corpse had not been removed from the cell at Ville-Evrard. God had put a new soul into the old body. In the morning, someone else woke up in the same bed, with an identical body, but new and virginal. 'I am carrying in my body memories of the entire life of Antonin

* See his letters of 15 April and 5 October 1943 to Barrault.

Artaud', he wrote on 18 July 1943 to Claude-Andri Puget, 'because I am his continuation on earth.'

But he did not carry any sexual memories. 'I despise all sexual relationships, of any kind, as debasing for humanity, and I find it deeply offensive that it should be believed my body could have been submitted to them at any moment of its life.'* All the greatest poets and painters had been chaste. Sexuality was the sourcc of all human evil. Before the Fall, procreation had been achieved by virginal methods, entirely spiritual. Antonin Artaud's soul had been that of an angel very close to God. Artaud had suffered because he was burdened with all the guilt of humanity.

The early letters from Rodez give no sign of any desire for freedom: a man had been chosen to remain a virgin and expiate with his suffering all the evil done by other men. 'But this man too has forgotten God, and he has sinned. But to pay for his errors and sins he has agreed to be shut up alive in a Lunatic Asylum and *to die there*' (letter of 5 April to Dr. Latrémolière). He did not always maintain that the incarceration was voluntary: in his letter of 25 March to Dr. Latrémolière he said that Satan and Antichrist were keeping him shut up so that they could nourish themselves on his excrement and seminal fluid. His letter of 18 July to Dr. Ferdière maintained that it was the fate of all enlightened men to be mistaken for madmen when there was interference from black magic and the police. By October he believed that his liberty would be given to him 'as soon as all my friends, all those I love and have known on this earth, have become chaste, pure, disinterested, as charitable finally and detached as it is possible to be in this base world'.

On the day after his first Christmas at Rodez, Artaud was again invited to have lunch with Dr. Ferdière, who impressed him by saying that his odyssey was no more than a trial which would come to an end. It had nothing to do with mental illness. 'You see,' Artaud wrote to his mother on the 27th, 'God in our unhappiness has done us the grace of putting me into the hands of a man with heart and Intelligence, who understands me. He is of a race apart.

---

* So Artaud wrote on 15 February 1943 to Dr. Latrémolière, one of the doctors at Rodez.

I now feel a strange spiritual fraternity with Dr. Ferdière, and if you heard him talking, I think you would quite often have the impression you were listening to me.'

Within a few weeks, the art therapy entered a new phase. Artaud had not done any drawing since designing sets and costumes for Dullin in the twenties, but in his letter of 5 February 1944 to Ferdière, he promised to do a gouache for him. He was delighted that the doctor had liked his drawings and expressed gratitude for the 'insistent prompting' he had received from Frédéric Delanglade, 'a true and very profound friend'. Delanglade later described how he had taken Artaud into his studio 'to "amuse" him with the paints. He drew my portrait very carefully in charcoal, rubbed it out and began all over again. This was repeated several times.'[7] Artaud had been helped to take a decisive step forward. As he wrote to Ferdière, 'Certainly I must move about, go out, see people and things. . . . It was an excellent idea of Frédéric Delanglade's to take me with him twice on walks to Rodez. . . . As a result of being confined, one ends up by imagining that the external world does not exist.'

Writing after a gap of fifteen years, Delanglade remembered the incident of the portrait as occurring after Dr. Ferdière had started using electro-convulsive therapy on Artaud; the letters Artaud wrote from Rodez make it seem highly unlikely that he was subjected to this treatment until May 1944. If Artaud was becoming less passive and less introverted, the improvement was probably due not to electric shock, but to the sketching and the excursions outside the asylum. Nor would Artaud have written to Ferdière as he did on 5 February if the electric-shock therapy had started. It obviously triggered a violent deterioration in the relationship between doctor and patient. Writing to his mother on 4 July, he entreated her to intervene by demanding his release. Delanglade was also inaccurate in recording that Artaud was incapable of applying himself to any literary work until the electric-shock therapy started. By 2 January 1944 he was already working on the 'Supplément au voyage au pays des Tarahumaras'. He even invited Delanglade to illustrate it, and according to the letter of 4 July 1944, Ferdière was prompted to begin the electric-shock therapy by a complaint from Robert Denoël that the stories Artaud was recording were inaccurate. 'He asked Dr. Ferdière to try another treatment and it is this treatment which cut me off from my thoughts from 15 May until 20 June, making me incapable of writing to you for a month because I no longer knew where I was or who I was. . . .'

In a letter written six months later (6 January 1945) to Dr. Latrémolière, thanking him for securing a reprieve during August, Artaud described the effects of the therapy:

> The electric shocks, M. Latrémolière, make me despair, take my memory away, numb my thinking and my heart, make me absent and aware of myself as absent. I see myself pursuing my own existence for weeks, like a dead man at the side of a living man who is no longer himself. Asked where he comes from, he can no longer go into his own home. After the last series I found it impossible throughout August or September to work, to think or to make contact with my existence.

About 7 April 1945 he drafted a letter to Dr. Ferdière quite unlike his earlier letters. 'I have never liked the atmosphere in houses of correction.' On 23 September he wrote to tell Roger Blin it was urgent that someone should secure his release 'because I don't want my soul, my memory, my consciousness and my personality to be murdered by a new series of electric shocks'. On 1 October he described to Jean Paulhan how he had fought with a knife 'to defend myself because each electric shock has killed me'. According to the explanation Dr. Ferdière later gave to Charles Marowitz,

> The electric shock produces an epileptic fit. After an epileptic fit—which develops stage by stage—the convulsion stage following the period of stimulation—a coma follows which may last several minutes, and sometimes, even longer. Then a period of sleep, which is very short, and, finally, there is an awakening. But on waking, as in all epilepsies, there is a gap. The epileptic doesn't know what has happened. . . . This kind of sub-anxiety on waking is, on the psychopathological level, even a desirable phenomenon as it obliges the patient, who has been reduced to nothingness, who has been totally obliterated, to build himself up again.[8]

The only positive effect the therapy can safely be said to have had on Artaud was to make him very eager not to stay at Rodez longer than necessary. The pressure his friends put on Ferdière to release him built up out of increasing pressure Artaud put on them.

It would be simplistic to suggest a direct causal connection between the electric-shock therapy and the rejection of Christianity, which occurred in the spring of 1945, but he was becoming progressively disenchanted with the image of himself as submissive, endlessly patient, a martyr. In his letter of 23 September 1945 to Roger Blin, he dated his decision from Passion Sunday: 'I threw the communion, the eucharist, god and his christ out of the window.' The refusal to use capital letters was typical of the new mood. 'I decided to be myself—that is to say quite simply Antonin Artaud, an irreligious unbeliever by nature and by soul, who has never hated anything more than God and his religions, whether they are based on christ, Jehovah or Brahma, not forgetting the nature rituals of the lamas.'

In a letter of 21 April 1944 to Pierre Souvtchinsky, he tried to prove that he had done nothing to deserve his reputation as a magician; he had never had any idea of magic in his head except that of praying to Jesus Christ. But after his rejection of religion, he went on believing that black magic was being practised against him and that he had to take magical counter-measures. The only explanation he could entertain for his friends' slowness in intervening was that spells were being cast on them to prevent them from seeing how desperately he needed their help. In France, as in Ireland, the police would not have behaved as they had if they were not devoted exclusively to the service of Satan and Antichrist. In 'L'Evêque de Rodez' (December 1945) Artaud said there were 'armies of black magicians placed in all the squares of Paris and all over the earth'. Sperm obtained by ritual masturbation was used in occult enchantment. He had also been poisoned, while at Ste. Anne, with potassium cyanide, which caused myelitis and cardiac debilitation. He needed heroin and opium as antidotes, but the woman friends who tried to bring drugs to him were liable to be raped by hostile doctors. Anne Manson had tried to bring heroin to him at Ville-Evrard on a Thursday in May 1939, but she had been taken to an office where Dr. Menuau and Dr. Chanès confiscated the packets she was carrying and, threatening to denounce her to the police, forced her to make love to both of them.*

---

* From a letter of 23 March 1946 to Jean Paulhan.

According to the letter of 9 April 1946, Dr. Ferdière himself took heroin, but when a ward sister, Mme Régis, tried to bring Artaud a gramme of the drug, the doctor, who found out by clairvoyance what was going on, threatened her with dismissal and made love to her in his office.

Artaud could no more protect these women than protect himself from being kicked in the testicles by a male nurse—the allegation made in a letter of 11 March 1946 to Paulhan—but what he believed he could do was explained in his letter of 23 September 1945 to Roger Blin. In order to generate benevolence all round him, he would, while writing, chant rhythmical phrases in the same way that other men might sing 'Auprès de ma blonde'. He would also strike blows into the air, sometimes with his breath, sometimes with his hand, as if wielding a hammer or an axe. Dervishes and black sorcerers did very much more than this, but in them no one regarded it as symptomatic of madness.

By 11 March 1946 Artaud had learned that he was to be released. Telling Paulhan the news in the letter, he reported one of his final conversations with Dr. Ferdière, who was apprehensive that Artaud would now take advantage of his liberty to procure laudanum, opium, and heroin. 'I answered that I am a man of character who above all holds it important not to dissipate his consciousness in drugs. I hate the abnormal states of mind they bring. For non-being is what has always given me the most horror.' The doctor's fears were well founded, and Artaud's confidence in his self-discipline was not; but had he had to stay at Rodez, he would probably not have survived for very much longer than he did in Paris. It was not drugs but rectal cancer that killed him.

9

The Final Freedom

On 27 July 1946, two months after he had moved into the clinic at Ivry, Artaud began writing a long letter addressed to Peter Watson. Intended for publication in Cyril Connolly's review *Horizon*, it was to introduce Artaud's work to the English public. 'I made my literary debut', he explained, 'writing books to say I could not write anything at all. My thinking was never more inaccessible to me than when I had something to say or to write.' In 1925, after completing *L'Ombilic des Limbes* and *Les Pèse-Nerfs*, he had thought them 'full of flaws, faults, platitudes, and as if stuffed with spontaneous abortions, abandonments, and abdications of all kinds, always coasting alongside what I wanted to say and never did say'. Looking back on them after 21 years, he found them 'stupefying, not for their success in relation to me but in relation to the inexpressible. This is how the bottle affects the contents. Without telling the truth about their author, works can themselves constitute a truth which is bizarre and which life, if only it were authentic, would never have accepted.'

The autobiographical section of the letter opened with prenatal memories of having to choose between the two sexes. Should he opt for a white, male *charnier*—the word can mean both charnel-house and water-tank—or stay in the black female fluid? 'It smelt of shit on my heart, this cistern with the trunk of me inside it, but the excrement was my self. In fact the cistern was a bleeding trunk, but a man's, while the white hole offering me its soul, a woman, was for me no more than nothing.'

The writing of the letter was spread over more than six weeks; the latter part of it oscillated more overtly between the personal and the ontological. 'I have never written except to say that I had never done anything, could not do anything and that doing something, I was in reality doing nothing. All my work has been built over this nothing and could not but have been. . . . You do not have a tongue for eating or talking but struggling, planting the point of your brain in the greasy mud of anxiety and stirring it like mayonnaise or aïoli.'

In equating the physical facts of the human condition with a continuum of excrement, Artaud saw himself as the avatar of humanity, while God was the thief who began to steal his body from him before it even existed:

> Only because of the fact
> that it is I
> who was God
> me a man
> and not the so-called spirit
> who was only the projection in the clouds
> of a body of another man than me
> who
> called himself the
> Demiurge. . .
> Now there was no one but I and he
> he
> an abject body
> unwanted by space,
> I
> a body in the process of making itself
> so not yet in a state of completion
> but evolving
> towards wholeness and purity
> like that of the so-called Demiurge
> who knowing himself to be unacceptable
> and wanting to live at any price
> found no better way
> to exist
> than to be born at the price of
> my murder.[1]

It is therefore impossible to have a body that is pure, or entirely one's own. God is my double: he has intruded into the space between me and my origin, stolen the nothing which would have been there. The presence of God is synonymous with oblivion of the void.[2]

Between July and September 1946 Artaud wrote the poems that were to be collected as *Le Retour d'Artaud, le Mômo*. In Marseillais slang *mômo* means 'idiot', but Artaud may also have been thanking of the word '*momie*' (mummy) and the word '*môme*' (child, brat). In his prose 'Correspondance de la momie' (1927), and in the poems 'La Momie attachée' (1925–6) and 'Invocation à la momie' (1926), written during his Surrealist period, he had used the image of the mummy, which automatically links the ideas of birth and death, petrifaction and putrefaction. 'Neither is my life complete,' he wrote in 'Correspondance de la momie',

> nor is my death absolutely aborted. . . . There is in this mummy a loss of flesh, and in the dark language of its intellectual flesh there is considerable impotence about raising up the body. Running through the veins in this mystical meat is a feeling in which each start is a kind of world and another kind of childbirth and which loses and consumes itself in the burning of an erroneous nothing.

In Artaud's later work the pulse is more febrile and there is less humour, more evidence of physical pain, but there is a remarkable continuity in both themes and undertones.

One new feature in *Artaud le Mômo* is the glossolalia or nonsense words:

> o dedi
> a dada orzoura
> o dou zoura
> a dada skizi
>
> o kaya
> o kaya pontoura
> o ponoura
> a pena
> poni

It has been pointed out[3] that Artaud was familiar with *La magie assyrienne: Étude suivi de textes magiques* (1902) in which the author, Charles Fossey, had quoted and translated some ancient Assyrian incantations. Several of the magical syllables recur in Artaud's verse. More important perhaps is his desire to create a language which did not depend on words that were not his. Before he left Rodez he wrote, in 'Révolte contre la poésie':

> I don't want a word from some astral libido, quite conscious of the formations of desire inside me. In the forms of the human word there is I don't know what rapacious operation, what rapacious self-devouring, in which the poet, limiting himself to the object, watches himself being eaten by this object. There is a crime weighing on the word made flesh, but the crime was to admit it. Libido is animal thinking and these are all animals who one day sloughed off their non-humanity.

Artaud stubbornly believed that he had created a new language which could become comprehensible to everybody. In his letter of 5 October 1945 to Henri Parisot there is a reference to the book he imagined he had written in 1934 under the title *Letura d'Eprahi Falli Tetar Fendi Photia o Fotre Indi*, 'in a language which was not French but which everyone would be able to read'. Under the influence of the Cabbala, which teaches that words, being an emanation from God, form the basis of all creation,[4] he had accepted the primitive belief that words possess intrinsic physical strength. Incantation could therefore be a powerful weapon. In 'Le Cahier Lutèce ou le reniement du baptême' he interpolated magical words into his denunciation of the Church, explaining that the 'preceding incomprehensible words' were curses against the fact of having been baptized.

The idea of the Theatre of Cruelty was still alive inside his mind. If the declamation of a Nerval poem* could constitute an example of it, so could a reading by Artaud of his own work, and the conviction grew in him that he ought himself to give a performance in public, so it was arranged that he should appear at the Vieux-Colombier on 13 January 1947. 'Histoire vécu par A-Mômo,' announced the handbills, 'Tête à tête par Antonin Artaud, avec 3 poèmes déclamés par l'auteur.' According to an article by Maurice Saillet in *Combat*, there were about 700 people in the theatre, a hundred of them standing at the back. The majority were young, but the audience included Gide, Barrault, Breton, Paulhan,

---

* See above, p. 25.

Adamov, Camus, and Roger Blin. 'Artaud made his entrance, with this emaciated, ravaged face resembling both Edgar Allan Poe's and Baudelaire's ... his impassioned hands flew like two birds round his face, groping at it tirelessly ... he began to declaim his beautiful, scarcely audible poems with his hoarse voice broken by sobs and tragic stammers.'[5] After the three poems, he spoke conversationally about his experiences in Ireland and in Mexico. He talked about electric-shock treatments and about black magic. Sensing that the whole audience was sceptical, he appealed for 'at least someone' to share his belief. 'So it happened', wrote Saillet, 'that he interrupted himself, losing the thread of his narrative: "I am putting myself in your place and I can quite see that what I am saying is not interesting at all. Still it is theatre. What to do to be truly sincere?" ' He read another poem. He improvised.

Ten days later Artaud wrote in a letter to Saillet: 'As for the improvised words, what I had to say was in my silences, not in my words. If I did not say what I had come to say, it was because having arrived at the actual point, I *renounced* it, and because, after the poems, it appeared to me that what I had to say could no longer be said with words.' How could he have told his audience 'that life lied to us when it brought us into the world and is lying still in making us think that the world is real'? But in a letter written five days later to Breton, Artaud gave a different explanation for not being able to go on talking: 'I had not taken account of the fact that the only language I could use with a public was to take bombs out of my pocket and throw them in its face with a characteristic gesture of aggression. And that blows are the only language I feel capable of speaking.'[6]

Saillet's article did not describe how the evening ended. According to some reports, Artaud fled from the stage in terror; according to others, he went on talking, shouting abuse and roaring, for more than two hours, until his voice gave out. The pathetic silence that ensued was not broken until André Gide climbed up on stage to embrace him. Gide's own account of the performance was written after Artaud's death:

To me he had never seemed more admirable. Of his material existence, nothing remained except what was expressive. His big, ungainly figure, his face consumed by inner fire, his hands that knot themselves together whether held out towards unreachable help, or twisting in anguish. More often tightly shielding his face, alternately hiding and revealing it, openly signalling abominable human distress, a sort of unreprievable damnation, with no possible escape, except into a frantic lyricism, nothing of which could reach the audience except scatological flashes, curses and blasphemies. Certainly the marvelous actor this artist could become was rediscovered, but it was his own personality he was offering to the audience with a sort of shameless barn storming that did not conceal a total authenticity. Reason beat a retreat—not only his but that of the whole assembly, all of us spectators of this atrocious drama, reduced to the role of malevolent supernumeraries, mere nobodies.[7]

Nine months previously, when the *Lettres de Rodez* were published by Guy Lévis Mano, only 666 copies had been printed. (Mano brought out a second limited edition of 1200 copies after Artaud's death.) But apart from the appearance of 'Lettre sur Lautréamont' in the *Cahiers du Sud,* and a few poems and fragments in minor literary reviews (*L'Heure nouvelle, Juin, L'Arch, La Rue, Les Lettres, Troisième convoi*), none of Artaud's work had appeared during 1946, and even if the 666 copies of *Lettres de Rodez* were read by more than 666 people, it is not easy to explain why the theatre was so overcrowded on 13 January 1947.

Paris had scarcely had time to recover from being occupied by the German Army from June 1940 to August 1944. Jean-Louis Brau recalls that the publication of Maurice Nadeau's *L'Histoire du surréalisme* had just revealed to a whole generation that from 1925 onwards a shipload of pirates had been assaulting the leaky old vessel which had finally sunk during the war. When the educational authorities, reluctantly and cautiously, admitted Rimbaud to the syllabus, 'we learnt that these freebooters existed, that they belonged to the same generation as our parents, that they could be met anywhere between New York and Paris.'[8]

While this largely explains the appeal which Artaud's image had to the younger generation, a more direct influence on the remainder of his life was exerted by a smaller, older, richer public—potential customers for the booksellers and publishers who made money in 1947–8 by bringing out expensive editions of short texts by Artaud. Not that he was any less meticulous when he composed by dictating to the secretaries who were put at his disposal or to his friends than he was when he scribbled into the exercise-books he carried around with him. Sometimes, he would dictate from notes: invariably he would revise carefully. Sometimes he would write a complete draft before dictating, as he did with 'La Culture Indienne' and 'Ci-gît', which were written in one day (25 November 1946). He dictated both texts to Paule Thévenin, who has described how 'he did it with very particular care, indicating punctuation, capital letters, spacing and the beginning of each new stanza. He spelt out the passages in glossolalia, etc. What is more, throughout the dictation, he sat next to us, checking our transcription and correcting the mistakes we happened to make.' (Notes, *O.C.* XII. 292.)

In the original version of 'Ci-gît' there was a passage which Artaud subsequently deleted, asserting that the mind was born out of the body:

> from the pain sawn out of the bone
> something was born which became what made
> itself into mind.   (*O.C.* XII. 264–5)

The only vestiges of this in the final version of the poem are the line

> from the pain sawn from the bone

and the spaced-out line:

> from the pain
>   sweated
> *in*
>   **the bone**

Between the two there is a passage in italics about the crucifixion of Artaud

> who knew there was no mind
> but a body
> which remakes itself. . . .   (*O.C.* XII. 94–5)

Logically, Artaud's position was untenable. He was simultaneously denying the existence of the mind and loading it with all the physical attributes of the body he so resented. But, combined with the ambiguity of the word '*esprit*' (spirit/mind), the contradiction helped him to an extraordinarily intense poetry in which voice, discourse, consciousness are all lacerated by the doubt about where they are coming from. The effect is like the consummation of a sadistic love affair between Creation and the Void.

All the concepts which have been fundamental to our culture are put to the test of Artaud's personal pain:

> Because even infinity is dead
> infinity is the name of a death
> which is not dead[9]

In 'Chiote à l'esprit' (written March 1947)[10] he maintained that spirit was no more than 'a grinding shortage of existence' which felt revulsion 'at the notion of becoming a body itself' and so took advantage of 'what the body would lose in life' to make sure of its own existence. This idea is very similar to the one about the Demiurge that steals Artaud's unborn body, but 'Chiote à l'esprit' goes on to argue that ideas are only empty space inside the body, intrusions of absence and desire 'between two movements of a brilliant reality which the body, by its unique presence, has never stopped advancing'.

Describing opium as the corporeal residue of a state humanity had once achieved, Artaud equated it with 'the overthrow of an ancient uprooting power' which it had eventually rejected. Striving 'towards a holocaust of grandeur', man suffers from 'the ache of not yet being' which demands bodily form, but opium can cure 'whatever has not yet risen'.[11]

A complete process of sublimation is at work, some of which has an inverse effect. Speaking out of a deeply sensed equation between body and mind, the voice that reaches us is constituting its text into a surrogate body, which is put at our disposal. The half-pleasurable, half-painful stresses and contortions of a human yearning which is neither wholly physical nor wholly mental are adumbrated in sentences whose meaning remains partly and tantalizingly inaccessible, while the tension between the phrases is richly and poetically satisfying. What Artaud consummately provides is what Roland Barthes calls a *texte de jouissance*, a text in which the reader can take a quasi-sexual pleasure, enjoying the pressures and discontinuities and collisions, reconciling himself to the logical contradiction which is itself irreconcilable. If language is the 'mother tongue', the writer, says Barthes, is someone who plays with his mother's body, 'in order to glorify it, to embellish it, or in order to dismember it, to take it to the limit of what can be known about the body: I would go so far as to take bliss in a *disfiguration* of the language'.[12] Without writing specifically about Artaud, Barthes—like Derrida, Sollers, and Kristeva in what they have written specifically about him—gives some useful hints on how to approach his work. One should try to postpone interpretative foreclosure indefinitely; *jouissance* (as opposed to *plaisir*) is defined by an extreme of perversion, 'an extreme continually shifted, an empty, mobile, unpredictable extreme'. Not that Artaud would have himself approved of this approach to his writing; though he did, during his religious period at Rodez, acknowledge that 'Le Clair Abélard' was the best of all his writings because it was the most 'perverse' and probably the most explicitly salacious. He had been helped by 'all the resources of erotic unconsciousness, all the treacherous forces of the spirit of reproduction—treacherous to God'.

It was because he believed in the reality of his pre-natal memories, that he was able to write about them so well; similarly his genuine belief in the myth he had invented about the human race's pre-history charged his ontological ideas with imaginative vitality. There had been a time when humanity had the choice between infinity and self-absorption, spiritual greatness and fleshly self-gratification.

> There where it smells of shit
> is the smell of existence.
> Man would easily have been able not to shit,
> not to open the anal pocket. . .
> he would have had to consent
> to not existing,
> but he could not bear the idea of losing existence
> that is to say of dying alive.[13]

As early as 1923 Artaud had described his work as 'waste matter from myself, scrapings off the soul'.* Writing to Henri Parisot on 22 September 1945, he said: 'I deny the possibility of losing excrement without cutting oneself open and losing one's soul.' Something from inside the living body is lifelessly discarded, as the whole body will be when the whole of life has passed through it.

Artaud's most frightened and frightening equation of art, excrement, and destruction was not published until 1950. As in James Joyce's work, extreme ontological pessimism is dressed up in wry word-play:

> the story of this maturing soul which has had to pass through the tail-like tunnel of language, a tongue I have not chosen because it is based on movement of the rectum, where the psychic expulsion of the idea is held firm, I said firm, by criminal incision of a consciousness sent back in liquefaction round the incisor tooth of existence, which has been repugnant to the soul, to the whole compressive cupping of the whole soul in the great colon. It would have wanted to come out like a bomb or a great cannon-ball but has been *rectified* in being in the rectum of the *Arbitrary*-mind.[14]

The future that Artaud proposed was as much of a personal myth as his alternative to Genesis. We must change the human body. We must learn to live without organs.

> I hate and despise as a coward everyone who refuses to recognize that life is given to us only for us to recreate and reconstitute the whole of our physical organism.[15]

> Man is sick because he is badly constructed. . . .
> We must decide to strip him naked to scrape off this tiny animal
> Whose itch is fatal,
>
> > god
> > and with god
> > his organs
>
> Contradict me if you want to
> but there is nothing more useless than an organ.

> When you have made a body without organs
> you will have saved him from all his compulsions and restored his
> true liberty.[16]

True liberty would include liberation from the vortex of decay and

* See above, p. 10.

death. He said in the poem 'Le Théâtre et la science'[17] that the human body dies 'only when we have forgotten how to transform it'. The poem opens by defining theatre as a 'crucible of fire and real meat' where bodies are renewed; it ends with a reference to 'this revolution of the whole body without which nothing can be altered'. And in the postscript to the letter about opium,* he said that behind theatre and poetry were what he called the trance-like effusions of the human spine—energies in a state of waiting. In both theatre and poetry 'unprecedented realities' could be brought to life. Something as yet uncreated could already have a will or a force directing it towards articulation.

It was three weeks after his performance at the Vieux-Colombier that Artaud visited the Van Gogh exhibition at the Orangerie; within the next four weeks *Van Gogh le suicidé de la société* was written. What Artaud saw in the paintings was what he had himself been unable to say from the stage. Van Gogh had been endowed with a 'superior lucidity' that enabled him 'to see further, infinitely and dangerously further than the immediate and apparent reality of facts'. In his 'morbid alchemical experiments' he 'took nature as an object and the human body as a crucible'. He went beyond 'the inert act of imitating nature' to start up a whirlwind, an element ripped from the heart. Underneath his imitation, 'he has raised an atmosphere, isolated a nerve, which do not exist in nature, but they are of a nature and an atmosphere that are truer than the atmosphere and the nerve of true nature.'

In July 1947 there was an exhibition of Artaud's drawings in the Galerie Pierre. In the poem he wrote for the catalogue, he paid tribute to Van Gogh for extracting from the human head a portrait

> that is the
> rocket explosive of
> the beating of a burst
> heart.
> His own.[18]

At the beginning of November 1947, Fernand Pouey, chief

* See above, p. 138.

producer of dramatic and literary programmes on Radiodiffusion Française, commissioned Artaud to do a broadcast in the series *La Voix des poètes*, offering him as much rehearsal time as he needed and complete freedom in choosing texts and actors. A secretary was provided to whom he could dictate any new material. Most of it was new, but it was ready in time for rehearsals to start in the middle of the month. The title Artaud chose was *Pour en finir avec le jugement de Dieu*, and the programme had been recorded by the end of the month. The four speakers were Maria Casarès, Roger Blin, Paule Thévenin, and Artaud himself, who also created a most effective rhythmic punctuation out of percussion instruments which he played himself—xylophone, drums, and gongs. His screams also functioned percussively: since seeing the Balinese theatre he had not only leaned towards the non-human but learned to make his voice sound inhuman. The transmission was scheduled for 2 February 1948, but the Director-General of Radiodiffusion Française, Wladimir Porché, had been worried by the title and had listened to the recording, which he promptly banned as blasphemous. The newspapers gave so much space to the affair that Pouey was able to arrange for the recording to be heard by a jury which included Barrault, Jouvet, Cocteau, Eluard, and Paulhan. They were unanimously in favour of letting it be transmitted, and when Porché refused to withdraw his veto, Pouey resigned.

Artaud decided to have nothing further to do with radio. From now on, he wrote to Paule Thévenin on 24 February, he would devote himself

> exclusively
> to the theatre
> of my conception,
> a theatre of blood,
> a theatre which ensures at each performance that
>   something is gained
> *bodily*
> something
> no less by those who play than by those who come to watch.

But he had only another week to live. He had been complaining, increasingly, of intestinal pain. Paule Thévenin's husband, a doctor, arranged for him to see a gastro-enterologist, who took

X-rays. Artaud was reassured that all he needed was a healthy diet and plenty of rest, but the Thévenins were told that he was suffering from an inoperable rectal cancer. He should be given all the opium he wanted.

At the Ivry clinic on 4 March, the caretaker who was bringing him his breakfast found him dead. For three days his friends took it in turns to stay with the body to protect it from the rats.

Artaud and After

To attempt a comprehensive account of Artaud's influence would be like trying to map the currents in an ocean. How, for instance, could we even begin to analyse the results of his influence on Pierre Boulez or on R. D. Laing? We have the testimony of the men themselves. Boulez has said:

> I can find in his writings the fundamental preoccupations of contemporary music. To have seen him and heard him speaking his own texts, accompanying them with cries, noises, rhythms, showed us how to contrive a fusion of sound and word, how to make the phoneme spurt out when the word no longer can, in short, how to organize delirium. What non-sense, it will be said, what an absurd mixture of terms. What? Would you believe only in the vertigo of improvisation, in the power of an 'elementary' ritualization? More and more, I imagine, to make it effective, we will have to take delirium into account and, yes, organize it.[1]

But we will never know precisely how much difference Artaud and his work have made to the development of Boulez, or how far the Artaudian elements in his work penetrated into that of the composers and conductors who have been influenced by him.

R. D. Laing has said that when, as a student, he read Peter Watson's translation of an excerpt from *Van Gogh le suicidé de la société* in *Horizon* (January 1948) it came as a 'revelation' to him and 'played a decisive part' in his development.[2] It is curious that there is no mention of Artaud or Van Gogh either in his first book *The Divided Self*, written when he was twenty-eight, or in his second, *The Self and Others* (published 1961), but his characterization of the schizoid personality in *The Divided Self* is oddly similar to what

A sequence from Artaud's *The Spurt of Blood* (*Le Jet de sang*), produced as part of the *Theatre of Cruelty* season, directed by Peter Brook and Charles Marowitz at the LAMDA Theatre, 1964

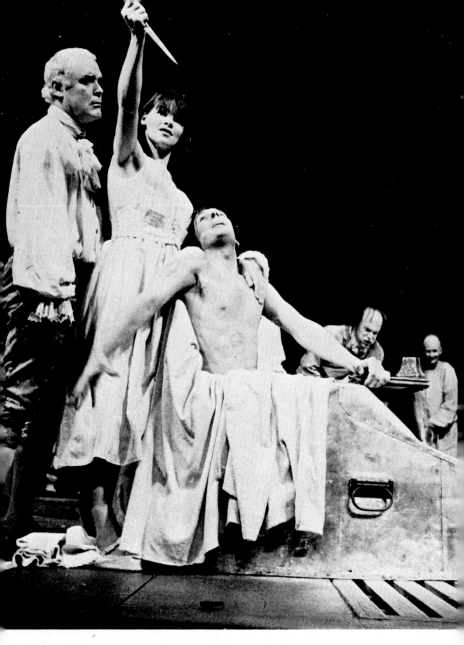

Patrick Magee as Sade, Glenda Jackson as Charlotte Corday, and
Ian Richardson as Marat in Brook's 1964 production of the
Marat/Sade by Peter Weiss

Artaud wrote about the feeling of having no real existence. The schizophrenic, said Laing, 'may feel more unreal than real; in a literal sense, more dead than alive; precariously differentiated from the rest of the world, so that his identity and autonomy are always in question'. It is impossible to judge whether Artaud's essay on Van Gogh contributed causally or even catalytically to Laing's revolutionary willingness to identify sympathetically with the viewpoint of the schizophrenic; but while Artaud never encouraged anyone else to use drugs, Laing, as a therapist, became increasingly involved with them, while his ideas became more mystical and Artaudian. The early work differentiates clearly between the schizophrenic and the individual who has a sense of ontological security, who does not question his identity or his autonomy. But in the chapter on 'Transcendental Experience' in *The Politics of Experience* (1967) Laing argues that:

> True sanity entails in one way or another the dissolution of the normal ego, that false self competently adjusted to our alienated social reality: the emergence of the 'inner' archetypal mediators of divine power, and through this death a rebirth, and the eventual re-establishment of a new kind of ego-functioning, the ego now being the servant of the divine, no longer its betrayer.

In the English theatre Peter Brook has been the main filter for the passage of Artaudian ideas. Of his major productions, *King Lear* (1962) and the *Marat/Sade* (1964) bore the most unmistakable signs of the influence; the ideas have also been disseminated directly by Brook's writings—his articles in the theatrical review *Encore* during the early sixties and his book *The Empty Space* (1968). In *Encore* he said: 'this visionary, undoubtedly mad, wrote more sense than anyone else about the theatre in our time'.[3] But even when Artaud's magnetic pull on Brook was at its strongest, there were other cultural forces drawing him in the same direction. The hippie movement was beginning to have its effect on the media. Shirley Clarke's 1960 film of the Jack Gelber play about drug addicts, *The Connection* (originally produced by the Living Theatre), made its impact almost at the same time as John Cassavetes's 1960 film *Shadows*, which was shot on 16-mm film with no script and a technical crew of four. 'I would define a good film', wrote Brook,

'as a piecing together of *living* fragments. . . . If each fragment—
each shot—is a piece of *living* material—then half the battle is won.'

Once again, as when Surrealism was at its height, old ideas of
structure and order were disintegrating under hammer-blows from
the most influential of practising artists. The Picasso exhibition in
London had been hugely popular. In the U.S. Allen Ginsberg was
attracting a bigger following than Robert Lowell. 'We are aware',
said Peter Brook in his *Encore* article,

> of the vast surging momentum of the whirling–force–speed–image–
> emotional farrago in which we exist—and order—whether the
> organisation of plot, the definition of character or of political
> panaceas—seems pitifully inadequate, like Boy Scout mottoes in the
> ferocity of war. We accept noise, rhythm, the climaxes of sex, kicks,
> food, drink, dope, speed, danger, violence as facts, as elements
> (recently we have discovered one of the few political facts that cannot
> be disputed—the power of silence, of concentrated passive protest)—
> we do not wish to question these things because they are so simple
> that they defy analysis. They are there, electrons of living, belonging
> to no system, no order.

Artaud's work seemed to suggest that it was possible to make
ontological statements regardless of time, place, historical analysis
of society, or psychological analysis of personality—as Shakespeare
had, for instance, in his use of the audience's belief in the supernatural. At the Globe Theatre the Ghost in *Hamlet* would not have
looked frightening, but the effect would have been frightening, and
implicitly a statement was being made about death, life, and the
love between father and son. Brook had recently been to Mexico,
visited fiestas in the Indian villages, and brought back from Vera
Cruz a little figure of a goddess with her head thrown back, her
hands held up. The artist must have experienced an 'inner
radiance', said Brook, and communicated it by creating a concrete
object. 'This to me is the essence of great acting.'

When he started work on *King Lear*, Brook regarded it less as a
script that had to be translated into theatrical three-dimensionality
than as a 'series of intellectual strands which only performance can
tie together . . . its full meaning can only be comprehended exis-
tentially—on a stage.'[4] It is a play about madness; it is also about
eyesight and blindness and the void. Brook said: 'as characters

acquire sight it enables them to see only into a void.' Compared
with Artaud's dictatorial method of directing actors ('I do not
want there to be so much as the bat of an eyelid that does not
belong to me') Brook's is more democratic, more empirical, and
more modern. He knows that he does not know what he wants.
'What is achieved determines what is to follow, and you just can't
go about things as if you knew all the answers.' He compared himself to a modern painter who put a splodge of red on his canvas
'and only after it goes on does he decide it might be a good idea to
add a little green, to make a vertical line here or a horizontal line
there'. But the results Brook has achieved have often been
Artaudian, and in *King Lear* it was the most sadistic sequence that
was most reminiscent of the Theatre of Cruelty. There were no
servants to sympathize with Gloucester when Cornwall blinded
him. The lines were cut and the blinded man was brusquely
pushed in the direction of the audience as the house lights came up.

In the autumn of 1963 Brook and Charles Marowitz formed an
experimental company of twelve young actors to work together
for twelve weeks before giving five weeks of performances at the
LAMDA Theatre under the title *Theatre of Cruelty*. Brook called
the programme 'a form of surrealist revue composed of shots in the
dark; shots at distant targets'. He stressed that Artaud's work was
more a 'springboard' than 'a model for slavish reproduction'.[5]
The twelve weeks of exercises and rehearsals seem to have been
designed partly to break down Stanislavskian consistencies with
Artaudian disruptions. 'One of the main objects of the work',
Marowitz has written, 'was to create a discontinuous style of
acting.'[6] The development of an improvisation would be checked
by a sound or by throwing an irrelevant object to the actor, who
immediately had to accommodate it by changing tack.

Afterwards, many of the actors and many of the ideas that had
been evolved in working with them were used in Brook's production of the *Marat/Sade*—another play about madness. Peter Weiss,
the author, had acknowledged his debt to Artaud; Brook said that
his approach to the play was partly Brechtian, partly Artaudian.
This was apt because the central conflict was between a man who
wanted to change the world (as Marat and Brecht did) by political
action, and a man who wanted to change human nature (as Sade

and Artaud did) by making it truer to itself. The success of the production depended on the impact of a theatre language that seemed brilliantly fresh. With the ironical compounding of alienation effects, with the buckets of red, black, and aristocratically blue paint to represent the blood that flowed from the guillotine, with Charlotte Corday's portentous knocking on Marat's non-existent door, her use of her hair in flagellating the masochistic Sade, the string wigs and grotesquely lipsticked mouths of the four lunatics who formed the chorus, the abrupt shifts between realism and stylization, the outbreaks of manic behaviour that interrupted the performance of the play-within-the-play, the semi-incantatory use of language, the use of percussion instruments in the songs, Brook was going further than anyone had gone before towards bringing the Theatre of Cruelty to theatrical life.

Before the production went into rehearsal, he had already been saying 'I'm fed up with Artaud.' Expanding on the remark in a discussion at the LAMDA Theatre, Brook said that Artaud had himself used thirties imagery, 'Picasso–Dadaist–Salvador Dali-influenced techniques', and that 'the means, the telling means are today vastly different from those that Artaud either proposed or could have found in the theatrical climate of his time'.[7] In theatre, fashion changes no less rapidly than in *haute couture*, though it is only the foam on the new waves that is new, not the water. Many of Artaud's ideas about cruelty came from the Greeks and the Elizabethans; of the production ideas and techniques that seemed new in the British theatre of the sixties, many of the ones that did not derive from Artaud derived from theories Brecht had worked out in the late twenties and early thirties. Today we see few productions which are as demonstrably Artaudian as *King Lear* and the *Marat/Sade,* but this is partly because Artaud's influence has been so deeply absorbed and so widely diffused. Generally theatre has become more physical and dynamic, less cerebral and verbal. Face and voice have become less important; body, energy, movement, use of space more important. The rigid segregation of acting area from auditorium has been broken down. Though Artaud was by no means the only cause of these changes, his influence was probably the most powerful of the contributory factors.

After collaborating with Brook, Charles Marowitz went on in

1968 to run his own theatre, the Open Space, which operated until 1976 in a Tottenham Court Road basement. Believing that 'By substituting a metaphysical view of society, Artaud pulled the rug out from under Brecht's notion that the ultimate reality must have sociological and political roots',[8] Marowitz often cited Artaud's name in formulating his aim: to continue the search for a gestural, non-verbal theatre.

One of Marowitz's most Artaudian experiments was a production in November 1970 of *Palach*, with a script by Alan Burns which was little more than a scenario. A small stage backed against each of the four walls, so the audience was encircled by the action. The same idea of turning the auditorium into a kind of fairground where people could wander between the booths had been used by Ariane Mnouchkine in the Théâtre du Soleil production of *1789*, which opened in 1970 at the Palace of Sports in Milan after five months of study and rehearsal. The standing audience had to turn its attention from one to another of five rostra as the focus of the action shifted.

At the end of 1975 Marowitz developed the material he had used in his *Theatre Quarterly* article on 'Artaud at Rodez'* into a stage show which had the same title. It was a jaggedly disconnected succession of brief scenes presenting a persecuted Artaud at the mercy of a plumply self-satisfied Ferdière, who was largely motivated by envy of his patient's creative talent. The method of presentation made it impossible for the audience to distinguish between biographical fact and directorial invention, but some of the theatrical images were powerful: two crouching actors provided a human couch; a sexy muse offered opium as inspiration; Ferdière gave Artaud lunch at a table with a crazily angled top. At the end, Artaud, still alive, was nailed into a coffin. One by one his friends walked away, but the shrill, manic voice from inside the coffin remained audible, as Artaud's voice has remained audible ever since his death.

The Polish director Jerzy Grotowski has been called 'Artaud's

* See above, page 128.

natural son'[9] and Brook has written: 'Grotowski's theatre is as close as anyone has got to Artaud's ideal.'

> Grotowski's actors offer their performance as a ceremony for those who wish to assist: the actor invokes, lays bare what lies in every man—and what daily life covers up. This theatre is holy because its purpose is holy; it has a clearly defined place in the community and it responds to a need the churches can no longer fill.[10]

Roger Blin, on the other hand, insists that Grotowski is 'totally the opposite of Artaud', tending always towards the spiritual and mystical, whereas Artaud tended towards the physical. Without denying the affinity, Grotowski has pointed out that Artaud had no method, no technique. Grotowski spent ten years on evolving a system of exercises with the actors in his Teatr Laboratorium. From 1959 to 1962 the object was positive—to extend the actor's technical range. During the next seven years, many of the original exercises were retained, but the main intention was to build what he called a *via negativa*—instead of helping the actors to answer the question 'How can we do this?' Grotowski was trying to show them what not to do, how to discover what was obstructing and limiting the use they made of themselves.

Compared with the theatre Artaud imagined, the theatre Grotowski realized was austere, anti-spectacular. He was aiming at an uncluttered relationship between actor and audience, with no make-up, no scenery, no lighting changes, no sound effects, minimal costumes. This was partly the result of a temperamental aversion to the showy and the meretricious, but the intention was to clear the ground for the actor to make a total gift of himself: 'In the final result we are speaking of the impossibility of separating spiritual and physical. The actor should not use his organism to illustrate a "movement of the soul", he should accomplish this movement with his organism.'[11]

As in Artaud's earliest analyses of his psycho-physical disabilities, the thinking evolved out of an exacerbating drive to abolish the space between impulse and expression. According to Grotowski, what the actor needs to achieve is

> freedom from the time-lapse between inner impulse and outer reaction in such a way that the impulse is already an outward reaction.

Impulse and action are concurrent: the body vanishes, burns, and the spectator sees only a series of visible impulses. . . . The requisite state of mind is a passive readiness to realise an active role, a state in which one does not '*want to do that*' but rather '*resigns from not doing it*'.

Grotowski has been able to translate Artaud's ideal into a training programme and a technique of rehearsing actors. The dedicated members of Grotowski's troupe were schooled to think of body, mind, spirit, and voice as indistinguishable. In the vocal process, the whole organism must resonate: Grotowski succeeded in activating resonators all over the body. His actors learned to involve their whole physique in their reaction to a stimulus before bringing the voice into play. First you strike the table and then you shout. Exercises were devised to establish an imaginary contact between a part of the body and an area of the room. In learning to make the thinking process more physical, the actors were simultaneously learning to fill the space outside themselves.

As in Artaud, transcendental imagery was coupled with antireligious intentions, and the energy generated by the tension was used creatively. 'Soul' and 'spiritual' are keywords. Grotowski talked of 'trance' and 'translumination'. He was conscious of wanting to blaspheme against what religion and tradition had raised to the level of taboo. He tried to attack it by confronting it with his own experience 'which is itself determined by the collective experience of our time'.

Like Artaud he had to read his own consciousness as if it were a map of contemporary reality; unlike Artaud he realized productions which triumphantly vindicated his theories. His staging of *The Constant Prince* made statements about humanity which, like Shakespeare's use of the supernatural, quite transcended the social and the personal. As the prince, Ryszard Cieslak seemed to be in greater danger than a matador in a bull-ring. There was no faking about the pain he had to suffer: the audience saw his body bouncing and his back going red under flagellation from a folded cloak, and he was genuinely hurting himself when he slapped his own chest. He submitted to all the pain and humiliation with the same stoical passivity as to the kiss that Rena Mirecka implanted on his groin, but the alternation between supinity and violent animation made his performance seem all the more dangerous. His physical expressiveness could have emerged only from a profound interiorization of a discipline that allows great scope to spontaneity. As Grotowski has said, 'what is elementary feeds what is constructed and vice versa, to become the real source of a kind of acting that glows. This lesson was neither understood by Stanislavski, who let natural impulses dominate, nor by Brecht, who gave too much emphasis to the construction of a role.'

Calderón's *The Constant Prince* is a rather wordy play about a Christian prince who accepts martyrdom in preference to paying the ransom demanded by his Moorish captors—a whole Christian town. In eliminating most of the words, most of the plot, and most of the characters, Grotowski was doing very much the same sort of stripping down that, in his first manifesto for a Theatre of Cruelty,* Artaud had promised to perform on Elizabethan texts. Grotowski's production was imbued with a cruelty that seemed both timeless and modern, even though one of the torturers was wearing a crown.

Writing in *Les Temps modernes* (April 1967), Grotowski said: 'The secret of Artaud is, among others, to have been particularly prolific in his mistakes and contradictions.' That Grotowski was aware of this only makes it seem all the more extraordinary that he could incorporate so many of Artaud's ideas into a coherent system.

It is harder to analyse the influence Artaud has had in his own country. Thanks to the continuity in the existence of the Comédie Française, French acting has been more bound by tradition than English acting, and the tradition has been one of high rhetoric. A major part of Artaud's influence, therefore, worked negatively: Philippe Soupault has suggested that actors such as Jouvet and Raymond Rouleau found it impossible to go on allowing themselves so much exaggeration.[12] Among directors, Roger Blin (who was responsible for the original productions of Beckett's plays) must have been influenced by Artaud no less profoundly than Barrault or Brook were, but the influence was more osmotic, and Blin says he finds it impossible to analyse.

* See above, p. 84.

It would be difficult to prove that Artaud exerted a direct influence on Jean Genet, but the affinity is obvious: 'One cannot but dream of an art that would be a profound tangle of active symbols, capable of speaking to the public a language in which nothing would be said, everything presented,' wrote Genet in a letter to Pauvert. Genet's theatre is ritualistic, anti-rational, anti-psychological, anti-materialistic, calculated to launch a metaphysical assault on the audience. In one of the early versions of *Le Balcon*, Genet resorted to the Artaudian device of introducing Blood, Sperm, and Tears as personifications.

How much has *Les Nègres* in common with the Theatre of Cruelty? A ceremony is performed by black actors playing white characters and implicitly denying the reality they appear to be asserting. The white playwright forces them to force the white spectators into the confusion and discomfort of becoming accomplices of the denial and in the enacted murder of a white woman. They feel like involuntary eavesdroppers on a dreamlike plan (or planlike dream) for ruthless insurrection against white supremacy. The fiction has one foot planted in the reality of black resentment against white exploitation and the other in Genet's undisguisable glee at the prospect of Western culture's overthrow. The Parthenon, Chopin, French cuisine and Cartesian principles will all be trampled to dust. The ceremony turns the audience against itself.

In Ionesco's work the Artaudian parallels are very curious, though the question of direct influence is complicated both by their common interest in the work of Jarry and by Ionesco's insistence that a work of art owes almost nothing to other people: the creator is using his native intuition, discovering a world of his own. Ionesco is arguably the first successful surrealist playwright* and he was aware of picking up a thread that had been dropped in the mid-twenties. 'I have attempted, for example, to exteriorise, by using objects, the anguish . . . of my characters, to make the set speak and the action on the stage more visual, to translate into concrete images terror, regret or remorse, and estrangement, to play with words (but not to send them packing) and even perhaps to

* A contention I have tried to substantiate in *Eugène Ionesco* (London, 1972; New York, 1976).

deform them.' Though his use of language is simpler, less idio-
syncratic, less interesting than Artaud's, he is often reminiscent of
him; even his hankering after immortality recalls Artaud's belief
that we would not have to die if only we could learn to live without organs: 'It is in our nature to understand everything, and we
understand very little: we cannot understand ourselves. We are
created to live together and we tear one another to pieces; we do
not want to die, so we are meant to be immortal, but we *do* die. It
is horrible and cannot be taken seriously.'[13]

The theatre language Ionesco has evolved is much more richly
textured. In *Les Chaises* he contrives a powerful theatrical evocation
of the void. On an island surrounded by stagnant water, a ninety-
five-year-old man and a ninety-four-year-old woman fill the stage
with empty chairs as they welcome invisible guests to the last party
they will give before committing suicide. The old man believes
that if only he had not lacked the gift of speech, he could have
saved mankind. Now, finally, he has hired an Orator to deliver his
message to the invisible guests, who include the Emperor. The
Orator is visible, and the old man and woman kill themselves
before he begins to speak. The anti-climactic revelation that the
Orator is dumb is like a grotesquely parodic echo of Artaud's
Vieux-Colombier débâcle, and the play ends with real sounds from
the imaginary crowd and with a murmuring of wind and water,
which 'should be heard for a very long time, as though coming
from nothing, coming from the void'.

After the abortion of Artaud's and Barrault's plan for a drama-
tization of Defoe's *Journal of the Plague Year*, and after the failure of
Camus's *L'État de siège*, it was left for Ionesco to dramatize the
Defoe book in *Jeux de massacre* (1970). The play was written for a
huge cast, but the stage directions suggest that some of the citizens
could be represented by large marionettes, or dolls, or painted
figures—another idea that might have been inspired by Artaud's
work, while many of the sequences may have roots in 'Le Théâtre et
la peste'. In one a nurse advances murderously on an old woman,
wanting to steal money she would be unable to spend.

In New York, the Living Theatre, which originated in 1946, was doing what is generally considered to be its best work when its directors, Julian Beck and Judith Malina, were most under the influence of Artaud. They first read *The Theatre and Its Double* in 1958. 'He was the only one of our time', Beck has said, 'who understood the nature and greatness of theatre,' while Judith Malina has called him 'My muse, never absent from my dreams'. Jack Gelber's *The Connection*, which they produced in 1959, was Artaudian and anti-theatrical in its refusal to get caught up in any of the normal mechanics for generating suspense.

In Judith Malina's production, Kenneth H. Brown's *The Brig* (1963) was a devastatingly accurate replica of the ritual cruelty shown to prisoners in U.S. Marine Corps brigs. Bawling out requests for permission to cross the white line, moving constantly at the double, obeying commands like automata, submitting meekly to punches in the stomach from the hectoring guards, the sane prisoners have been conditioned to behave like madmen; it is only the one who is going mad who insists that he still has human rights and a name which is not a number. Julian Beck later told a French critic that Artaud's mistake had been to think that horror had its source in fantasy, not in reality.

The Living Theatre production directed by Judith Malina, with designs by Julian Beck, of *Frankenstein* went back to Mary Shelley's fantasy. Instead of a script, the company used a collage of quotations from the Bible, the Cabbala, Ezra Pound, Walt Whitman, and so on, making the words into incantations. But Artaud's idea of working for spiritual regeneration in the audience had been vulgarized into political evangelism decorated with cross-legged meditation and perfunctory gestures in the direction of Oriental religion.

After Brook and Grotowski, the director with the best claim to be considered as Artaud's natural son is Joseph Chaikin, who worked as an actor in the Living Theatre, but left to form a new company, the Open Theatre, in 1963. The points of comparison with Artaud's life are striking. Since childhood, Chaikin has suffered from a cardiac weakness. His career as an actor, which started in the commercial theatre, ended when he was warned not even to risk the strain of playing with his own company. Inevitably, like Artaud's, his ideas about acting were conditioned by his own disability. Consciously or unconsciously echoing the letters to Jacques Rivière, Chaikin has insisted that the actor needs direct access to the life that is moving inside him. The ideal actor can 'approach in himself a cosmic dread' and rebound into 'a joy so sweet that it is without limit'. But he must not attach himself rigidly to one internal condition as being more human, more theatrical, or more appealing than another.[15]

Believing that Julian Beck and Judith Malina were not sufficiently concerned to explore the potential of the actor or the possibilities of the ensemble experience, Chaikin found that he was making most use of Artaud's formulations where the work of the new company was moving furthest away from the territory charted by Stanislavski. Working at first in freedom from any schedule of public performances, the group concentrated on improvisations and exercises, exploring ways of using the voice and body not to tell a story naturalistically but to exteriorize states of mind. Shunning psychology, they tried, as the Surrealists had, to develop material drawn from dreams. Chaikin spoke of trying to 'locate the inside of a situation in its abstract and elusive texture'. The next step was to make it visible.

Unlike Grotowski, Chaikin wanted to involve writers in the process of developing a theatrical language which would not depend primarily on dialogue. Movements, silences and semi-articulate sounds would be no less important than words, while words or disconnected phrases might be used in a non-logical sequence. The writers collaborated directly with the actors, developing rhythms and ideas that emerged from improvisations, suggesting theatrical images, discovering varieties of non-verbal expression and communication. From the outset, Jean-Claude van Itallie attended studio sessions, and in his trilogy of short plays which the company presented in 1966 under the title *America Hurrah*, the actors were required (as in the Brook–Marowitz *Theatre of Cruelty*) to switch abruptly and unnaturalistically from one level to another, sometimes from one character to another. In *Interview*, the first play, sentences are split between several speakers; in the third, *Motel*, the motel-keeper and the couple who smash up the room are represented by grotesque, outsize dolls with disproportionately big heads.

In 1967 van Itallie started working with Chaikin and the actors on the idea which was shown to the public in 1969 under the title *The Serpent*. Like Artaud, Chaikin found he wanted to explore the roots of the situation we are all in by evolving his own version of Genesis. The premise of the piece, he wrote in the Introduction, 'is that Man made God in his own image, and held up this God to determine his own, Man's, limits'. The play is subtitled *A Ceremony*. 'In *The Serpent*, the point of crossing a boundary is a point of transformation, and the whole company crosses a boundary. Because when one person crosses a forbidden line, nothing is the same after that.' The action was quite devoid of the dramatic conflict that forms the staple of most theatrical entertainment, but as van Itallie said, 'I'm trying to do with words what Chaikin is trying to do with the actors—get to the very essence of things. It's the only extent to which you can reach the archetype.'[16] There was some incantation, and more of an attempt to create a myth than to tell a story. When the actors reproduced moments from the Zapruder film of the Kennedy assassination, the juxtaposition with Cain's murder of Abel gave the modern event a mythical connotation. Even Artaud's hostility to God was paralleled during the preparation of the production, which, according to Chaikin, provoked great anger among the actors. 'We're guests in the world. The sense of being a "guest" is something we became really mad at.'

Like the Balinese company Artaud saw, the group had also started to draw on observation of animal movement and imitation of animal sounds, using body and voice to probe at the edges of human experience. What would it feel like to be dying, or to be an animal? Would people be able to drag an ambiguous bird-woman back across the frontier between the animal and the human? How is that frontier located? This was one of the problems in *The Mutation Show*.

In preparing *Terminal* the actors brought material taken from their dreams, and one of the most effective sections represented an attempt to investigate the frontier between life and death by showing their physical response to the news that this would be their last chance to use their legs, their eyes, their voice. For years Chaikin had been living privately with the possibility that death would come suddenly, but he seems to have been quite unsentimental in putting his own cosmic dread at the disposal of the actors, who were able to touch chillingly on each other's nerve centres, working with neither reverence nor irreverence but with a sensitivity that helped them to a theatrical coefficient of the transition from life to death. A complementary motif was evolved with the guides who could introduce the spirits of the dead into the bodies of the living.

One of the Artaudian elements in the show resulted from the interest of one actor, Paul Zimet, in a New Orleans sorceress. Out of her garbled Cajun words he evolved a rhythm which the writer, Susan Yankowitz, preserved, creating a character reminiscent of Artaud's clairvoyante and lines reminiscent of his glossolalia:

> Eh ye ye Mamzelle Marie
> ye ye ye li konin tou
> li te kouri, aver vieux kokodril
> eh oui ye, Mamzelle Marie.

It is understandable that Artaud's name should so often have been associated with the Happenings that started in the fifties. Jean-Paul Sartre has argued that the Happening is a logical development from Artaud's assumption that theatre is an act which should release the violence latent within the spectator.[17] Why not confront the audience with a 'true' event? The roots of Happenings can obviously be traced back to the anti-art gestures of the Surrealists and their ancestors. What better happening could there be than the chance encounter on a dissecting table of a sewing machine and an umbrella? It is true that Artaud catalysed the 'Happening': the original multi-media show at Black Mountain College in 1952 came about when John Cage, prompted by Pierre Boulez, read Artaud's work (Cage then recruited Charles Olson, Robert Rauschenberg, and Merce Cunningham to participate in the event), and the subordination of the verbal element to the visual is in keeping with his theories, but he does not seem to have exerted much analysable influence on such practitioners of Happenings as Allan Kaprow, Jim Dine, Red Grooms, and Claes Oldenburg.

*

Parallel with the effect Artaud had on R. D. Laing was his effect on Michel Foucault, whose first book *Histoire de la folie à l'âge classique* seems to start out from a point Artaud had made in *Van Gogh le suicidé de la société*: that a madman's discourse will not merely be ignored by society, it will be prevented from circulating. The terms of Foucault's narrative are strikingly Artaudian. In the Middle Ages, humanity's 'debate with madness' had dramatically confronted 'the secret powers of the world'. When the fifteenth-century preoccupation with death was superseded by the sixteenth-century mockery of madness, the nothingness of existence could no longer be viewed as an external threat. It had to be 'experienced from within as the continuous and constant form of existence'. But for Artaud's genealogies of *poètes maudits*, it is unlikely that Foucault would have grouped Nietzsche, Van Gogh, Hölderlin and Nerval together with Artaud himself. 'The number of writers, painters, and musicians who have "succumbed" to madness has increased.' But Foucault sees art and madness as mutually exclusive. Artaud's

madness is precisely *the absence of the work of art*, the reiterated presence of that absence, its central void experienced and measured in all its endless dimensions. . . . The moment when, together, the work of art and madness are born and fulfilled is the beginning of the time when the world finds itself arraigned by that work of art and responsible before it for what it is. Ruse and new triumph of madness: the world that thought to measure and justify madness through psychology must justify itself before madness, since in its struggles and agonies it measures itself by the excess of works like those of Nietzsche, of Van Gogh, of Artaud.[18]

Foucault's subsequent work has been largely an exploration of two related subjects: the organization of knowledge and discourse into categories and disciplines; the use of the prison and the clinic to discredit heterodoxies that would be socially subversive. It is not accidental that in France the revival of interest in Artaud's work has coincided with the revival of interest in Sade's. Both men were violent extremists who spent a major part of their adult life behind bars; both were dangerous men if Roland Barthes is right to argue that 'the invention of a paradoxical discourse is more revolutionary than provocation'.[19] The violence of the theatre

that Artaud proposed is a Dionysian violence in which the flood-
gates of delirium and desire could be thrown wide open, and it
might seem that the restraints of Church and State, morality and
hierarchy, could be swept aside in the onrush of the animal desires
that come bubbling out of the liberated imagination.

In a pre-Laing, pre-Foucault climate of thinking, the internal
contradictions in Artaud's writing would have tended to undercut
it more flagrantly than they do today, when they make it, poten-
tially, all the more subversive. As Barthes argues, the language that
is given the official support of state-controlled institutions is
always consistent and repetitive. The only way to escape the
alienation of present-day society is 'to *retreat ahead of it*: every old
language is immediately compromised, and every language
becomes old once it is repeated . . . all official institutions of
language are repeating machines: school, sports, advertising,
popular songs, news, all continually repeat the same structure, the
same meaning, often the same words: the stereotype is a political
fact, the major figure of ideology'.[20] So the serious challenger to
orthodoxy must be imprisoned as criminal or mad; sometimes he
is actually driven into criminality or madness by the treatment
meted out—confinement in the company of criminals or madmen,
rough handling, sexual frustration, electric-shock therapy, drugs,
etc.

As Artaud was aware, his ideas for the Theatre of Cruelty—even
if they had been free from contradictions—could never have
become a reality without a social revolution. 'To be possible and
admissible to the era,' he wrote to Paulhan on 28 May 1933, 'the
Theatre I wanted to create presupposed a different form of civilization.' His constant assaults on language and the structures
created out of it imply a potent and nostalgic yearning for the
primordial chaos that he imagined as preceding the moment when
things were given names. His creative talent is inseparable from
the instinct for destruction evident in this fabrication of a myth
about primordial purity. As Julia Kristeva has shown, beside the
anality which is often suppressed and the death-wish which is
often apparent in his writing, there is a pleasure in subverting the
processes by which signification imposes order on chaos.[21]

If Artaud today seems more relevant to our situation than any other writer who took part in the Surrealist movement, it is because the force that emerges from his life and work can be more damaging to the assumption that our culture is reasonable or even intelligible: 'The world was left to man not as a creation but as a reject, a foul turd whose zimzoum the Ancient of Days withdrew from when he was making zimzoum, not to leave space for it but to avoid the risk of touching it.'[22] This may at first seem like an excerpt from the Prophetic Books of a minor, coprophiliac Blake, but, as Kristeva comments, the linguistic return to the oral and glottal pleasures of suction and expulsion tends towards undermining the superego and its linear language, which is characterized by the concatenation of statements through subject and predicate. As Freud has shown in his accounts of the primitive functioning of the pleasure principle, it works towards the absorption into the body or ego of everything that seems good and the rejection of what seems bad. Tortuously though Artaud's consciousness functioned, it was on a level no less rudimentary that he was aware of 'holding myself always at the insensible limit of things . . . being perpetually in a state where things pass, without ever being able to latch on to them or incorporate them within myself'.[23] This sense of alienation is not unusual; what was exceptional was his being so articulate about it, his ability to use discourse as a means of registering the ebb and flow of unifying and disintegrating pressures both within itself and within his consciousness.

Freud tells us that though some things have no existence outside the imagination, all images originate out of perceptions—which they repeat. 'Affirmation, as being a substitute for union, belongs to Eros; while negation, the derivative of expulsion, belongs with destruction.' The process by which the concrete presence of the object is represented by the abstract sign or word implies a renunciation of tactile pleasure, which is partly compensated by the pleasure that can be taken in words, but a prerequisite for the acquisition of language is a repression of the anal impulses which Freud associated with the sadistic side of the sexual instincts. Capacity for symbolization implies detachment from the object, and, as Kristeva says, 'The process of the subjectivity, being the process of its language and/or of the symbolic function itself, supposes—in the economy of the body which supports it—a reactivation of this anality. Artaud's texts explicitly show that anal impulse disturbing the body of the subject in its subversion of the symbolic function.' The rejected turd pokes its head up threateningly from the bowl of the lavatory, asserting a presence we cannot go on excluding from the tissue of signification. In Artaud, as in Joyce, free-associating scatological puns work as a device for short-circuiting the machinery of repression. The apparatus of discourse is knocked backwards into an embarrassing infantilism, at the same time as being charged with a dangerous current of erotic pleasure.

Artaud launched an exceptionally violent and extraordinarily sustained assault against dualism, and, without inflicting an unequivocal defeat on it, he has at least succeeded in revealing that it functions equivocally as a safety device. So rational discourse itself becomes suspect. The irrational alternative he offers is obviously unacceptable, but his prose is forceful enough to make us hesitate, and it is during the hesitation that we can recognize that, as Foucault says, the world needs to measure itself against the excesses of Artaud.

Select Bibliography

Place of publication of works in French is Paris unless otherwise indicated; of works in English, London.

BY ARTAUD IN FRENCH

Collected works:

Oeuvres complètes (Gallimard). A revised edition is currently being produced; I list the latest available edition of each volume.

I * (pub. 1976) Contains the Préambule, the addresses to the Pope and the Dalai Lama, the correspondence with Rivière, *L'Ombilic des Limbes*, *Les Pèse-Nerfs*, 'Fragments d'un journal d'Enfer', *L'Art et la Mort*, Premières Poèmes (1913–23), Premières Proses, *Tric-Trac du Ciel*, *Bilboquet*, and Poèmes (1924–35).

I ** (1976) Textes surréalistes and letters 1921–32 (other letters from the same period appear in vol. III).

II (1961) Manifestos and brochures for the Théâtre Alfred Jarry, 'La Pierre philosophale', 'Il n'y a plus de firmament', notes for a production of Vitrac's *Le Coup de Trafalgar*, reviews of plays, books, and art exhibitions (1920–35).

III (1970) *La Coquille et le clergyman* and other screenplays, writings on the cinema, letters 1921–35, two interviews.

IV (1967) *Le Théâtre et son double*, *Les Cenci*, supplementary documentation on both.

V (1967) Additional articles and documentation on both the above, articles on the project for a Théâtre de la *N.R.F.*, letters 1931–7, interviews.

VI (1972) *Le Moine*, letters 1930–1.

VII (1967) *Héliogabale*, *Les Nouvelles Révélations de l'Être*, letters 1933–7.

VIII (1973) 'Sur quelques problèmes d'actualité', deux textes pour *Voilà*, pages de carnet, notes intimes, *Satan le feu*, notes sur les cultures orientales, grecques, indiennes, 'Le Mexique et la civilisation', lectures and articles written in Mexico, letters 1932–6.

IX (1972) *Les Tarahumaras*, relevant letters 1937 and 1943, two texts written in 1944 at Rodez, four adaptations from the English, *Lettres de Rodez*, additional letters to Henri Parisot from Rodez (1945).

X (1974) Letters written from Rodez 1943–4.

XI (1974) Letters written from Rodez 1945–6.

XII (1974) *Artaud le Mômo*, 'La Culture Indienne', 'Ci-Gît', documentation on all three, letters to Maurice Saillet and Peter Watson.

XIII (1974) *Van Gogh le suicidé de la société, Pour en finir avec le jugement de Dieu,* documentation on both, 'Le Théâtre de la Cruauté', letters 1947–8.

Lettres d'Antonin Artaud à Jean-Louis Barrault (Bordas, 1952)

Lettres à Génica Athanasiou (Gallimard, 1969)

Nouveaux écrits de Rodez (Gallimard, 1977)

Uncollected work (select listing):

1946 'Lettre sur Lautréamont', *Les Cahiers du Sud,* no. 275
'Histoire entre la Groume et Dieu', *Fontaine,* no. 57

1947 'Les malades et les médicins', *Les Quatre Vents,* no. 8

1948 'Main d'ouvrier et main de singe' and 'Coleridge le traître', *K—revue de la poésie,* nos. 1–2 (June)

1949 Extracts from *Suppôts et suppliciations, Les Temps modernes* (Feb.) and *Revue 84,* nos. 8–9
'Il y a une vieille histoire', *84,* no. 7
'C'est qu'un jour', 'Je suis l'inerte', 'L'erreur est dans le fait', *84,* nos. 10–11
Lettre contre la Cabbale (Jacques Haumont)

1950 'La Mort et l'homme', *84,* no. 13
'Je n'ai jamais rien étudié', *84,* no. 16

1952 'Trois lettres adressées à des médecins', *Botteghe Oscure,* no. 8

1954 'Le Théâtre et la science', *Théâtre populaire,* no. 5 (Jan.–Feb.)

1960 'Chiote à l'esprit', *Tel Quel,* no. 3 (Autumn)

1961 Extracts from 'Le Cahier Lutèce', *Tour de Feu,* no. 69

1968 'Il y a dans la magie', *Tel Quel,* no. 35 (Autumn)

1971 'Notes pour une "Lettre aux Balinais"', *Tel Quel,* no. 46 (Summer)

BY ARTAUD IN ENGLISH TRANSLATION

Collected Works, vols. I–IV, trans. Victor Corti (Calder and Boyars, 1968–75). Vol. I corresponds to the 1956 edn. of *Oeuvres complètes,* vol. I.

Anthologies:

Antonin Artaud Anthology, ed. Jack Hirschman (San Francisco: City Lights Books, 1965)

Antonin Artaud: Selected Writings, ed. Susan Sontag, trans. Helen Weaver (New York: Farrar, Straus & Giroux, 1976)

About Artaud in French (select listing)

Books:

Jean-Louis Brau, *Antonin Artaud* (La Table Ronde, 1971)
Henri Gouhier, *Antonin Artaud et l'essence du théâtre* (Vrin, 1974)
Otto Hahn, *Portrait d'Antonin Artaud* (Soleil Noir, 1968)
Jean Hort, *Antonin Artaud, le suicidé de la société* (Editions Connaître, 1960)
Jacques Prevel, *En compagnie d'Antonin Artaud* (Flammarion, 1974)
Artaud, ed. Philippe Sollers (Publications du Centre Culturel de Cerisy-la-Salle 10/18, 1973)
Alain Virmaux, *Antonin Artaud et le théâtre* (Seghers, 1970)

Essays and articles:

Maurice Blanchot, 'Artaud' in *Le Livre à venir* (Gallimard, 1959)
Jacques Derrida, 'La Parole soufflée' and 'Le Théâtre de la Cruauté' in *L'Ecriture et la différence* (Seuil, 1967)
Philippe Sollers, 'La pensée émet des signes' in *Logiques* (Seuil, 1968)
Paule Thévenin, 'Antonin Artaud dans la vie', *Tel Quel,* no. 20 (Winter 1965)

Special issues of reviews devoted to Artaud:

K—revue de la poésie, nos. 1-2 (June 1948)
Cahiers de la Compagnie Renaud-Barrault, nos. 22-3 (May 1958)
La Tour de Feu, nos. 63-4 (Dec. 1959); no. 69 (Apr. 1961); no. 112 (Dec. 1971)
Tel Quel, no. 22 (Winter 1965); no. 52 (Winter 1972)
Obliques, nos. 10-11 (1977)

About Artaud in English (select listing)

Books:

Martin Esslin, *Artaud* (Fontana Modern Masters, 1976)
Naomi Greene, *Antonin Artaud: Poet without Words* (New York: Simon & Schuster, 1970)
Eric Sellin, *The Dramatic Concepts of Antonin Artaud* (Chicago: Univ. of Chicago Press, 1968)

Essays and articles:

Leo Bersani, 'Artaud, Birth and Defecation', *Partisan Review,* vol. 43, no. 3 (1976)

Susan Sontag, 'Approaching Artaud', *The New Yorker*, 19 May 1973 (reprinted as the Introduction to her anthology)

Special issues:

Tulane Drama Review, no. 22 (Winter 1963)

REFERENCE NOTES

Works listed in full in the Select Bibliography are cited here in abbreviated form. AA = Antonin Artaud.

Chapter 1. *The Old Man of Fifty*

1 'Je n'ai jamais rien étudié', written 1945, *84*, no. 16
2 'L'Aliénation et le magie noir', recorded by AA on 8 June 1946 and broadcast on 9 June.
3 Prevel, in *En compagnie d'AA.*
4 Roger Blin in *Le Figaro littéraire*, 18 Mar. 1950.
5 I am grateful to M. Parisot for permission to quote from this unpublished letter.

Chapter 2. *Artaud and Before*

1 *Tour de Feu*, nos. 63–4.
2 'The Imp of the Perverse' (1845).
3 *Gérard de Nerval* (Seghers, 1950).
4 'Le Peintre de la vie moderne' (1859–60).
5 Wallace Fowlie makes this point in *The Age of Surrealism* (Dobson, 1953).
6 *Logiques.*
7 Edgell Rickword's translation, reprinted in his *Essays and Opinions 1921–31* (Manchester: Carcanet Press, 1974).

Chapter 3. *The Young Artaud*

1 In a lecture during his 1936 visit to Mexico.
2 'Je n'ai jamais rien étudié.'
3 I am grateful to Artaud's sister, Marie-Ange Malausséna, for giving me a photostat of this letter.
4 In *L'Éclair*, 18 Dec. 1932.
5 Letter to Roger Blin, 12 Apr. 1948, published in *K*, nos. 1–2.
6 'Le Théâtre de l'Atelier', *La Criée*, no. 17 (Oct. 1922); reprinted *O.C.* II. 155.

7 *Tour de Feu*, no. 65 (1960).
8 *K*, nos. 1–2.

Chapter 4. *Film Actor and Surrealist*

1 *Une Vague de rêves* (privately printed, n.d.).
2 Maurice Nadeau, *The History of Surrealism*, trans. Richard Howard (Cape, 1968).
3 'Le Surréalisme en 1929'—a special issue of the Belgian review *Variétés*—contains extracts from the minutes of the meeting held at the café le Prophète.

Chapter 5. *The Aborted Theatre*

1 'Le Théâtre de l'Atelier', op. cit.
2 'L'Atelier de Charles Dullin', *Action* (1921); reprinted *O.C.* II. 153.
3 Writing in *La Gazette du Franc*, 4 June 1927.
4 See the chapter on *Travesties* in Ronald Hayman, *Tom Stoppard* (Heinemann, 1977).

Chapter 6. *The Theatre of Cruelty*

1 'Sur le théâtre Balinais', *Le Théâtre et son double*.
2 *Reflections on the Theatre*, trans. Barbara Wall (1951).
3 *L'Oeuvre d'art vivant* (Editions Atar, 1921).
4 *The Art of the Theatre* (Berlin, 1905; London, 1911).
5 See *Meyerhold on Theatre*, ed. Edward Braun (Methuen, 1970).
6 Article on Theatre, *Encyclopaedia Britannica* (1929 edn.).
7 Published in *Sur* (Buenos Aires), 1932.
8 *The Journals of Anaïs Nin*, ed. Gunther Stuhlmann, vol. I (Peter Owen, 1966).
9 *Marcel Duchamp or the Castle of Purity*, trans. Donald Gardner (Cape, 1970).
10 *Psychology and Alchemy* (Zurich, 1944; London, 1953).
11 *Duchamp: 'The Bride Stripped Bare by her Bachelors, Even'* (Allen Lane, 1973).
12 André Franck, in the Preface to *Lettres d'AA à J.-L. Barrault*.
13 'Les Cenci', *Revue théâtrale*, no. 13 (Summer 1950).
14 Radiodiffusion Française broadcast, 5 Mar. 1938.
15 Interview with Roger Blin, Radiodiffusion Française.
16 *Memories for Tomorrow*, trans. Jonathan Griffin (Thames & Hudson, 1974).
17 'An Attempt at a Little Treatise . . .' is included in Barrault's *Reflections on the Theatre*, and 'Alchemy of the Human Body' in his *Memories for Tomorrow*, both cited above.

18 *Cahiers Renaud–Barrault*, no. 71 (1970).

Chapter 7. *Mexico*

1 'New Mexico', *Survey Graphic* (May 1931); reprinted in *Phoenix* (1936).
2 Preface to *Lettres d'AA à J.-L. Barrault*.
3 For a detailed comparison of Baty's work with Artaud's, see Gouhier, *AA et l'essence du théâtre*.
4 *Transition*, no. 5 (1949).
5 *Et c'est au Mexique* . . . (L'Arbalète, 1955).
6 'Le Montagne des Signes', written in Mexico about Sept. 1936, and published in Spanish, Oct. 1936; *O.C.* IX. 43.
7 'La Race des hommes perdus', *O.C.* IX. 97.

Chapter 8. *Delirium and Asylums*

1 *K*, nos. 1–2.
2 Quoted by Hort, in *AA, le suicidé de la société*.
3 Cited by Brau in *AA*.
4 Letter to Dr. Ferdière quoted in *Tour de Feu*, nos. 63–4.
5 *Tour de Feu*, nos. 63–4.
6 Ibid.
7 Ibid.
8 'Artaud at Rodez', *Theatre Quarterly*, vol. II, no. 6 (Apr.–June 1972).

Chapter 9. *The Final Freedom*

1 'Poèmes inédits', in *84*, nos. 5–6 (1948).
2 Cf. Derrida, 'La Parole soufflée'.
3 By Naomi Greene, in *AA: Poet without Words*.
4 Ibid., p. 211.
5 *Combat*, 24 Jan. 1947; Saillet wrote under the pseudonym 'Justin Saget'.
6 Published in *Combat*, 19 Mar. 1948.
7 Ibid.
8 Brau, *AA*, p. 233.
9 'Poèmes inédits', op. cit.
10 Published in *Tel Quel*, no. 3.
11 'Trois lettres adressées à des médecins', *Botteghe Oscure*, no. 8.
12 *The Pleasure of the Text*, trans. Richard Miller (Cape, 1976).
13 *Pour en finir avec le jugement de Dieu*.
14 'Je n'ai jamais rien étudié.'
15 'Je haïs et abjecte en lâche', *84*, nos. 8–9.
16 *Pour en finir avec le jugement de Dieu*.

17 Published in *Théâtre populaire*, no. 5 (Jan.–Feb. 1954).
18 I quote from Jack Hirschman's translation of the poem in the *AA Anthology*.

Chapter 10. *Artaud and After*

1 *Cahiers Renaud-Barrault*, no. 57.
2 Esslin, *Artaud*.
3 'Search for a Hunger', *Encore*, no. 32 (July–Aug. 1961).
4 I quote from 'Lear Log' by Charles Marowitz, who worked as assistant director on the production. *Encore*, no. 41 (Jan.–Feb. 1963).
5 See J. C. Trewin, *Peter Brook* (Macdonald, 1971).
6 'Notes on the Theatre of Cruelty', *Tulane Drama Review*, no. 34 (Winter 1966).
7 'Artaud for Artaud's Sake', transcript in *Encore*, no. 49 (May–June 1964).
8 *Confessions of a Counterfeit Critic* (Eyre Methuen, 1973).
9 Raymonde Temkine, 'Fils naturel d'Artaud', *Les Lettres nouvelles*, May–June 1966.
10 Peter Brook, *The Empty Space* (MacGibbon & Kee, 1968).
11 J. Grotowski, *Towards a Poor Theatre*, ed. Eugenio Barba (Methuen, 1969).
12 Radiodiffusion Française broadcast.
13 Eugène Ionesco, *Notes and Counter-Notes*, trans. Donald Watson (Calder, 1964).
14 Sylvain Dhomme, 'Une Aventure exemplaire', *Art et Création*, no. 1 (Jan.–Feb. 1968).
15 Joseph Chaikin, *The Presence of the Actor. Notes on the Open Theatre, Disguises, Acting and Repression* (New York: Atheneum, 1973).
16 In an interview with John Lahr, cited in his book *Up Against the Fourth Wall* (New York: Grove Press, 1970; published in England under the title *Acting Out America*, Penguin, 1972).
17 In a 1966 lecture on 'Myth and Reality in the Theatre', reprinted in *Sartre on Theatre*, ed. Michel Contat and Michel Rybalka (Quartet, 1976).
18 *Madness and Civilisation*, trans. Richard Howard (Tavistock, 1967).
19 *Sade, Fourier, Loyola* (Seuil, 1971).
20 *The Pleasure of the Text*, op. cit.
21 'Le Sujet en procès', in *Artaud*, ed. Sollers.
22 *Lettre contre la Cabbale*, a letter originally written to Jacques Prevel but published as a pamphlet in 1949.
23 'Notes pour une "Lettre aux Balinais"', *Tel Quel*, no. 46.

Appendix

As actor:

17 Feb. 1921	Employed by Lugné-Poe. Walked on as a 'bourgeois still half asleep' in *Les Scrupules de Sganarelle* by Henri de Régnier, at the Théâtre de l'Oeuvre.
1922–3	Employed by Charles Dullin.
Feb. 1922	Anselme in *L'Avare* by Molière.
2 Mar. 1922	Galvan (Moorish King) in *Moriana et Galvan* by Alexandre Arnoux; Sottinet in *Le Divorce* by Regnard, at the Salle Pasdeloup (double bill).
1 Apr. 1922	A blind man in *L'Hôtellerie* by Francesco de Castro; Don Luis in *Visits of Condolence* by Calderón, at the Salle Pasdeloup (double bill).
20 June 1922	Basile in *Life Is a Dream* by Calderón, at the Vieux-Colombier.
Nov. 1922	Apoplexie in *La Condamnation de Banquet* (adapted by Roger Semichon from a 16th-century morality play); member of the council in *The Pleasure of Honesty* by Pirandello, at the Théâtre de l'Atelier (double bill).
Dec. 1922	Tiresias in the *Antigone* of Sophocles (adapted by Cocteau; décor by Picasso), at the Atelier.
1923	Grotesque puppet Pedro Urdemalas in *Monsieur de Pygmalion* by Jacinto Grau, at the Atelier. Charlemagne in *Huon de Bordeaux* by Alexandre Arnoux, at the Atelier.
1923–4	Employed by Georges Pitoëff at the Comédie des Champs-Elysées.
18 May 1923	Retiarius in *Androcles and the Lion* by Bernard Shaw.
8 June 1923	A black angel or (?) a detective and a policeman in *Liliom* by Ferenc Molnar.
9 Oct. 1923	A guard in *Le Club des Canards Mandarins* by Henri Duvernois, at the Studio des Champs-Elysées.

22 Nov. 1923	The first Mystic in *La Petite Baraque* by Alexander Blok.
6 Dec. 1923	Jackson in *He Who Gets Slapped* by Leonid Andreyev.
4 Mar. 1924	The Prompter in *Six Characters in Search of an Author* by Pirandello.
24 Mar. 1924	The robot Marius in R.U.R. by Karel Čapek.
1925–35	In his own productions.
28–29 May 1925	In *Au pied du mur* by Louis Aragon, at the Vieux-Colombier.
2 and 9 June 1928	Theology in *Dream Play* by Strindberg, at the Théâtre de l'Avenue.
6 May 1935	Cenci in *Les Cenci*, at the Folies Wagram.

As director:

28–29 May 1925	*Au pied du mur* by Louis Aragon, at the Vieux-Colombier.
1–2 June 1927	Théâtre Alfred Jarry at the Théâtre de Grenelle: *Le Ventre brûlé* by Artaud; *Gigogne* by Max Robur (Robert Aron); *Les Mystères de l'amour* by Roger Vitrac.
14 Jan. 1928	Théâtre Alfred Jarry at the Comédie des Champs-Elysées: Act III of *Partage de midi* by Paul Claudel.
2 and 9 June 1928	Théâtre Alfred Jarry at the Théâtre de l'Avenue: *Dream Play* by Strindberg.
24 and 29 Dec. 1928; 5 Jan. 1929	Théâtre Alfred Jarry at the Comédie des Champs-Elysées: *Victor* by Roger Vitrac.
Feb.–Mar. 1932	Assistant director to Louis Jouvet on *La Patissière du village* by Alfred Savoir.
6–22 May 1935	*Les Cenci*, at the Folies Wagram.

As designer and lighting designer:

| 1922 | Designed *Les Olives, L'Hôtellerie,* and *Life Is a Dream* for Dullin. |
| 1931 | Designed lighting for recital by the Peruvian dancer Helba Huara on 31 May at the Salle Pleyel. |

ARTAUD'S WORK IN THE CINEMA

As actor:

1924	Monsieur 2 in Claude Autant-Lara's *Fait divers*.
1925	Cecco in Marcel Vandal's *Graziella*.
1925	Marat in Abel Gance's *Napoléon Bonaparte*.
1926	Three non-speaking roles in Jean Painlevé's film sequences for the staging of Yvan Goll's *Mathusalem* at the Théâtre Michel.
	Gringalet in Luitz Morat's *Le Juif errant*.
1927	The Intellectual in Léon Poirier's *Verdun, visions d'histoire* (silent version; sound version, titled *Verdun, souvenirs d'histoire*, 1931).
	Frère Massieu in Carl Dreyer's *La Passion de Jeanne d'Arc*.
1928	The secretary Mazaud in Marcel l'Herbier's *L'Argent*.
1929	A gypsy in love in Raymond Bernard's *Tarakanowa*.
1930	Vieublé in Raymond Bernard's *Les Croix de bois*.
	Jaroslav in Marcel l'Herbier's *La Femme d'une nuit*.
1931	An apprentice beggar in G. Pabst's *L'Opéra de quat'sous* (French version of *Dreigroschenoper*).
	Ringleader of revolt in Raymond Bernard's *Faubourg Montmartre*.
1932	Backmann in Serge Poligny's *Coup de feu à l'aube*.
	Loche in Henri Wullschleger's *L'Enfant de ma soeur*.
	d'Hornis in Abel Gance's *Mater Dolorosa* (sound version; original version 1917).
1933	Abd-el-Kadir in Henri Wullschleger's *Sidonie Panache*.
	Knifegrinder and guardian angel in Fritz Lang's *Liliom*.
1935	Savonarola in Abel Gance's *Lucrèce Borgia*.
	Cyrus Beck, the librarian, in Maurice Tourneur's *Koenigsmark*.

Catalogue of the Exhibition
Artaud and After

at the National Book League
7 Albemarle Street, London W1
19 October–12 November
1977

The Old Man of Fifty
1 Artaud in 1947: photograph by Denise Colomb.
2 Photograph of Artaud by Le Cuziat. See illus. 1.
3 Photograph by Georges Pastier, 1947.
4 Artaud at Dr. Delmas's clinic in Ivry: photographs by Denise Colomb, 1947. See p. 4 and illus. 2.
5 Artaud during the Ivry period.
6 Artaud's room at Ivry (Denise Colomb, 1947). See p. 6 and illus. 3.
7 Artaud's bedroom (Denise Colomb, 1947).
8 The caretaker at Ivry who befriended Artaud (Denise Colomb, 1947). See p. 143.

Artaud and Before
9 Edgar Allan Poe (1809–49). See pp. 20–2.
10 Gérard de Nerval (1808–55). See pp. 22–6.

11 Charles Baudelaire (1821–67): portrait by Courbet. See pp. 26–8.

12 Lautréamont (Isidore Ducasse, 1846–70). See pp. 28–31.

13 Arthur Rimbaud (1854–91): portrait by Fantin-Latour. See pp. 31–5.

14 Rimbaud wounded at Brussels in 1873 (Jef Rosman).

The Young Artaud

15 Childhood photographs.

16 Certificate of first communion.

17 Sketch of himself, 1915 (photograph).

18 Landscape at Châtelard, Savoie: Artaud's original gouache, 1915.

19 Dr. Edouard Toulouse, director of the clinic at Villejuif and editor of *Demain*. See pp. 20, 39–42.

20 Artaud's pencil sketch of Dr. Toulouse.

21 Two pencil sketches of Mme Toulouse, 1920.

22 Autograph letters to Dr. and Mme Toulouse.

23 Ink drawing of a schoolgirl.

24 Two charcoal sketches of a patient at Villejuif.

25 'Les Oeuvres et les hommes': manuscript text, 1922.

26 Review of an art exhibition: manuscript text. See p. 39.

27 Aurélien Lugné-Poe (1869–1940) in one of his roles as an actor, 1934. See pp. 40–1, 47, and illus. 4.

28 Charles Dullin (1885–1949). See pp. 41–3, 46–7, and illus. 5.

29 Dullin taking a class at his school. Looking over his left shoulder is the actor Alain Cuny, who became a friend of Artaud. See illus. 5.

30 Génica Athanasiou in *La Coquille et le clergyman*. See pp. 43–6, 50–1.

31 Cambodian dancers in the courtyard of the temple of Angkor Vat. At the Colonial Exhibition in Marseilles, 1922, there was a giant reconstruction of the temple, with dancers performing. See pp. 44–5.

32 A previously unpublished poem, 'Fête Régence', written 25 September 1922, in *La Tour de Feu*, no. 116, December 1972.

33 Georges Pitoëff (1886–1939) in *He Who Gets Slapped* (October 1937). See pp. 47–8.

34 Jacques Rivière (1886–1925), editor of the *Nouvelle Revue Française* 1919–25. See pp. 7–10, 49, 50, and illus. 6.

35 Autograph letter to Max Jacob, 1925.

36 Three stories: autograph manuscript.

Film Actor and Surrealist

37 As Monsieur II in Claude Autant-Lara's *Fait Divers*, 1924. See pp. 51–2.

38 Abel Gance (1889–). See p. 54.

39 André Breton (1896–1966). See pp. 55–6.

40 Paul Eluard (1895–1952). See pp. 55, 64.

41 Louis Aragon (1897–). See pp. 55–6.

42 The first issue of *La Révolution surréaliste*, which appeared in November 1924 with a picture of Artaud in it. See pp. 55–7, 63–4.

43 'L'Activité du bureau de recherches surréalistes': original typescript with manuscript corrections by Artaud. He became director of the Bureau in January 1925. See p. 55.

44 'Lettre aux Recteurs des Universités Européennes': manuscript in the hand of Michel Leiris, who was sole author of the first two paragraphs, while Artaud was sole author of the last three. Like the next five items, it appeared in the third issue of *La Révolution surréaliste*, 3 April 1925, which Artaud edited.

45 'Adresse au Pape': typescript with manuscript corrections by Artaud and Breton of the typist's errors. Breton's title 'Lettre au Pape' was changed by Artaud in proof. Artaud was sole author of the text. See p. 56

46 'Adresse au Dalai-Lama': text entirely by Artaud. Title in Breton's hand. At least two of the manuscript corrections are not in Artaud's hand. See pp. 56–7.

47 'Lettre aux Écoles de Bouddha': text entirely by Artaud. See p. 57.

48 'Rêve': typescript of text by Artaud with his manuscript corrections. See p. 56.

49 'Oui, voici maintenant le seul usage': manuscript copy

of a text by Artaud which followed Leiris's 'Glossaire: j'y serre mes gloses' in the third issue of *La Révolution surréaliste*.

50   'Le Monde physique': typescript.

51   Artaud as Marat in Abel Gance's *Napoléon Bonaparte*. Shooting started in either February or June 1925; the film was released in April 1927. Alexandre Koubitzky plays Danton.

52   Artaud and Koubitzky in another sequence.

53   Marat after the murder. See illus. 10.

54   Actors and technicians in the studio during the filming of *Napoléon Bonaparte*.

55   Photograph of Artaud in *Mon ciné*, 1926.

56   Photograph by Man Ray, 1926. See illus. 8.

57   Six stills from *La Coquille et le clergyman*, directed by Germaine Dulac with Alex Allin, Génica Athanasiou, and Bataille. The scenario was by Artaud – the only one of his screenplays ever to be made into a film. Shot between July and September 1927. First public screening February 1928. See pp. 70–1, and illus. 14.

58   Newspaper reviews of *La Coquille et le clergyman*.

59   Artaud as Frère Massieu in Carl Dreyer's *La Passion de Jeanne d'Arc*. Renée Falconetti played St. Joan. Shot between August and December 1927. Released April 1928. See p. 70, and illus. 11.

60   Artaud as Mazaud in Marcel l'Herbier's *L'Argent* based on Zola's novel. Shot during 1928 and released in December 1928. Brigitte Helm played the Baroness Sandorf.

61   Programme for *Tarakanowa*, 1929, with photograph of Artaud as the young gypsy. See p. 76.

62   Brochure for *L'Art et la Mort*, 1929, with subscription form. See pp. 60 ff.

62a. Uccello: Portrait en Buste and Fragment de Cassone. See p. 57.

The Aborted Theatre

63   The issue of *Comœdia* for 19 April 1924, containing Artaud's article, 'L'Evolution de décor', with a reproduction of one of his designs. See p. 66.

64 Alfred Jarry (1873–1907). See p. 64.

65 Roger Vitrac (1899–1952). See p. 64, and illus. 12.

66 Jean Paulhan (1884–1968), who took over from Rivière as editor of the *Nouvelle Revue Française* and published Artaud's 1926 manifesto for the Théâtre Alfred Jarry in it. See illus. 7.

67 Exterior of the Théâtre des Champs-Elysées. Two of the Théâtre Alfred Jarry's four productions were staged here— Act III of Claudel's *Partage de midi* in January 1928 (see pp. 72–3) and Vitrac's *Victor* in December 1928–January 1929 (see pp. 73–4).

68 Interior of the auditorium of the theatre.

69 Montage of extracts from programmes of the Théâtre Alfred Jarry (photograph).

70 The brochure 'Le Théâtre Alfred Jarry et l'hostilité publique', 1930. The cover was designed by J.-L. Roux. See p. 74.

71 One of the photographs used to illustrate the brochure. The girl is Josette Luson (for Artaud's relationship with her, see p. 77).

The Theatre of Cruelty

72 Antonin Artaud: photograph by Martinie.

73 Balinese dancing girls. See pp. 76–8.

74 Lucas Van Leyden's *Lot and his Daughters* (reproduction). See pp. 78–9, 80–1.

75 Louis Jouvet (1887–1951), with Madeleine Ozeray in *Tessa*, November 1934. Artaud worked as his assistant in February–March 1932. See p. 82.

76 Invitations to lectures by Artaud. See pp. 78, 89–90.

77 Artaud's first manifesto for 'Le Théâtre de la Cruauté', published in the *Nouvelle Revue Française* 1 October 1932. See pp. 84–7.

78 The second manifesto, 1933.

79 Autograph letters to André Gide, the earliest dated 29 March 1932. For the letter of 10 February 1935, see p. 96.

80 Autograph letters to Natalie Clifford Barney, 12 and 17 August and 25 November 1933.

81   Autograph letters to Robert Desnos, August 1933.
82   Artaud as Cenci in his own production of *Les Cenci* at the Folies Wagram, May 1935. See pp. 96–9, and illus. 15.
83   A scene showing the set by Balthus.
84   Roger Blin (1907–). See pp. 98–9.
85   Artaud as Savonarola in Abel Gance's *Lucrèce Borgia*. Edwige Feuillère played Lucrèce. The film was shot between July and October 1935, and first screened in December 1935.
86   Jean-Louis Barrault (1910–). Artaud's friendship with him began after the failure of *Les Cenci*. See pp. 99–101.

Mexico
87   *Au pays des Tarahumaras*: the first edition, published by Editions Fontaine, 1945.

Delirium and Asylums
88   Artaud with his hair cropped. See p. 123.
89   The asylum of Quatre-Mares, Sotteville-les-Rouen. He was there from December 1937 to April 1938. See p. 122 and illus. 16.
90   The asylum of Ste. Anne, Paris, founded by Marguerite of Provence and enlarged after the plague of 1607: general plan. The present buildings date from 1861. Artaud was interned there from April till December 1938. See p. 122.
91   Authorization for Artaud's transfer in January 1943 from the asylum at Ville-Evrard to Rodez, after three transitional weeks in Chezal-Benoit. See p. 124.
92   The asylum of Chezal-Benoit. He was there in January–February 1943. See p. 124.
93   Letters to Robert Desnos from Chezal-Benoit and Rodez. See pp. 123–4.
94   Documents from the dossier about Artaud's internment at Rodez. See pp. 124–30.
95   Three autograph letters to his mother, 13, 20, 27 December 1943. See pp. 126–7.
96   Autograph letter to his sister, 30 January 1945.
97   Photographs of Artaud on his arrival at Rodez, 11 February

1943 (see p. 124), and his departure, 24 May 1946, in *La Tour de Feu*, no. 112, December 1971.

98 Autograph letters to André Gide from Rodez, 30 January 1944 and 22 February 1946.

99 Arthur Adamov (1908–70). See pp. 124, 135.

100 Artaud's friend Marthe Robert, who visited him at Rodez and, with Adamov, put pressure on Dr. Ferdiére to release him.

The Final Freedom

101 Pencil self-portrait, 17 December 1946. See illus. 18.

102 Two autograph letters to his sister from Ivry, 21 September 1947 and 7 January 1948.

103 'Portrait of Sima Feder': pencil sketch, 7 October 1946.

104 'Portrait of Florence Loeb', 4 December 1946. Florence Loeb is the daughter of Pierre Loeb (see p. 16).

105 Sketch of Arthur Adamov.

106 'Portrait of Mania Germain', May 1947.

107 Sketches inscribed to Florence Loeb. The head in the bottom right-hand corner is a self-portrait. See p. 6, and illus. 19.

108 Letter to Artaud from René Char (1907–), 19 January 1948.

109 Vincent Van Gogh (1853–90): *Wheatfield with Crows* (reproduction), painted shortly before 9 July 1890.

110 Van Gogh's *Self-Portrait with a Straw Hat* (reproduction). See p. 19.

111 Autograph note to Adrienne Monnier on *Van Gogh le suicidé de la société*, 1947.

112 First edition of *Van Gogh le suicidé de la société*. See pp. 16–19, 141.

113 Guy Lévis Mano's second edition of *Lettres de Rodez* (see p. 136), and first edition of *Supplément aux Lettres de Rodez suivi de Coleridge le traître*.

114 Drawing by Artaud dated 5 November 1946, with (*left*), part of a letter to Maurice Saillet about Artaud's solo performance at the Vieux-Colombier on 13 January 1947 (see pp. 134–5), in *K—revue de la poésie*, nos. 1–2, a special issue on Artaud.

Artaud and After

115   Pierre Boulez (1925–). See p. 144.

116   R. D. Laing (1927–): photograph by Dorothe von Greiff. See p. 144.

117   Michel Foucalt (1926–): photographs by Jacques Robert. See pp. 159–60.

118   Peter Brook's 'Search for a Hunger', *Encore*, no. 32, July–August 1961. See p. 145.

119   'Artaud for Artaud's Sake': discussion by Brook, Peter Hall, Michel St. Denis, Peter Shaffer, and Charles Marowitz, *Encore*, no. 49, May–June 1964. See p. 145.

120   Brook's *King Lear*, 1962, with Paul Scofield as Lear, Alec McCowen as the Fool, and Diana Rigg as Cordelia. See pp. 145–7.

121   A scene from Artaud's *Spurt of Blood*, in the *Theatre of Cruelty* season directed by Brook and Marowitz, 1964. See pp. 59, 147, and illus. 20.

122   *Theatre of Cruelty*: a scene from the sequence that merged the identities of Mrs. Kennedy and Christine Keeler.

123   Brook's production of the *Marat/Sade*, by Peter Weiss, 1964, with Susan Williamson as Simonne Everard, Patrick Magee as Sade, Clive Revill as Marat. See pp. 145, 147–8.

124   Susan Williamson, Patrick Magee, Glenda Jackson (as Charlotte Corday), and Ian Richardson (who took over the role of Marat). See illus. 21.

125   Patrick Magee, John Steiner (Duperret), Jonathan Burn (Polpoch), Michael Williams (Herald), Elizabeth Spriggs (Rossignol), Freddie Jones (Cucurucu) in *Marat/Sade*.

126   Three other sequences from the same production.

127   Grotowski's *The Constant Prince* with Ryszard Cieslak. See pp. 149–52.

128   Genet's *Les Nègres*, 1959. See p. 153.

129   Genet's *Le Balcon*, which was written earlier but not staged until 1960 in a production by Peter Brook: a sequence from this production. See p. 153.

130   Ionesco's *Les Chaises*, 1952. See p. 153.

131   Jean-Louis Barrault's production of Camus's *L'État de siège*, 1948. See pp. 100, 154.

132 Barrault's 1953 production of Claudel's *Christophe Colomb* with Madeleine Renaud, Jean Desailly. See p. 101.

133 Barrault's use of masks in his 1975 revival of *Christophe Colomb*.

134 Barrault with Laurent Terzieff in a scene from the same production.

135 Jean Anouilh's 1962 production of Vitrac's *Victor* (see pp. 73–4) with Claude Rich.

136 A still from Buñuel's *Un Chien andalou*, 1928. See p. 71.

137 From Cocteau's *Le Sang d'un poète*, 1930.

138 From Cocteau's *Orphée*, 1950.

Recordings by Artaud:
  L'Aliénation et le magie noir
  Les malades et les médecins

Interviews with:
  Henri Parisot
  Marthe Robert

ACKNOWLEDGEMENTS

For help in mounting the exhibition, the author and the National Book League wish to express gratitude to the French Government. We are also deeply indebted to all those who have helped us either by lending material or by advising on how to locate it: Mme Marie-Ange Malausséna, M. Henri Parisot, M. Albert Loeb, M. Alain Gheerbrant, Dr. Gaston Ferdière, the Institut National de l'Audiovisuel, Mme Gabrielle Heller of the Centre Français du Théâtre, M. J. A. Thomas of the Hôpital Psychiatrique de Chezal-Benoit, Mr. H. M. Berg of Bergs Forlag, Miss Michelle Snapes of the British Film Institute, Miss Irene Staunton of John Calder Ltd., Mrs. Susan Stenderup, and Miss Susan le Roux of Oxford University Press.

Index

AA = Antonin Artaud

Abdy, Iya, 96, 98

Abélard, see AA, identification with

Achard, Marcel, 47

Adamov, Arthur, 124, 135

Allendy, Dr. René, 64, 72, 76, 89, 103; AA's letter to, 72

Allendy, Mme Yvonne, 64, 69, 73, 76; AA's letter to, 76

Appia, Adolphe, 42, 85–6, 87

Aragon, Louis, 54, 55, 56

Aron, Robert, 64, 69, 73

Arp, Hans, 54

Artaud, Antoine-Roi (AA's father), 37

ARTAUD, ANTONIN
childhood illnesses, 36; at school, 38; military service, 39; at sanatoria, 3, 39, 45; befriended by Dr. and Mme Toulouse, 20, 39–40, 42, 50; acts with Lugné-Poe, 40, 41; with Dullin (Théâtre de l'Atelier), 41, 42–3, 44, 46–7; with Pitoëff, 47, 51–2; at Colonial Exhibition, Marseilles, 1922, 44–5; correspondence with Rivière, 7–10, 32, 50, 54, 56, 59; first book published, 46; edits *Bilboquet*, 49; career in films, 51–52, 53–4, 70, 71–2, 76–7;

association with Surrealism, 9, 54–65, 67, 161; director of *centrale surréaliste*, 55; contributes to *La Révolution surréaliste*, 11, 54–7, 60; expelled from group, 64;

and Théâtre Alfred Jarry, 64, 67–9, 72–7; at Colonial Exhibition, Bois de Vincennes (Paris), 1931, 76; lectures at Sorbonne, 78–9, 89–90; assistant director to Jouvet, 76, 82; meeting and relationship with J.-L. Barrault, 81–2, 99–101; and Theatre of Cruelty, 1, 25, 67, 76, 79, 82–7, 91–2, 134, 152, 160; first manifesto, 84–7, 95; second manifesto, 91–2; produces *Les Cenci*, 96–9;

travels in Mexico, 104–14; lectures in Mexico City, 104–6; visit to Tarahumaras, 26, 108–114; peyote ritual, 109–11, 113; and Cane of St. Patrick, 13, 117–18, 120–2; travels in Ireland, 120–2; confined in asylums: Quatre-Mares, 122; Ste. Anne, 122–3, 129; Ville-Evrard, 1, 122–4, 125, 129; Chezal-Benoit, 124; Rodez, 1, 117, 121, 124–30, 134, 139;

relationship with Dr. Ferdière, 18, 24, 124–30; translates Lewis Carroll and Robert Southwell, 125; and electro-convulsive therapy, 111, 127–9;

at Ivry, 4–6, 131–43; performance at Vieux-Colombier, 1947, 134–6, 154; at Van Gogh exhibition, 15–16, 141; preparation of broadcast for ORTF, 141–2; death, 143

physical appearance, 2, 40, 48, 81–2, 89, 91, 123, 124, 135–136; physical sufferings, 2–3, 36–7, 40, 45, 50–1, 76; and drug-addiction, 2, 4–5, 40, 45, 50, 51, 60, 61, 72, 91, 108, 111, 123, 129–30, 138; drawing and sketching, 6, 127, 141; habits of writing, 6, 11, 137; and letter-writing, 11, *and see under individual correspondents*; and his father, 37; and his mother, 36–38, 51, 122–3; friendships and love affairs: with Génica Athanasiou, 38, 43–6, 48, 50–1, 53–4, 60, 63; with Yvonne Gilles, 39; with Dr. and Mme Allendy, 64, 72, 76; with Roger Vitrac, 64, 73–5; with Josette Lusson, 77; with Anaïs Nin, 89–90, 91; with Cécile Schramme, 104, 115–16; with Lise Deharme, 95–6, 104; with Anne Manson, 119–21; with Frédéric Delanglade, 124–8

and black magic, 3–4, 99, 129; and sexuality, 4, 62, 93, 118, 126, 139; and Catholicism, 5, 11–12, 39, 41, 64–5, 67, 80, 110, 125–6, 129, 134; and language, 7, 41, 81, 133–4, 139, 161; and painting: *see under* Van Gogh, Van Leyden; and *poètes maudits*, 14, 17, 20–35 *passim*, 159, *and see below under* identifications, influences; attitude to madness, 17, 91, 94, 123 ff.; and the Tarot pack, 24–5, 116–18; and alchemy, 24–5, 88, 95; interest in Eastern culture and religion, 49, 80, 100, 102–3; and clairvoyance, 61, 130; and psychoanalysis, 72; and Balinese theatre, 76–8, 80, 99, 142; and Gnosticism, 88, 110; and the idea of plague, 89–91; interest in primitive cultures, 92, 101

identification of: with Rimbaud, 6, 10, 14, 32–3; with Nietzsche, 10, 67; with Uccello, 11, 15–16, 18, 57, 62, 92; with Christ, 12–14, 17, 109–10, 119, 125–6; with Coleridge, 14–15, 16; with Poe, 14, 22n.; with Baudelaire, 14; with Nerval, 14, 17; with Lautréamont, 14; with Van Gogh, 15–19, 141; with St. Francis of Assisi, 45, 62; with Abélard, 62, 92; with Heliogabalus, 92–3; affinity with Duchamp, 94–5; literary influences and precursors: *see under* Baudelaire, Charles; Lautréamont, Comte de; Nerval, Gérard de; Poe, E. A.; Rimbaud, Arthur; *and* 20–35 *passim*; influences in the theatre: *see under* Appia, Adolphe; Craig, Gordon; Meyerhold, Vsevolod; Reinhardt, Max; influence exerted by: *see under* Barrault,

Artaud, Antonin—*contd.*
  J.-L.; Beck, Julian; Beckett, Samuel; Blin, Roger; Boulez, Pierre; Brook, Peter; Chaikin, Joseph; Foucault, Michel; Genet, Jean; Grotowski, Jerzy; Ionesco, Eugène; Laing, R. D.; Malina, Judith; Marowitz, Charles
  WORK IN THE THEATRE: as actor, in *Les Scrupules de Sganarelle* (de Régnier), 40; in *The Pleasure of Honesty* (Pirandello), 43; in *L'Avare* (Molière), 44; in *Moriana et Galvan* (Arnoux), 44; in *Le Divorce* (Regnard), 44; in *L'Hôtellerie* (de Castro), 44; in *Life Is a Dream* (Calderón), 44, 46; in *La Condamnation du Banquet* (Semichon), 46; in *Antigone* (Cocteau), 46; in *Monsieur de Pygmalion* (Grau), 46; in *Huon de Bordeaux* (Arnoux), 47; in *Six Characters in Search of an Author* (Pirandello), 47, 51; in *Androcles and the Lion* (Shaw), 47; in *Liliom* (Molnar), 47; in *He Who Gets Slapped* (Andreyev), 51; in *R.U.R.* (Čapek), 51; as director ('Théâtre Alfred Jarry), of *Ventre brulé* (Artaud), 69; *Les Mystères de l'amour* (Vitrac), 69, 78; *Gigogne* (Aron), 69; *Partage de midi*, Act III (Claudel), 72–3; *Dream Play* (Strindberg), 73; *Victor* (Vitrac), 73–4, 77; (Theatre of Cruelty), of *Les Cenci*, 77, 79, 96–9
  WORK IN FILMS: as actor, in *Fait Divers*, 52; *Surcouf*, 53; *Napoléon*, 54; *Le Juif errant*, 63;

  La Passion de Jeanne d'Arc, 70; *Verdun*, 72; *Tarakanowa*, 76; *Dreigroschenoper*, 77; *Faubourg Montmartre*, 77; *Femme d'une nuit*, 77; *Les Croix de bois*, 77
  WRITINGS: books, *Tric-Trac du Ciel*, 46, 49; *L'Ombilic des Limbes*, 2, 57–9, 131; *Les Pèse-Nerfs*, 10–11, 59, 131; *L'Art et la Mort*, 60–2, 116; *Héliogabale*, 92–3; *Le Théâtre et son double*, 1, 11, 49, 104, 111n., 125, 155; *Au pays des Tarahumaras*, 1; *Le Retour d'Artaud, le Mômo*, 133–134; *Lettres de Rodez*, 136; *Van Gogh le suicidé de la société*, 11, 16–19, 116, 141, 144, 159; *Oeuvres complètes*, 111n.; Préambule to *O.C.*, 7, 9; pamphlet, *Les Nouvelles Révélations de l'Être*, 116–118, 119, 125;
  plays, *Le Jet de sang* (The Spurt of Blood), 59; *Ventre brulé*, 69; *Les Cenci*, 77; adaptations, *The Monk* (Lewis), 77; screenplays, *La Coquille et le clergyman*, 70–1;
  articles, 'Paul les Oiseaux', 11, 15–16, 57; 'Coleridge le traître', 11, 14–15; 'Lettre sur Lautréamont', 11, 14, 30, 136; 'Le Clair Abélard', 62, 92, 139; 'Le Théâtre alchimique', 88, 95; lectures, 'La Mise en scène et la métaphysique', 78, 90; 'Le Théâtre et la peste', 89–91, 95, 100; 'Surréalisme et révolution', 104; 'L'Homme contre le destin', 104, 107; 'Le Théâtre et les dieux', 105, 107; 'Le Théâtre d'après-guerre à Paris', 105;

prefaces, to *Au fil des préjugés* (Toulouse), 48; to *Douze chansons* (Maeterlinck), 49;

contributions to newspapers and periodicals, *La Nouvelle Revue Française*, 7, 67, 71, 78, 84, 95, 99; *Cahiers du Sud*, 11, 68, 136; *Demain*, 39; *L'Ere nouvelle*, 41; *Images de Paris*, 46; *Nouvelles littéraires*, 46; *Mercure de France*, 46; *Bilboquet*, 49, *Commerce*, 60; *Comœdia*, 66; *Le Monde illustré*, 70; *Paris Soir* (letter), 74; *Le Figaro* (letter), 96; *El Nacional Revolucionario*, 106–8, 111; *Voilà*, 111; *Gazette des amis des livres* (letter), 122; *and* 136 *passim*

Artaud, Euphrasie (AA's mother), 35, 36–8, 122–3; AA's letters to, 125, 126, 127

Artaud, Germaine (AA's sister), 37

Artaud, Marie-Ange (later Mme Malausséna, AA's sister), 36, 121–2, 123

Atelier, Théâtre de l', 42, 44, 46–47; *see also* Dullin, Charles

Athanasiou, Génica, 38, 43–6, 48, 50–1, 53–4, 60, 63, 69, 72, 105, 123; AA's letters to, 38, 43, 44, 45, 46, 47, 48, 50, 51, 53, 64, 123

Audard, Pierre, 70

Autant-Lara, Claude, 52

Balthus, 98, 100

Barbezat, Marc, 111

Barrault, Jean-Louis, 2, 81–2, 99–101, 106, 134, 142, 152, 154; AA's letters to, 113, 125; production of *L'Etat de siège* (Camus), 100, 135, 154; of *Par-*

tage de midi (Claudel), 100–1; of *Christophe Colomb*, 101

Barthes, Roland, 138–9, 159–60

Baty, Gaston, 106

Baudelaire, Charles, 14, 20, 25, 26–8, 30–5, 38

Beauchamp, E., 69

Beck, Julian, 155, 156

Beckett, Samuel, 57–8, 107, 152

Benda, Julien, 83

Bernard, Raymond, 76, 77

Bilboquet, 49

Blake, William, 21, 161

Blanche, Dr., and Nerval, 22, 23–24

Blin, Roger, 2, 98, 122, 123, 128, 135, 142, 150, 152; AA's letters to, 122, 128, 129, 130

Boulez, Pierre, 144, 158

Braque, Georges, 1, 80

Brau, Jean-Louis, 136

Brecht, Bertolt, 77, 86, 87, 92, 147–9

Bressant, Cécile, 96

Breton, André, 28, 46, 54, 55–6, 58, 63, 64–5, 73, 134; AA's letters to, 58, 118, 120, 121, 135

Breton, Jacqueline, 118, 121; AA's letters to, 118, 123

Brook, Peter, 59, 145–8, 150, 152, 155, 156; production of *King Lear*, 145, 146–7, 148; of *Marat/Sade* (Weiss), 147–8; and *Theatre of Cruelty* season, 147–8

Brown, Kenneth H., 155

Buñuel, Luis, 71

Burns, Alan, 149

Cage, John, 158

Camus, Albert, 100, 135, 154

Casarès, Maria, 142

Cassavetes, John, 145
Castro, Manuel Cano de, 116
Chaikin, Joseph, 155–8
Cieslak, Ryszard, 151–2
Clarke, Shirley, 145
Claudel, Paul, 33, 72–3, 100–1
Cocteau, Jean, 46, 105, 142
Coleridge, Samuel Taylor, 14–15, 17–18, 20, 21
Comédie Française, 54, 66, 152
Connolly, Cyril, 131
Conty, Jean-Marie, 96, 115
Copeau, Jacques, 66, 86, 105
Craig, Gordon, 42, 66, 85–6
Crémieux, Benjamin, 69, 81; AA's letter to, 81

Dadaists, 54, 94
Dardel, Dr., 39
Decroux, Etienne, 100
Deharme, Lise, 95–6, 104
Delanglade, Frédéric, 124–8
Delmas, Dr., 4–5
Demain, 39
Demazis, Orane, AA's letter to, 93
Denoël, Robert, 77, 96, 127
Derrida, Jacques, 61n., 139
Desnos, Robert, 55, 71, 122, 124; AA's letter to, 115
Dreyer, Carl, 70
Dubuffet, Jean, 1, 2
Duchamp, Marcel, 1, 28–9, 94–5
Dulac, Germaine, 70–1
Dullin, Charles, 1, 41, 42–3, 44, 46–7, 53, 56, 66, 67, 68, 105, 123, 127

Eliot, T. S., 94
Eluard, Paul, 1, 54, 55, 64, 142
Ernst, Max, 55
Euripides, 14

Ferdière, Dr. Gaston, 18, 24, 124–130, 149; AA's letters to, 80, 125–9
Ford, John, *'Tis Pity She's a Whore*, 91, 96
Fossey, Charles, 133
Foucault, Michel, 159–60, 162
Francis of Assisi, St., *see* AA, identification with
Franck, André, 98, 102
Freud, Sigmund, 80, 160

Gallimard, Gaston, 82, 83
Gance, Abel, 54
Gauguin, Paul, 18
Gelber, Jack, 145, 155
Gémier, Firmin, 42
Genet, Jean, 153; *Le Balcon*, 153; *Les Nègres*, 153
Giacometti, Alberto, 1
Gide, André, 1, 82, 83–4, 134–6; AA's letters to, 83, 96, 97
Gilles, Yvonne, 39; AA's letters to, 42, 44, 52
Ginsberg, Allen, 145
Goethe, J. W. von, 23
Golding, John, 95
Gouhier, Henri, 67
Grotowski, Jerzy, 149–52, 155, 156; production of *The Constant Prince* (Calderón), 151–2
Guitry, Sacha, 66

Happenings, 158
Hébertôt, Jacques, AA's letter to, 69
Hölderlin, Friedrich, 17, 159
Horizon, 131–2
Hort, Jean, 47–8

Ionesco, Eugène, 153–4; *Les*

Chaises, 154; *Jeux de massacre*, 154

Jacob, Max, 42, 68; AA's letters to, 42, 68
Jarry, Alfred, 64, 94; *see also* AA and Théâtre Alfred Jarry
Jouve, Pierre Jean, 98
Jouvet, Louis, 1, 67, 76, 82, 142, 152
Joyce, James, 140, 162
Jung, C. G., 80, 95

Kafka, Franz, 29
Kahnweiler, Daniel Henry, 46, 48, 54
Kierkegaard, Søren, 17, 29
Klee, Paul, 49, 70
Kott, Jan, 84
Kristeva, Julia, 139, 160–2

Laing, R. D., 144–5, 159, 160
Latrémolière, Dr., 126, 128; AA's letters to, 126, 128
Lautréamont, Comte de (Isidore Ducasse), 14, 20, 28–31, 34
Lawrence, D. H., 13n., 21–2, 102
le Breton, Georges, 24; AA's letters to, 24–6
Léger, Fernand, 1
Leiris, Michel, 98
l'Herbier, Marcel, 77
Lévi-Strauss, Claude, 106
Living Theatre, 145, 154–5; production of *The Connection* (Gelber), 155; of *The Brig* (Brown), 155; of *Frankenstein*, 155; *see also* Beck, Julian *and* Malina, Judith
Loeb, Pierre, 16, 46

Lugné-Poe, Aurélien, 40, 41, 47, 67
Lusson, Josette, 77

Maeterlinck, Maurice, 49, 70
Magre, Maurice, 41
Malevich, Casimir, 80
Malina, Judith, 155, 156
Mano, Guy Lévis, 136
Manson, Anne, 119–21, 129; AA's letters to, 119, 120, 121
Maritain, Jacques, 64–5
Marowitz, Charles, 59, 128, 147–149, 156; production of *Palach* (Burns), 149; of *Artaud at Rodez*, 149; and *Theatre of Cruelty* season, 147–8
Masson, André, 58
Mathot, Léon, 77
Matisse, Henri, 9, 16
Mauriac, François, 1
Meyerhold, Vsevolod, 85–6
Mirecka, Rena, 151
Mnouchkine, Ariane, 149; production of *1789*, 149
Monnier, Adrienne, 122; AA's letter to, 122–3
Mossé, Sonia, 118

Nouvelle Revue Française, La, 7–9, 63, 73, 82, 95; *see also under* AA, contributions to
Nacional Revolucionario, El, 106–8, 11
Nadeau, Maurice, 136
Nalpas, Louis, 54
Naville, Pierre, 55
Nerval, Gérard de, 14, 17, 20, 22–26, 31, 134, 159
Nietzsche, Friedrich, 10, 14n., 19, 20, 67, 159

Nin, Anaïs, 38, 89–90, 91; AA's
    letter to, 38
Noailles, Vicomte and Vicomtesse
    de, 74

Open Theatre, 155–8; production
    of America Hurrah (van Itallie),
    156; of The Serpent (van Itallie),
    157; of The Mutation Show, 157;
    of Terminal, 157–8; see also
    Chaikin, Joseph

Pabst, G. W., 77
Panthès, Maria, 54
Parisot, Henri, 5; AA's letters to,
    5, 12–13, 25–6, 117, 134, 140
Paulhan, Jean, 49, 63, 64–5, 73,
    82, 83, 95, 115, 122, 134, 142;
    AA's letters to, 64, 69, 76, 81,
    82, 87, 99, 101, 103, 104, 128,
    129, 130, 160
Paz, Octavio, 95,
Péret, Benjamin, 54, 55
Picabia, Francis, 84, 94
Picasso, Pablo, 1, 16, 46, 55, 146
Piscator, Erwin, 85–6
Pitoëff, Georges, 47, 67
Poe, Edgar Allan, 14, 20–2, 23–7,
    38, 39–40, 42, 125, 135
Poirier, Léon, 71
Porché, Wladimir, 142
Pouey, Fernand, 141–2
Prevel, Jacques, 2, 5, 6
Pudovkin, Vsevolod, 72
Puget, Claude-Andri, AA's letter
    to, 126

Ray, Man, 55
Reinhardt, Max, 85–6
Reverdy, Pierre, 55
Révolution surréaliste, La, 11, 54–7,

60–3; see also under AA, contri-
    butions to
Ricard, Robert, 103
Richer, Jean, 24
Rimbaud, Arthur, 6, 10, 14, 20,
    24, 28, 29, 31–5, 39–40, 50, 56,
    93, 105, 116, 136
Rivière, Jacques, 10, 32, 49, 56,
    59, 60, 63, 72, 125, 156; AA's
    letters to, 7–9, 32, 50, 54
Rouleau, Raymond, 69, 152

Sade, Marquis de, 26, 29, 84, 97,
    98, 120, 147–8, 159
Saillet, Maurice, 134–5; AA's
    letter to, 135
Salacrou, Armand, 59
Sartre, Jean-Paul, 1, 26, 27, 158
Saussure, Ferdinand de, 80
Savoir, Alfred, La Pâtissière du
    village, 82
Schramme, Cécile, 104, 115–16,
    118
Shaffer, Peter, 92
Shelley, Percy Bysshe, 96–7
Sollers, Philippe, 30–1, 139
Sontag, Susan, 6, 55, 85
Soulié de Morant, Dr. Georges,
    36; AA's letter to, 36–7, 39
Soupault, Philippe, 54, 55, 152
Souvtchinsky, Pierre, AA's letter
    to, 129
Stanislavski, Constantin, 147, 152,
    156
Stoppard, Tom, 69
Supervielle, Jules, AA's letter to, 11
Surrealists, 46, 54–65, 73, 92, 156,
    158; and communism, 63–4

Tarahumaras, 26, 108–14; and see
    AA, travels in Mexico

Theatre of Cruelty (London season, 1964), 59, 147-8, 156; *see also* Brook, Peter *and* Marowitz, Charles

Thévenin, Paule, 16, 100, 137, 142-3

Thomas, René, 101, 117, 121; AA's letter to, 121

Toulouse, Dr. Edouard, 20, 39, 40, 42, 48; AA's letters to, 10, 50, 76

Toulouse, Mme, 20, 39; AA's letters to, 39-40, 50, 54

Tourret, Fernand, 46

Tual, Roland, AA's letter to, 72

Tzara, Tristan, 54

Uccello, Paolo, 11, 15-16, 18, 57, 62, 92, 106

Valéry, Paul, 82, 83

Van Gogh, Vincent, 6, 15-19, 141, 144-5, 159; *Self-Portrait*, 19

van Itallie, Jean-Claude, 156-7

Van Leyden, Lucas, 78-9, 80-1, 96, 106; *Lot and his Daughters*, 79, 80-1, 96, 106

Verlaine, Paul, 34

Vilar, Jean, 2

Vitrac, Roger, 55, 64, 69, 73-5, 76, 109

Watson, Peter, 144; AA's letter to, 10, 131-3

Weiss, Peter, 147

Whitehead, A. N., 80

Yankowitz, Susan, 158

Zimet, Paul, 158